# Beyond The Title

## The Yearbook

## Josh Barry

## Dedication

This is dedicated to the continued work and legacy of the writer, journalist and broadcaster John Hannam who inspired me to enter the wonderful world of entertainment journalism and despite never being able to emulate his body of work I can still try...even if I can't make the perfect cup of tea!

# Contents

## Foreword

What can one say about the man, Josh Barry?
As one Barry to another, I find I carry,
A happy responsibility,
To salute a man who's rare ability
To communicate, despite his apparent disability,
I say "apparent" because you are never aware
Of it - he is always eager to share,
The experiences of those he interviewed,
And so I happily now conclude,
My foreword - onward, forward!
Read this book and I guarantee,
You'll be enthralled by him, like me
Read on - I envy you.

**Barry Cryer OBE**

i

# Acknowledgements

A book of this kind doesn't just happen and in completing it I have had the support of some remarkable people. Firstly, my overwhelming thanks goes to the legendary Barry Cryer for his wonderfully original foreword. When devising the concept for this book there was just a few names that I could only hope would do me this great honour and Barry was right at the very top, so I'm very thankful that he was so obliging. If you had told the thirteen-year-old Josh Barry that one day, Barry Cryer would provide a foreword for his book on entertainment I expect he would have laughed his head off. Yet that's just one of the many examples of how bizarre and incredibly lucky my life has been and I can't thank him enough.

The second and perhaps most obvious group of people I have to thank are my celebrity subjects who have each kindly given their time to be interrogated by my frequently bizarre lines of questioning. Through this great project I have met some of the nicest and most generous people and all are shining ambassadors for the entertainment industry. Everyone from first to last have enthusiastically entered into the spirit in which my podcast is intended and that has made for fascinating listening. No matter where my career takes me hereafter, I shall forever remember the selfless gestures of these people in making my dream into a reality. To me, they're all superstars in so many ways!

Finally and dare I say most importantly, I feel I owe a massive debt of gratitude to my amazing team of personal assistants who along with my devoted family and friends, are absolutely vital to all my successes. My personal assistants have been pivotal not just in the creation of this book but everything I do. Working with me isn't always easy and the demands I put on these highly talented people often forces them to go above and beyond their call of duty. Although I don't always say or show it, I remain thankful for their positive input in my life and they are truly the heroes behind *Beyond The Title*. A combination of this, together with the love and support from my adoring family and friends, makes me one of the luckiest people in the world and I can't think what I would do without any of them.

# Introduction

Firstly, thanks for purchasing this book, I hope you love reading it as much as I have loved writing it. You see, books on entertainment are always difficult to perfect. Not just from an author's perspective but also the very basis of the Arts relies upon subjectivity, catering for different tastes and moods. So in this instance, the old saying is probably right and 'you can't please all the people all the time'. When developing an entertainment based podcast, I knew I would always struggle to find the balance between only interviewing subjects who were personal favourites and broadening my search to include those who the public had a great fascination with. I concluded that if I didn't necessarily have a vested interest in these people then I wouldn't do them justice in a set of ten questions and besides, the entertainment industry is so vast and wide ranging that it would be almost impossible to pick subjects who are universally popular and with so much selection available this gets increasingly more difficult as the years go by.

Yet my story within entertainment is arguably bigger and more difficult than that (as you're about to find out) and in a world where diversity remains a hot topic on political agendas, it poses the question: can disabled people really function within the realms of mainstream society? Although in no way is this book any sort of crusade against disability. Mainly because very rarely does my Cerebral Palsy even arise in any of my work. However, I am always aware that my subject may be a little startled when they walk into the room and find a man in a wheelchair making undecipherable noises and spasming. It is only when we get into the crux of the interview do they realise that, although I can't speak clearly, I am in full command of my work and frankly excited about how they tackle my questions.

With that said, allow me to introduce myself: I'm Josh Barry, I have Cerebral Palsy and for the last four years I've been running an entertainment based podcast website called www.beyondthetitle.co.uk where I interview significant figures from the world of entertainment. Having a severe disability which results in my speech being difficult to understand to the untrained ear is a substantial hurdle when attempting to interview someone for a podcast. In fact out of all the possible mediums which I could immerse myself in, radio is probably the most challenging as it doesn't allow for miscommunication and all participants are required to have an impeccable command of the spoken word. If I attempted to do any sort of radio broadcast, listeners would be excused for believing it was the return of Bill and Ben, or a vague tribute to Rowley Birkin from The Fast Show - if I can't understand myself, how can I expect anyone else to understand me!

Although my disability is an obvious bargaining tool which could encourage people to be more generous with their time, it would be naive of me to think that I have never secured a big interview merely out of pity. I would like to think that as soon as people meet me, they realise that I'm a fellow media professional and frankly there to do a job.

Through the journey I've met some remarkable people who have offered me an insight into their life, career and what has made them supremely successful in their chosen field. The release of this book coincides with the fourth anniversary of *Beyond The Title*. I felt it was the perfect opportunity to reflect on and celebrate the many people who have given their time to help me get such a mammoth project off the ground and, with continued cooperation, I hope the project will flourish for many years to come. This is my opportunity to relive some of my favourite interviews and to tell you a little more about the real-life stories of the people who dominate our television screens. In short, this is 'my tale of my time' with some of the most prolific figures of the 20th and 21st centuries.

I've always been fascinated by the magical and enigmatic world of entertainment. I don't actually remember watching that much television as a kid but what I did watch instantly filled me with awe and wonder. It was then that I felt a sense of connection with these stars and I wanted to know more about them. By the time I was twelve, Michael Parkinson had returned with his iconic talk show back to their spiritual home on BBC1 and was thriving on meeting the new stars of the nineties. Watching his show, I realised that stars could appear on it in a different way. Instead of the usual 'personas' presented to the public, they were talking very candidly to Parky in a manner that I never thought I would see. It was raw and in a completely different setting with a host in full command of the conversation, gently unpicking the contributing factors which made them unique.

In later years, whenever I saw the 'King of Chat' get interviewed himself, he always explained that his interviews as a collective, charted the rise and fall of the second great Hollywood/showbiz era. Such a comment was able to stir an unbelievable reaction in me and each and every time Parkinson said it, I could sense my brain going into overdrive. Not that I thought I could ever rival or emulate the legendary Sir Michael Parkinson, but I started to wonder … that if I had my own collection of interviews, what would they say as a collective entity and how would they chart the changing face of entertainment?

In the celebrity obsessed world of 2020 with the rise of Social Media, stars are more accessible than ever before and contact with them could be only a tweet away. No longer is it necessary to send off postal forms in order to join the fan club of your favourite star or to wait at the stage door of a theatre armed with a pocket sized autograph book in the hope that the star is able to draw a squiggle on it. Today with email and social media, it's easier than it's ever been to get in touch with our favourite TV stars, yet there's still a big appetite to learn more about the people in the spotlight.

I have always been fascinated by the way stars were represented in the media and this goes back to my early childhood when my family and I would sit down to watch Light Entertainment shows of the day. Growing up in 90s Britain, I benefitted from the rebirth of big budget Light Entertainment shows which were all about vibrancy and fun. Everyone from Brian Conley to Cilla Black had their own unique take on shiny floor family entertainment. So before we move on I feel that I should let you into my own TV taste, so that you have a little background about my entertainment perception. If I would have to select one comedian who I favoured above all else it would probably have to be the late, great Bob Monkhouse for his impeccable command over the English language; here was not just a master of delivery but also comedic construction. He made each line of each joke feel absolutely natural and despite having a team of carefully nurtured writers on hand, Monkhouse had the unique ability to make every performance bespoke to that audience. He was a complete encyclopaedia of comedy and always had his finger firmly on the pulse when it came to new stars. Therefore every generation from the early 50's to the early noughties could say that they owned a little piece of him and this made him devoid of fashion and fad. In my mind Monkhouse was the full comedy package.

Within the world of sitcom my taste covers the whole breadth of the genre and I appreciate ground-breaking shows such as *Hancock's Half Hour* just as much as I love the magic of *Gavin and Stacey*. Yet if I was pressed for an answer to my all-time favourite sitcom I guess it would have to be *Fawlty Towers* for it's perfectly constructed farcical scenes together with its quintessential British snobbery which makes for indulgent TV watching. The character of Basil Fawlty constantly sits vicariously on the thin line between sanity and madness brought on by his own impunity as a man. Away from sitcom this story would be one of vast tragedy and mental torment but Cleese and Booth were able to gage the character of Basil in a way that exposed the right amount of psychological torment without playing on the negative undertones. I believe this is why *Fawlty Towers* still remains one of Britain's best sitcoms.

So with an awareness of Britain's rich cultural heritage, I set about attempting to record and celebrate the significant figures who have had a dominant effect over our popular culture over the last sixty years. I believe these insights are vital to us understanding the world we live in today and with so much selection, they go some way to answering the real purpose of the arts. It was my aim to attempt to uncover the real people behind our favourite TV and understand their importance in the evolution of the genre.

Before I could go full steam ahead and contact everyone on my interview hit list (and believe me there were a lot!) there were a few vital components which I was required to perfect before I could jump in at the deep end. What 'style' was *Beyond The Title* going to be? How was I going to maintain the calibre of guest I attracted? And how would I pitch the idea to noteworthy figures who frankly were a hundred times more successful than me? My great friend and local broadcaster, John Hannam began interviewing stars during the mid-1970's when the Isle of Wight played host to Summer Seasons in Sandown and Shanklin starring some of the biggest names in British television. John would avidly wait outside the stage door in the hope of getting five minutes with them for his showbiz article in the

Isle of Wight Evening Post. Everyone from Cilla Black to Tommy Cooper crossed the Solent to perform and it wasn't long before John secured his iconic Sunday lunchtime entertainment slot on the newly formed Isle of Wight Radio. He started in 1990 and remained there for the next quarter of a century until he turned the now legendary, *John Hannam Meets* into a podcast series available on a variety of media outlets. The veteran broadcaster can be heard all over the world...this gave me a lightbulb moment. Could I create my own interview based platform?

A major difference between today's entertainment fraternity compared to when John began his trip through showbiz is that Social Media has changed the way people interact. Creating a successful Social Media outlet can often have a dual purpose, in that if you're followed by the right people, it could be a very appealing proposition to be featured on a platform which might be seen by influential people in the industry. Likewise I'm not that naïve to not recognise a picture with a disabled person still has the unique power to assist in reversing negative stereotypes surrounding a public figure so in such cases, this becomes mutually beneficial for both parties. Still, whatever their motive, I'm just glad to have them grace the *Beyond The Title* microphone and hope that by the end of the interview they realise that my disability is totally irrelevant to what I do.

I realised that simplicity would have a big part to play in the success of the podcast. After all, I knew that it would be a big enough task to entice some of the country's biggest stars to give me their time, so everything needed to be kept as simple as possible. It occurred to me that if I couldn't encapsulate the essence of a person in a maximum of ten questions then I was doing something wrong. Obviously there are exceptions to this rule and admittedly I still get carried away when my subject is someone who I really admire, but ten questions is always my benchmark and gives me a much needed style and focus. Without this, I truly believe that *Beyond The Title* wouldn't be what it has become.

So with my concept assured, all I needed was to create an individual style and tone. This was going to be a lot more difficult than it sounded as I knew that I would have to rely on those around me to adhere to the style I wanted. After all, if I couldn't contribute to the on air interviews then surely I could develop everything that went with it? I didn't want a jazzy, informal conversation like a magazine type programme, instead I wanted the integrity of Melvyn Bragg but with the relaxed tone of Graham Norton (I know, I didn't want much but if you don't aim high then you'll never reach the stars!). Once I had decided on this, all I needed to do was convey this to my personal assistants in the hope that they would understand what I was trying to do, as it was them who would be required to carry it out. Thankfully they did, *Beyond The Title* became my creation and the rest is history!

So come with me on a journey of discovery as I share my memories of my time spent with some of the most popular faces in British entertainment.

## Chapter One - Showbiz legends

In this age of 360 degree content, we have grown accustomed to having bespoke entertainment at our fingertips. Seemingly unlimited channels constantly gives birth to new stars and challenges the very way that we perceive the Arts. Yet sixty years ago, the box in the corner of the living room was considered a luxury and frequently was shared not just with the whole family but in some circumstances the whole street. Television had yet to gain momentum and the BBC were conservatively adhering to the fixed trinity established by their first Director General Lord John Reith, to "inform, educate and entertain". Occasionally putting less importance on that third aspect which had severe consequences for the audience. Yet by 1955 the British government had approved the license for commercial television and suddenly the corporation had strong competition. Arguably this gave birth to Britain's first wave of national stars and entertainment never looked back.

The devastating effects of the Second World War were still being felt by a large percentage of the population and this influenced the socioeconomic landscape. Britain was only coming to the end of rationing in 1954. At such a bleak time entertainment was more important than ever before and entertainers had the difficult task to raise morale inside theatres which oft times still required rebuilding from heavy bomb damage. For entertainers who had honed their craft in theatres and music halls across the country, the concept of television seemed a million miles away from their skill set but it slowly loomed, large like a cloud of uncertainty, over their long theatrical careers. For performers who had been recycling the same act for theatre audiences, this was a very daunting time and in many cases such entertainer's careers sadly perished in the new fast-paced world. Of course others triumphed in this brand new medium and shone brighter than ever before.

Being such a new concept brought challenges. Very few studios, limited experience in production values and entertainers who were not yet ofay with the disciplines of television were all factors in the slow development of the medium in its early years. Executives who had grown up with full-on theatrical variety shows, attempted to replicate it for the televisual audience. Some had grown up in the theatre either performing themselves or had been agents for variety stars. As a result theatre was in their DNA, they could smell variety and vaudeville was what they had been bred on. They understood the magic and power that theatrical variety had on the audience and believed that if television entertainment could have just a slice of this, it would be a success. On the 25th September 1955 ATV was launched and one of the first shows in the schedule was *Val Parnell's Sunday Night at the London Palladium* which unbeknown to all would go on to revolutionise television for generations, giving birth on the way to some of the pioneers of modern popular culture. No longer did audiences have to flock to theatres or variety halls when you could get it all in your living room for the modest price of a licence.

As with any discipline, the pioneers remain the most prominent because they were the people who contributed to the birth of the genre. They were doing something that had never been attempted before and had no idea how they would be received. Piece by piece this generation created a showbiz firmament which is still thriving today. Once it had generated a following, it wasn't long before the small screen became a vital part of British life and these stars would enjoy vast longevity, with some of them becoming almost another member of the family. Their enduring appeal made them timeless in their appearance and devoid of any fashion or fad in popular culture. They were just ever present.

The influx of Beatlemania during the mid-sixties would have a dominant effect on the world of entertainment and suddenly television stars no longer needed to speak with Received Pronunciation BBC English. Northern accents became in vogue. Liverpool was the unofficial culture capital of the world and gave birth to a whole generation of lower middle class young people who had the desire to escape the glum shackles of post war Britain and make a better future for themselves. This social revolution united the nation and provided inspiration for a swathes of sixties pop culture.

Pop icons such as Cliff Richard became overnight symbols of a better life and gave people invaluable hope that they could escape from the mundane rat race and dream of something better. They were somehow more relatable than the transatlantic stars like Elvis Presley and Bill Haley. These home-grown stars were easily accessible and you didn't have to wait for British television to show an infrequent broadcast of a CBS special to see them. Such familiarity became one of the most significant aspects of shows such as *Sunday Night at The London Palladium* and developed an emerging rapport between the public and these entertainers which has never really gone away.

This is a subject which has always fascinated me for its incredible resonance with the people who lived through it and it was this emotion that first sparked my passion for the art of Light Entertainment. I always assumed that my chances of making contact with anyone from this period was just impossible. Yet as the following subjects explain, I was able to do the unthinkable and for that I shall forever be grateful.

## Barry Cryer OBE

Now, as this is a book about my favourite interviews, this one definitely earns its place at the top (I'm not just saying that because the great man wrote the foreword!). Not that I actually rank my interviews, as the Arts is subjective and the concept of talent is sometimes confused with fame. In fact my appreciation for this man goes much deeper and as I make my journey through entertainment, I become increasingly aware of the substantial impact which Barry Cryer has had over the history of British comedy and Light Entertainment.

When I was young and my fascination with the art of British comedy, grew, it was always my ambition to attempt to one day meet the people who influenced my passion. It's an incredible feeling to think that I have actually achieved something that I set out to do when I was so young. As an avid fan of the history of Light Entertainment, I have always felt more comfortable talking to a celebrated figure of British comedy than I do attempting an interview with the latest reality star. Not that entertainment should be elitist in any way as the very purpose of entertainment is to appeal to the masses and just as the influx of multi-channel and multi-platform content has expanded our choices I feel that as a journalist, it's my responsibility to capture the whole breadth of the arts. Reality television obviously caters to a broad section of the TV demographic and it would be naïve of me to trivialise it. Yet as a British comedy buff, sometimes I find it is acceptable to indulge my fascination of the early days of the genre and interview an icon. For any aspiring writer and television historian like myself, the ultimate treat was to spend a few moments with an icon of the art of comedy script writing. Legendary writer and comedian Barry Cryer has been on the cutting edge of British comedy for over sixty years and has worked with many of the prominent figures in British Light Entertainment, but arguably his own career rivals any comedy royalty.

It makes me extremely proud (and quite smug!) to say that this interview wasn't my first encounter with the comedy legend. In fact my interest in him dates back to when my parents took me to the Isle Of Wight leg of his nationwide tour. I was a mere teenager but was already besotted with the history of British comedy, so I was very excited to see the entertainment legend perform. The first time I became aware of Cryer's wider contribution to comedy was when he presented the 1999 *Two Ronnie's Night* celebrating the magic of Corbett and Barker. It was here I learnt the remarkable story of how Ronnie met Ronnie and the vast array of figures who contributed to their story. Barry presided over this special show and having known both of them for over forty years he was the perfect anchor for a programme of this kind. When I found out that he was performing in my local town I just knew I had to witness his live show for myself. Unbeknown to me this would be the first of many associations with Mr Cryer in the coming years which eventually resulted in this wonderful opportunity to interview one of my heroes in person. Yet at this stage of my journey through entertainment, it was just enough to have been able to say that I had seen the legend of comedy perform. Had you asked me back then I would have rated my chances of coming into further contact with him as almost impossible. I was just happy to tick him off my comedy bucket list.

Fast forward five years, I was undertaking my Masters at Bournemouth and for my major project I wrote a screenplay based on the life and work of celebrated television executive Sir Bill Cotton. In order to get a fair representation, I was required to obtain personal accounts of him from people who knew him best. I already knew the huge love and respect for Sir Bill which united everyone who ever came into contact with the great man so I knew that my chances of obtaining these insights were higher than just a mere interview. By coincidence Mr Cryer was once again on tour, bringing his new show, *That Reminds Me* to the Tivoli Theatre in Wimborne alongside the celebrated pianist and his long-time friend Colin Sell. I instantly bought a ticket.

This got me thinking about how I might be able to interview him the night before he took to the stage. Unfortunately this wasn't possible but instead he offered me a phone interview where I could quiz him on his friend and former boss, Sir Bill. I couldn't believe it, I was going to interview one of my all-time heroes and the fact that it was on the phone seemed totally irrelevant. I clearly remember being absolutely overwhelmed as I listened to my assistant John deliver my questions to the showbiz god, not being able to speak because I was just completely gobsmacked that Barry Cryer was at the other end of the phone. He ended the conversation with an invitation to come backstage at the Tivoli Theatre on the Friday night where I would have the opportunity to meet the man himself. I was so excited as my carer and I took our seats for what we hoped would be a fantastic evening of comedy. We weren't let down. The veteran comedian was still on fire and treated his audience to over an hour of quick witted hilarity. Sure enough, after the show Barry stuck to his word and had a quick chat with us while he got his things together to leave the theatre.

It would be another seven years before our next meeting at the Museum Of Comedy when we were both attending a Writer's Guild event celebrating the work of legendary comedy writing partnership Lawrence Marks and Maurice Gran. As I sat waiting for the event to start, in walked Barry. By this time I was a year into *Beyond The Title* and instantly thought how great it would be to have him as a subject for a podcast. After the event, myself and my PA, Ben made our way to the foyer and started to mingle where I was lucky enough to catch his eye. He immediately interrupted the person he was talking to and gave me his full attention. It was here that I asked him about the possibility that I could interview him again for my podcast to which he replied with those exciting words, "Let's do it!" Within just a few weeks, my PA, James and I found ourselves ready to fulfil a lifetime ambition; to interview the legendary Barry Cryer in person.

There was so much I wanted to ask him; from his early days at the Windmill Theatre, writing scripts for Danny La Rue and Ronnie Corbett at the legendary nightclub *Winston's* before going on to be the driving force behind some of Britain's most successful comedy stars. How did he make the smooth transition from full on theatrical variety to cutting edge satire?

Indeed from there, how did he adapt himself yet again to compliment the anarchic world of Kenny Everett and make the zany DJ acceptable for television? It was these questions and more which I was determined to discover in this special interview with a veteran of comedy.

When we arrived, Barry stood in the doorway of his Tudor detached house in shorts and t-shirt. I was in disbelief as he showed us into his conservatory. Despite being a minute from one of the busiest motorways in Britain, the house seemed full of peace and tranquillity as James set up the sound equipment. Like most of my subjects, Barry was extremely intrigued by me and what I did and for a moment it seemed like he had turned the interview tables. Yet I wasn't going to waste this precious time talking about myself so I promptly asked James to get the interview underway. There was no doubt that we were in for half an hour of the most amazing tales from an unparalleled career in entertainment.

Born in Leeds in 1935, Barry quickly realised that his aspirations for the world of comedy would not be satisfied within his home community. After failing an English Literature degree at the University of Leeds, he uprooted to London to seek success and fame. After a series of unsuccessful attempts to enter the world of showbiz, Barry was resigned to the fact that he would be forced to return to Leeds. Yet the day before he was due to leave he received an invitation to audition at the famous or perhaps infamous, Windmill Theatre. Astonishingly, in a couple of hours following that audition, Barry found himself on stage entertaining an audience, performing a staggering 6 shows a day, 6 days a week. The Windmill Theatre was the perfect grounding for a life in entertainment under the supervision of theatrical impresario Vivian Van Damme.

Van Damme was a master of knowing what an audience wanted and took meticulous care in every aspect of production. He would instinctively know what material would work for which comic and how to deliver it, often providing feedback about whether a gag was delivered too quick or too slow. Although he wasn't on stage it was very clear that Vivian was the heart and soul of the Windmill Theatre and was responsible for the popularity of the theatre throughout London. Frequently criticised by contemporary entertainment critics for being vulgar and sexist, 'The Windmill' played host to some of the best nude artists in the world and Barry is adamant that these performers were so much more than seedy figures of lust. This common misconception has put a significant negative shadow over the Windmill and in a lot of ways has devalued the influential impact that it had over the course of British comedy.

With Van Damme as its formidable impresario, The Windmill became responsible for many of Britain's best loved comics and entertainers. It was here that Barry met the stick-thin force of nature, Bruce Forsyth who was doing a residency. Feeling despondent and frustrated, Bruce told Barry that if showbiz didn't work out he intended on opening a cafe in Edmonton. This became a running joke between Bruce and Barry and even in later years, each time the pair met, they would joke about the fictional cafe which fortunately for British entertainment never opened. It wasn't long before producers saw Boy Bruce, The Mighty Atom and gave him a shot at presenting duties on *Sunday Night At The London Palladium.* Yet it was clear to Cryer that Forsyth was always destined to be a star and this was the start of a friendship that would last a lifetime.

From the Windmill, Barry honed his talent as a scriptwriter and then became the resident writer at the Winston's nightclub, penning sketches for the comedy sections of the cabaret show. This shall forever hold an extra significance for him as it proved the setting of the meeting between him and his future wife Terri. In fact he often joked that he met Terri and Ronnie Corbett on the same day and flipped a coin, marrying her instead of his pint sized fellow comedian. In 1964, after Winston's, Danny La Rue established his own club on Hannover Square and his whole repertoire company followed him, creating a showbiz family made up of future icons of the genre including Ronnie Corbett and Barbara Windsor. The club itself opened the night after the final show at Winston's. This was invaluable experience for Barry as he was able to hone his talents as a writer forced as he was to deliver new scripts for new shows every few weeks with an ever changing cast. Indeed when Danny was otherwise engaged with summer seasons and pantomime it fell to Barry and Ronnie Corbett to create a show of their own. He believed that it was this experience that he was able to nurture as both a writer and a performer.

Danny's club was such a success that it wasn't long before it generated quite a cult following among showbiz circles and promptly the great and the good wanted to be in the audience of the late night show. One evening in particular the great dancer, Rudolph Nureyev was in attendance and was so impressed by the performance that he booked the club for a private show. For Cryer, this was just one high in a career that has spanned decades. It was also here that Barry met a man who would prove to be influential in his, and many other's careers, David Frost. Following an impromptu drink one night, he accepted an offer to become a part of the writing team on a brand new show called The Frost Report. Frost (or "the Practicing Catalyst" as Barry refers to him) had just set the comedy world on fire with his satirical series, *That Was The Week That Was (TW3)* but now wanted to create a new programme which combined the talents of old school Variety with university review. It would take a satirical and irreverent look at significant themes of British life, including language and class. Such a revolutionary process pitted old school comedy writers such as Cryer, Dennis Norden and Anthony Jay up against university review writers that included Michael Palin, Terry Jones and Graham Chapman who would of course go on to form Monty Python. The Frost Report starring Ronnies Corbett and Barker alongside another 'front of camera' newcomer, John Cleese, was first broadcast on Thursday 10th March 1967 and ran for twenty eight episodes on BBC1. It saw the blossoming union between the two men who would go on to play a dominant role in Barry's career. Barry insists that only the magic of David Frost's organisation and people power would have made such a revolutionary show a success. Nurturing writers from two separate backgrounds wasn't easy and it would have been difficult to create a cohesive ethos throughout the programme, but under Frost's leadership the two separate groups became one. Not only creating unlikely partnerships within the programme but forming a union which would last for the next half a century.

Today television comedy is packed with writing teams that assist in the development process but forty years ago this approach was revolutionary. The continuing developing monologue (CDM for short – also known as Cadbury's Dairy Milk!) was put in place to give the writers focus and to structure each episode under the stewardship of the script editor Anthony Jay (who later created, "Yes Minister"). At eight thirty each Thursday evening, The Frost Report was broadcast live from the BBC and made stars of Ronnie Corbett, Ronnie Barker and John Cleese. The show survived for just one series on the BBC before Frost moved the team to London Weekend Television (LWT). *Frost On Sunday* perfectly united the talents of Corbett and Barker for just one series until Bill Cotton did a deal with David Frost, following an impromptu performance at the BAFTA's, which led to Corbett and Barker or The Two Ronnies as they were now known, being

BBC bound. Nevertheless, Barry remained a vital part of *The Two Ronnies* writing team up until their eventual sign off on Christmas Day 1987 and was present at every pivotal landmark moment in the series. One example of his contribution is the show's iconic opening sequence. When devising the concept of *The Two Ronnies*, it was proving very difficult to think of a way to start the show. After all, with Ronnie Barker being a straight actor, they were unable to have the same comedic patter of Morecambe and Wise and were crying out for a way that both Ronnies could feel comfortable. At a production meeting, Barry had a brainwave and just uttered the words "News At Ten" and the rest, as they say, is history. The legendary news items bookended each Two Ronnies show and became the ultimate shorthand for the series.

Hearing Barry wax lyrical about this special time it is obvious that he treats his vast accomplishments with a large amount of modesty. Indeed it's easy to forget that here is a man who has been vital to a large percentage of comedy landmarks of the last half century. It was Barry who first reacted to the revelation that Ronnie Barker was in fact Gerald Wiley, anonymously contributing to the majority of *The Frost Report* and *The Two Ronnies*.

Not content with just one legendary comedy act Barry Cryer also started to write sketches for Morecambe and Wise on their ATV series before they returned to the bedrock of the BBC. At the BBC Barry also became their warm up act and frequently had the pleasure of introducing the pair to the studio audience. Together with writing partner John Junkin, Barry wrote for Eric and Ernie up until the late seventies, alongside main writer Eddie Braben. This period Barry holds very dear and he recounted that it was great working with one of the most influential figures in comedy history. As he states, 'Eric always had a line' and this proved very easy for a writer to work with as once you knew the patter between Eric and Ernie, you could give them anything and they would be able to turn it into comedy gold. Having worked with such kings of British comedy it was very easy for Barry to be pigeon-holed as a traditional variety writer and performer. Yet another comedy powerhouse was about to emerge from a completely different avenue which would shake the very foundation of the art.

Anarchic DJ turned darling of Light Entertainment, Kenny Everett had an interesting transition following a controversial exit from Radio 1 and required a team of experienced comedy writers to make him relevant for the fast paced world of television. Alongside Ray Cameron, the late father of Michael McIntyre, Barry wrote for Everett throughout his Thames Television supremacy. Barry insists that Everett was a one off and a performer who was impossible to categorise. It was Cryer who refined the highly dubious female character of Cupid Stunt, who appeared on The Parkinson Show originally as the one word Cupid, but when asked by Michael Parkinson to supply a full name so that he could give her a proper introduction, Barry replied "Cupid Stunt!" Consequently, Parky promptly was forced to heavily rehearse the introduction to avoid making the obvious mistake. Barry remained one of Everett's main writers throughout his television success on both the BBC and Thames and developed a strong friendship which lasted until Kenny's untimely death in 1995.

Alongside his substantial writing credentials, Barry remains one of only two surviving original members of the formidable Radio 4 comedy series, *I'm Sorry I Haven't a Clue* along with Graeme Garden. Beginning as a "filler" in the 1972 Boxing Day schedule, the impromptu panel show currently attracts an average weekly audience of 2.5 million listeners. In 2008, *ISIHAC*, tragically lost its versatile chairman, Humphrey Lyttelton at the age of 86, covering the future of the show in a cloud of doubt. However, with the dry-witted Jack Dee being appointed as 'Humph's' replacement, the show continues to entertain audiences up and down the British Isles. Today it is as popular as ever, with live episodes filmed on location around the country. As Barry says, "Next is the O2!"

It is only when discussing his career that I realise the truly mammoth contribution he made to comedy over the last sixty years and the comedy landmarks he has been present at. It was him who uttered the phrase, 'No one likes a smart arse!' on hearing Ronnie Barker's shock revelation that he was the real Gerald Whiley who was submitting scripts to The Frost Report. From the late 1950's to the multi-platform landscape of the late 2010s, Barry Cryer has seen it all. Forever updating for new audiences, admiring the biggest stars of the day and having the new and contemporary crop of comedy stars queuing up to collaborate with this icon of entertainment. On the subject of how he wants to be remembered, Barry doesn't care. He is, he says, just content with doing what he does and mixing with the new generation. He likes talking about the past but doesn't want to live there. Still in high demand on both TV and radio, the Barry Cryer I interviewed in 2017 was as energetic and sprightly as ever and it was obvious that he still had a great love for what he did.

It was an honour to spend the morning with him and if I have half the career that Barry Cryer has had, I'll definitely die a very happy man!

## Tim Brooke-Taylor OBE

This is a really personal interview for me. Not only because Tim Brooke-Taylor was one of my heroes who I was fortunate enough to meet during this journey through entertainment, but because unbeknown to both of us, in the space of a few months, Tim would tragically be taken by the Coronavirus outbreak of 2020.

Starting my podcast in 2016, I subconsciously assumed that my chances of featuring the true icons of British entertainment would be almost impossible. Added to that, time marches on and has of course tragically robbed British comedy of some of the most original and innovative figures in the history of television. As this golden generation slowly fades away, their insights and stories become increasingly invaluable. As a budding comedy historian, I find it fascinating to attempt to piece together some of this history and it is only when I am in the presence of a veteran entertainer that I am able to attain this. Therefore I am forever on the lookout for opportunities to interview the original class of such a comedy revolution and when I discover these veterans on my doorstep it becomes too much of an opportunity to miss.

Such an event was to take place in the autumn of 2019 when I was perusing the website of Shanklin Theatre on the Isle of Wight and realised that the great Tim Brooke-Taylor was bringing his conversation tour there in a few weeks' time. Ever since my fascination with British comedy began, Tim Brooke-Taylor had been a constant face on my radar as a result of his formidable contribution to the comedy scene of the 1960's and 1970's. From *The Frost Report* to *The Goodies*, Brooke-Taylor's contribution to the story of entertainment is remarkable and the opportunity to interview him is one I have contemplated many times, but never in my wildest dreams did I think it would ever become a reality. So with him making a trip to the Isle of Wight I knew I had to seize my chance.

As always I relied on my full proof technique of attempting to find a contact for his agent but when I accessed the website for the specific agency it somehow looked extremely corporate, which didn't fill me with much hope. But, as usual, I thought I would give it a go! A few days went by and I heard nothing so I had started to resign myself to the fact that I can't win them all and I would just have to attend the show like any other punter. Yet three days before the show I was in a meeting with a kitchen fitter about designing my new kitchen when I heard the email tone on my iPad. Without being rude I checked the message only to find that the legendary writer and comedian had actually contacted me himself to accept an interview before his show on the Sunday. I wanted to scream in elation but I thought I might scare the kitchen fitter! Instead, I maintained my dignity only to scream, shout and dance around my kitchen in celebration at the precise moment he left.

After my celebrations it was time to get down to work as I knew that with such a formidable figure I needed to get everything absolutely perfect. The research for the interview was possibly the most enjoyable I have ever conducted as I personally find the era of the 60's a fascinating period to study and Tim was involved in the majority of pivotal events during this part of comedy history. I never thought I would ever be able to ask someone first-hand what it was like to star in ground-breaking sketch shows such as *At Last The 1948 Show* but suddenly I was writing questions about some of the most influential programmes of the 1960's and it felt so good!

On the day of the interview, myself and my PA, Will got to the theatre 10 minutes early in order to set up the sound equipment. All of a sudden I heard the voice of Tim Brooke-Taylor echoing down the corridor. It is very rare for me to become star struck but as he came into the room, I couldn't speak. I was in the presence of a comedy legend. Ever calm and collected, Will ignored my nervous disposition and commenced with the interview.

As the interview started to flow I began to relax and it allowed Will to take the reins. However, at the third question one of my worst nightmares took place. I had asked about *The Frost Report* and as a result of my knowledge of the programme I thought I would ask a bit of challenging question about the differences between writers from different backgrounds and how that benefited the success of the show. Being one of the first sketch shows to combine writing and performing talent from both University revue and mainstream Variety, *The Frost Report* rewrote the rule book in terms of the submission of material from an endless supply of different comedy minds. I was interested to learn how this technique benefited the quality of the material. This was a question that I had asked Barry Cryer some two years previously and had been delighted by his detailed answer. Yet unfortunately, due to the way I had written it, the question was difficult to comprehend and for a moment I was face to face with one of my heroes feeling stupid and flustered. I wanted the ground to swallow me whole. This was Tim Brooke-Taylor and I had made myself look a right idiot in front of him. It took me a while to get myself together and explain what I actually meant whilst getting over my utter embarrassment. We quickly moved on to the next question with my face still as red as a beetroot!

Thankfully, that aside, throughout the interview and indeed for the entirety of his one-man show, Tim was in fantastic form and you could see that he truly loved looking back. It seems almost inconceivable that in the space of a few months, this giant would be taken away from us. On 12th April 2020, Britain woke to the tragic news that Tim had passed away from Coronavirus in the midst of the worldwide pandemic. Graeme Garden and David Walliams led the tributes to the legendary writer and comedian who had been at the forefront of British comedy for over half a century. But for me, this news had an added emotional element given that I had, so recently, enjoyed an intimate interview with him. And what an interview it was!

The Cambridge Footlights has become globally renowned for giving a platform to some of Britain's best loved writers and performers. Yet it was the early sixties when the society nurtured an unprecedented amount of comedy talent. Footlights alumni of those years included Peter Cook, David Frost, John Cleese and Graham Chapman, all of whom came to define British comedy for generations and spawned a TV culture which still remains. Tim Brooke-Taylor became president of The Footlights in 1964 when he embarked upon an international tour alongside Bill Oddie, Graeme Garden, Eric Idle, John Cleese and Graham Chapman. This resulted in the group securing their own BBC Radio series *I'm Sorry I'll Read That Again* in 1964 which helped to spark a comedy revolution.

At just twenty three years old, Footlights alumni and friend David Frost had just landed the first of many television triumphs in the shape of the satirical juggernaut, *That Was The Week That Was* and was looking to follow up its success with a brand new sketch show combining the irreverent tone of university revue with the vaudeville nature of full on variety. With the main cast featuring theatrical stalwarts Ronnie Corbett and Ronnie Barker (who prior to this had never worked together), alongside 'front of camera' newcomer, John Cleese, the series provided a fantastic testing ground for young writers and it was here that Tim honed his comedic writing voice. Surrounded by the cream of UK writing talent including Barry Cryer, Dennis Norden, Anthony Jay, Bill Oddie, Graeme Garden and almost the entire team who would go on to create *Python, The Frost Report* focused on a particular subject each week. Despite coming from different backgrounds, *The Frost Report* team was comprised of likeminded individuals who took an irreverent look at the establishment. This was an influential part of the success and legacy of the show.

Despite showcasing his writing dexterity on *The Frost Report,* Tim had yet to display his talents as a performer which he had developed during his time with The Footlights. But all this was about to change when he was cast alongside John Cleese, Marty Feldman and Amy McDonald for *At Last The 1948 Show.* Responsible for classic sketches including *The Four Yorkshireman, At Last The 1948 Show* toiled with the concept of logic in the class obsessed society of the 1960's. Tim has since grown tired of forever reinforcing ownership over *The Four Yorkshiremen* sketch and feeling the need to correct the fallacy that it's from *Monty Python.* Yet this doesn't bother him as much as it once did. Tragically due to the BBC's "unsacredness" policy of the time, recordings of the show were carelessly wiped and only a few episodes remain. Yet in 2019 Tim was invited to BFI Southbank for a special screening of recently rediscovered episodes which meant a great deal to him.

His next comedy vehicle was for the still relatively new station BBC2 in the irreverent sketch show entitled *Broaden Your Mind* alongside Michael Palin, the late Terry Jones, Graeme Garden and Bill Oddie. This was the first time that the future *Goodies* had shared the screen together and the chemistry between them was instantly on point. Consisting of thirteen half hour episodes, *Broaden Your Mind* proved another opportunity for the cream of UK writing talent to come together to create a surreal sketch show centered on a cast made up of Tim Brooke-Taylor, Graeme Garden and Bill Oddie. Yet as soon as the phenomenon of Python fully took hold, the comedy landscape changed and the three actors were looking to create a platform which contained the unashamedly silliness of their contemporaries.

While Python rewrote the comedy rule book in terms of the structure of the sketch show, *The Goodies* instead created an overarching storyline which interlinked the sketches. First broadcast on the 8th November 1970, the series loosely followed the bizarre lives of heightened versions of Oddie, Garden and Brooke-Taylor as they enjoyed adventures on their famous three-seated 'tandem'. When thinking up the title of the show, a whole host of names were in the reckoning yet promptly the three men settled on *The Goodies*. The only reservation that Tim had surrounding the name was that there was a chance that it would conjure up images of Goody-Two-Shoes and Goody Goodies, neither of which represented what the series was about and could create the illusion that it was twee and tame. Yet when the format was explained and Tim realised that in each episode, the three of them would overcome the odds and defeat an enemy, the title seemed to make sense. Thus *The Goodies* stuck and became a weekly half hour of anarchic stupidity for over a decade.

As he chatted to me, he recounted how he had, for as long as he could remember, two life goals. One being to play football for a sell-out crowd at Wembley and the other to appear on *Top Of The Pops*. Unfortunately the opportunity to play at Wembley escaped him but on the 24th March 1975 he achieved his second ambition when The Goodies appeared on *Top Of The Pops* performing their top five hit *The Funky Gibbon*. This was a dream come true for born performers Tim and Bill but for academic Graeme Garden, it was just about as far away from his comfort zone as one could possibly get. Despite this, the trio created a grand total of four studio albums, five compilation albums, twelve UK singles and one EP. That's quite a substantial musical repertoire for a group of comedy actors.

Beyond *The Goodies*, since 1972, Tim has been involved in another comedy institution. First broadcast on Boxing Day 1972, *I'm Sorry I Haven't a Clue* has been delighting audiences up and down the land for almost half a century. Yet Tim vividly recalls being in a bar with the late Humphrey Lyttelton as they both promised to never record another episode. Of course in this case, promises are there to be broken as *Clue* spawned legions of diehard fans who loved to hear Tim and co doing what they did best. Today *Clue* is as popular as ever, with live episodes filmed on location around the country and at the time of the interview Tim was looking forward to recording an episode in Portsmouth alongside his old friend Barry Cryer. It's clear that what originally started as a filler in the radio schedules has now become a radio juggernaut and Tim couldn't be more proud.

Returning to TV in 2000, Tim secured a role in David Renwick's seminal sitcom *One Foot In The Grave*. Playing the part of the Meldrews' new next door neighbour, Derek who had made a cameo in the 1997 episode *Endgame,* now producers had the desire to make him a recurring character. Derek was just as cantankerous and grumpy as Victor and yet the two men found each other completely unbearable. This role became a poisoned chalice for Tim when he discovered that this series was to be the last for *One Foot In The Grave,* but he still got the opportunity to appear in such an iconic series and for that he was grateful.

Long since achieving legendary status amongst both public and peers, Tim Brooke-Taylor thrived upon his longevity across a whole host of mediums as a true pioneer of modern British comedy. Whether it was his quick witted responses on *I'm Sorry I Haven't a Clue* or his conversational tours of Britain, Tim Brooke-Taylor was still in high demand six decades after starting out. Eloquent, sharp and supremely intelligent, it was a real joy to be in his company and despite his advancing years, he possessed the vigour of someone half his age. It seems strange that audiences will no longer admire his incredible improvisational skills on *I'm Sorry I Haven't a Clue* or be able to witness his great flare as a natural raconteur. Yet thanks to his formidable contributions to British comedy which has been immortalised in archive form, Tim Brooke-Taylor may be gone but will never be forgotten.

# Jimmy Tarbuck OBE

Light Entertainment has always been a driving force of my career and was the sole reason for me creating *Beyond The Title*. It was my aim to meet my heroes and chart their careers in real time so that I had a collection of time capsules from some of the people I respected most. Without getting too philosophical about it, I found it absolutely incredible how I could have an audio record of some of my all-time favourite stars and obtain their insight into how they saw themselves in that precise moment and to think that I would be able to do this with some of my idols was an incredible accolade.

As an avid fan of the history of British entertainment, nothing gets my heart racing like when I meet one of my heroes, so you can imagine the excitement I felt when I found myself at a distinguished golf club preparing to interview Jimmy Tarbuck. Now I'm not going to pretend that I'm a friend of the stars or a strange comedy groupie but I have met Mr Tarbuck on a number of occasions and he has kindly helped me on a range of different projects throughout the years, so when I was stuck for a special Christmas guest of 2017, I knew just the person I wanted. It was June 2017, the sun was beaming and I was in shorts and t-shirt so it was bizarre to think I was about to record my Christmas interview, but I guess if you want big stars you have to work around their big schedules and this star was probably busier than most.

For over half a century, Jimmy Tarbuck has been a vital part of the showbiz establishment and has been a constant face on our television screens and even in 2017 he was still pulling in theatre audiences with his Liverpudlian lilt and cheeky chappie sense of humour. When we arrived we discovered that Tarbuck was currently out doing his daily round of eighteen holes. We were shown into a lounge and treated to a drink and biscuits. However it soon became apparent that we were not the only people waiting for Jimmy. Two production staff from BBC Radio 2 were also waiting for the golf crazed comedian to return from the course so they could interview him for a documentary celebrating the 90th birthday of fellow Liverpudlian comedy great, Ken Dodd.

The crew from the BBC took one glance at me and my PA Will and promptly positioned themselves right at the front of the entrance in order to nab Jimmy before we even set our eyes on him. This was the first and only time that I had ever been in direct competition with the BBC and being extra polite and amiable, Will made it clear that we didn't have anything against them having 'first dibs' on Jimmy. However I wondered if Jimmy would see it their way and, sure enough when he finally appeared from his golf buggy he shook their hands, promptly walked over to me and said 'Right let's do this guys!' I think that's the only time I will ever get one over on the BBC.

We recorded the interview in a big reception room with a dividing wall where we could shut out the prying eyes of those pesky BBC folk as they recovered from getting their noses put out of joint. It was obvious that Jimmy didn't have long so we just got down to business. It was here I realised how eloquent and succinct the entertainer could be as Will fired the questions at him. It was like he could just reel it off from a mental script and the roll call of names who were dropped into the conversation was unbelievable.

Forever content with being portrayed as the boy from Liverpool who did good, it's easy to forget just how big a star Jimmy Tarbuck was during the sixties and seventies. The roll call of stars whom he calls friends is remarkable and includes, Tom Jones, Harry Secombe, Sean Connery, Billy Connolly, Shirley Bassey, Cilla Black and Bruce Forsyth. Tarbuck is, most definitely, a vital part of the showbiz establishment.

Making his debut on Sunday Night at the London Palladium on the 27th of October 1963, Jimmy went on to have a career defining association with the legendary theatre which still survives to this day. Originally only scheduled for a six minute act, Tarbuck overran by three minutes and garnered rave reviews which changed his life. Two years later, he was honoured to take the reins from host Norman Vaughan as the Palladium's main man. Jimmy insisted becoming famous at such a young age had enormous benefits as he had the strength and energy to fully embrace and enjoy it. Surrounded by legends of entertainment who were already established stars themselves, Jimmy wasn't short on receiving advice and it was Harry Secombe who offered him the best piece, the old saying that *'it's very nice to be big but you don't have to be big to be nice'*, this is something that has kept him grounded throughout his career and may explain his humility.

As host of Sunday Night at the London Palladium, Jimmy welcomed the likes of Rudolph Nureyev, Judy Garland and Dame Antoinette Sibley onto what was now one of the biggest shows on British television, making him one of the most famous men in Britain. As he states, "becoming famous when you're young gives you the time, energy and opportunity to enjoy your successes" and Jimmy Tarbuck has enjoyed more successes than most. Rising to fame in the midst of the Merseybeat phenomenon of the mid-sixties, Jimmy found himself surrounded by many of his childhood friends who had all been transformed into overnight superstars, thanks in part to music mogul Brian Epstein. The Beatles, Cilla, Gerry and The Pacemakers and Freddie and The Dreamers to name but a few. Unfortunately music wasn't Jimmy's forte and while he could hold a tune, his real talent lay in the ability to make an audience laugh.

After Sunday Night at the Palladium, Jimmy was among a select few entertainers to be given their own game show format. *Winner Takes All* was broadcasted by ITV from 1975 to 1984 and remains one of his favourite programmes. He was later lured back to the art of the game show in 1996 with the golfing centred game, *Full Swing* yet the over complex rules of the game lead to its premature demise. Ever modest, Jimmy remains quick to highlight that he could never reach the standards of his own game show heroes, Bob Monkhouse and Bruce Forsyth, but his laid back and amiable approach to the games forced people to have a vested interest in the contestants which was only been possible thanks to the Tarbuck charm.

With an obvious sea change in comedy during the eighties, established comics such as Jimmy wrongfully got labelled as unfit for modern Britain. There was a perceived huge divide between alternative comedy and traditional variety and with it came a negative backlash against the showbiz establishment. Jimmy was flung into this group with the likes of Stan Boardman and Bernard Manning whose material was racist, sexist and xenophobic. This was factually incorrect but there was very little that Jimmy could do about the misconception, so spent the majority of the decade being portrayed as old fashioned and out of date. Yet Jimmy is always one to see the funny side of life and when he came in contact with the comics who targeted him in their routines they were always extremely respectful and treated him as a hero. The biggest irony is that today most of these people are actually presenting game shows which was one of their original sources of criticism for Jimmy. Something which is layered with irony.

Still favoured by TV executives for his experience, popularly and professionalism, the versatile comedian returned to the *Sunday Night at the London Palladium* format in 1983 for *Live From Her Majesty's* which reunited Jimmy with the art that possibly suits him best; compering a live entertainment show. Yet this was tinged with sadness in that it was on this show that the genius who was Tommy Cooper passed away in front of a live audience and with millions watching at home on the 15th April 1984. As the old saying goes, "the show must go on" and while medical staff treated his long-time friend, Jimmy was forced to do one of the most difficult things he has ever had to do; returning to the stage and carrying on with the remainder of the show knowing his friend was dying. This event not only illustrates his emotional strength as a man but also his utter professionalism as a performer.

In 1994 Jimmy Tarbuck was honoured when ITV asked him to star in his own *Audience With...* special. A packed studio of sportsmen, musicians and entertainers came together to see a one man show from a performer who was now entertainment royalty. From his comedy mentor Harry Secombe to long-time friends Bruce Forsyth and Cilla Black, the audience read like a who's who of British television and they were all there for one man. To end the show, Jimmy made his own super group consisting of The Shadows' Hank Marvin on guitar, The Moody Blues' John Lodge and Justin Hayward on guitar and bass covering the Chuck Berry classic *Johnny Be Good*. For both cast and crew this was a very special moment and for the musical director Mike Dixon it was a dream to be arranging the music for such a supergroup.

In 2016 the Variety Club honoured Jimmy with a lifetime achievement award presented by his long-time friend Sir Michael Parkinson. Friends and family gathered at the Hilton Hotel in Central London to pay tribute to the man who's done just about everything and when we met him at the age of 77 there seemed to be no sign of him slowing down. Through his love of golf, he continues to arrange charity fundraisers raising much needed funds for disadvantaged children both here and in the most deprived areas of the world. This is something that he remains extremely proud of and as he's been so lucky in his life, Jimmy feels that it's important to give something back.

It was an absolute pleasure to spend the afternoon with Jimmy Tarbuck and long may he reign over Britain's entertainment landscape.

# Dame Esther Rantzen

Some of our best loved stars remain ever present in our lives and in many ways become like part of the furniture. Somehow they have the unique ability to transcend the times we live in and act as a natural commentator to the events which surround us. For over half a century, writer and broadcaster Esther Rantzen has remained at the cutting edge of public service broadcasting, specialising in live consumer affairs television. Being one of the most prominent female figures in the history of broadcasting, Rantzen's television heritage spans the very history of the medium. Her father, Henry Barnato Rantzen was hired by first BBC Director General Lord John Reith as Head of Lines and Design Department at the corporation and in charge of the Outside Broadcast at Windsor when Edward VIII made his abdication speech. Yet Esther always knew that her talents lay elsewhere.

The first time I became aware of her work was on the nineties BBC1 dream-making series *Hearts Of Gold.* For some reason as a youngster I always thought Esther encapsulated everything the BBC represented. I associated her with shiny floor spectaculars which the BBC could do better than anyone else (in the halcyon days of TV Centre). Yet unbeknown to that young version of me, a decade later I would meet the lady herself at a media event at Solent University Southampton. I was invited by a group which I'd joined just a year previously in the last year of my BA which organised events surrounding broadcasting and the arts. When myself and my PA Tom arrived I realised that instead of being a formal lecture, this would be an informal seminar where she would be interviewed by the most senior member of the media group. As Esther arrived she just happened to sit right opposite me and was in my eye line as we exchanged polite glances. There was no time for anything more than that as before long we were called to the lecture theatre where she was welcomed to the stage as the event commenced. The broadcasting icon was on top form as she waxed lyrical about her glittering career and the future of television which she was extremely passionate about. As I listened intently to her enthusiastic responses to questions, there was so much more I wanted to know about her career and I could only hope that our paths would cross again.

Such an opportunity took place on my Masters' course when I was writing my major project based on the life and career of television executive Sir Bill Cotton. Esther very kindly took part in an email question and answer form which gave me invaluable insight into Sir Bill's tenure as controller of BBC1. To glean such first-hand experience from a figure of Esther's calibre was absolutely incredible and I felt this offered my project more weight. Yet thankfully this wasn't my last contact with the broadcasting legend…

When I began to think about the concept of *Beyond The Title*, there were a few people who I thought would make fantastic interview subjects and Esther was near the top of my list. But for some reason she had escaped my radar for the first two years and it took a chance listing in a celebrity PR database to remind me of my ongoing quest to quiz her. I sent a request to her agent and received a lovely email inviting me to Esther's apartment in London to interview her in person. Unfortunately the apartment was on the first floor of a tower block with no lift and I thought it would look highly unprofessional to be carried into the flat so it was decided that a telephone interview would be more appropriate… and a little safer!

Beginning her career as a junior director on the seminal documentary and current affairs programme *Man Alive*, Esther was one of just a handful of women to be in a production role. At a time when women were sparsely represented on either side of the camera, she was offered trainee director on *Man Alive* following a string of unsuccessful considerations for roles which she believes were denied her as a direct result of her gender. *Man Alive* proved a catalyst in Esther's relationship with fellow television producer Desmond Wilcox whom she married in 1977. This began a successful union which would last up until Wilcox's untimely death in September 2000. Remaining on *Man Alive* until the mid-1960's, Esther's career path was to change dramatically with the arrival of Canadian born actor and comedian Bernard Braden.

Braden moved his successful ITV satirical entertainment series *On The Braden Beat* to the BBC in 1967 under the new title *Braden's Week*. Originally contracted as a junior director, it didn't take Braden long to realise that Esther's talents didn't lie behind the camera but in front of it. This made Esther even more determined to succeed in this male dominated business, not just for her own career prospects but for every female who came after her. Indeed it could be said that standing up for a cause would be something that would ultimately surround her whole career.

When Braden decided to return to his native Canada in 1972 the BBC was forced to replace the show with a similar consumer affairs programme and Esther was chosen to front it. *That's Life* reigned supreme on the BBC from 1973 to 1994 and helped to bridge the gap between consumer affairs and Light Entertainment dealing with everything from high food prices to talking dogs. The first series of *That's Life* didn't do terribly well in the ratings which forced Esther to ask the then controller of BBC One, Alistair Milne if she could have increased editorial control over the show's output. Milne accepted and *That's Life* regained the raw approach which made *Braden's Week* so successful. Working with the same producer, John Lloyd it was relatively easy for both the cast and crew to return to original values which had served them well. Beyond entertainment, *That's Life* also had a strong conscience for standing up to human poverty and in the days before lavish television appeals, raised awareness for those who needed support. In 1986 the series was responsible for the creation of a brand new charity campaign inspired by the death of a toddler from starvation whilst locked in a bedroom. Esther was appalled and quickly set about a charity which would offer children a lifeline. ChildLine has gone on to help and support over four million children in the UK and was a major factor in Esther's damehood in the 2015 New Year's honours.

Esther's determination to take a stand and support children with ChildLine wasn't her first major contribution. Previously, in November 1980, following a successful Christmas Day television appeal the year before, *BBC Children In Need* was launched. The seven hour extravaganza was broadcast live from the BBC and was ground-breaking for the corporation. Yet things didn't start smoothly as seconds into transmission all the equipment went down and Esther and her co-host Terry Wogan were faced with the real prospect of having to fill for what would have been the next seven hours. Luckily the production crew was able to restore everything back to normal and the show continued. In the hands of more inexperienced broadcasters it may have been in serious doubt as to the show's recovery. Esther and Terry provided safe hands to steady the ship, eventually making it one of the corporation's greatest accomplishments.

Pioneering new format shows had been a feature of her career. Back in 1976 Esther fronted the documentary series *The Big Time* which followed the lives of members of the public attempting to fulfil their dreams. In an era before reality television, the series provided a platform for potential entertainers to showcase their talents in a bid to mimic the show's title and hit the big time. Among the line-up was a singer called Sheena Easton who captured the audience's imagination and achieved a Number One hit with *9 To 5* in 1980. Yet Easton wasn't the only entertainer to be given a platform by Esther as following a successful performance on ITV's *New Faces,* future comedy powerhouse, Victoria Wood became the resident pianist on *That's Life* performing her now legendary repertoire of comedy songs. This combination of consumer affairs mixed with Light Entertainment was something revolutionary for its day and paved the way for the topical consumer programmes which we see today.

After *That's Life*, the BBC were determined to keep Esther's unique talents as a broadcaster and had already begun planning new challenges for her. Yet Esther has always been blessed with a substantial level of foresight and had already launched another successful entertainment series. *Hearts Of Gold* honoured members of the public for their good deeds by arranging life changing surprises. In the days before *The Pride Of Britain Awards* this gave a platform to some of Britain's unsung heroes. Running for six years, the series was Esther's brainchild and was something she felt extremely proud of.

In 1996 Esther stepped into the talk show format for her self-titled afternoon vehicle. Determined to steer clear of the outlandish and chaotic structure of Jerry Springer, Esther used her journalistic pedigree to explore the lives of her guests and maintain a light hearted tone throughout. Unlike Jeremy Kyle and his contemporaries, Esther was adamant to keep the show light in order to get everyone on her side. Although *Esther* was classed as a talk show, her vast experience as a journalist and broadcaster allowed her to get an in-depth and accurate portrait of her guests. This in turn made it more enjoyable for both the audience and guests alike as there was a universal positivity that transcended the whole studio. This formula proved popular up until the show's final airing in 2002.

Slowly becoming an elder statesperson of entertainment, Esther once again identified with another vulnerable group in our society who required assistance. In 2012 she founded *The Silver Line,* a 24-hour helpline for all senior citizens to assist with issues from loneliness to financial support. With the slogan, 'No problem too big, no question too small, no need to be alone', *The Silver Line* has quickly become an invaluable helping hand to those in their twilight years. When she's not campaigning for age discrimination, Esther hadn't quite given up her TV career and her Channel 5 series *Esther Rantzen's House Trap* cemented this. It was clear that the veteran broadcaster wasn't going anywhere any time soon. It was great to speak with Dame Esther Rantzen and I can but thank her for so generously giving up her time to talk to me.

# George Layton

For the first two years of *Beyond The Title*, I was essentially flying by the seat of my pants sending out hundreds and hundreds of interview requests in the hope that someone would accept the opportunity to talk about their life and career. Sometimes after receiving an inbox full of polite messages from agents explaining why their client couldn't take part, it was easy to become deflated by the whole process. Yet every so often it was (and still is) so rewarding when someone actually offers me an interview just because they like what I'm attempting to do. This was exactly what happened when I received an email offering me an interview with the legendary George Layton. It is very seldom that I get people offering interviews to me and to be offered this opportunity was too good to turn down. Ever-present within Britain's TV landscape, it felt as though Mr Layton had been a familiar face in my early television selection. Yet it was only when I embarked on the research for this interview that I realised just how much iconic TV Layton had been involved with.

In a glittering career spanning over half a century, actor, writer and director George Layton has remained a permanent fixture on our television screens and helped to define the 1960's kitchen sink generation. We arranged to meet at BFI Southbank where we were lucky enough to be able to use their press room to record the interview. However, it would appear that on that specific day, technology wasn't on our side as towards the end of the interview my PA James realised that the tape recorder had turned itself off, meaning that the fantastic interview which we'd just done had been for nothing. Luckily George agreed to stay around in order to do it all over again and thankfully it proved to be second time lucky! It's a real art to remember everything you've said and make it come over as if this is the first time you've said it, so it was here that I realised I was in the presence of a master of eloquence.

Attending the prestigious Royal Academy of Dramatic Arts (RADA) for two years in 1960 at the age of just eighteen, George was able to hone his craft. Being presented the Emile Littler award for most promising actor, worth £25, and the Dennis Blakelock award for outstanding performance in a minor role which earned him £30, he had enough to buy his first personal telephone. This had severe consequences when sharing a house with two fellow jobbing actors. When waiting to hear back from an audition it would be pot luck as to who would be the first to the phone to accept a role and sometimes roles would be accepted by actors who were never auditioned for the part. This is exactly how George landed his first TV role in *Z Cars* when he answered a call from the legendary Ken Loach at BBC TV Centre who had originally wanted to offer the part to John Lowe but as the old saying goes, 'The early bird catches the worm' and George was able to reap the benefits of being an early riser. Yet Lowe was able to get a part in the same episode which maintained harmony within the house.

His first professional theatre job came when George enrolled in rep at the Belgrade Theatre Coventry. Fresh from RADA, this was invaluable experience as it gave him an insight into the life of a true actor and the gruelling turnaround of performance was frequently rapid. The Belgrade Theatre based itself on the Shakespearean format where a play would be on for a limited amount of time before you were forced to learn a new one. From *Twelfth Night* to *A Midsummer Night's Dream*, George spent six months learning and enjoying the unique disciplines of classical theatre before returning to television. In 1964 he auditioned for the part of Terry Collier in a *Comedy Playhouse* pilot for a new BBC2 sitcom entitled *The Likely Lads* written by future comedy powerhouses Dick Clement and Ian Le Frenais. Unfortunately the pair concluded that George wasn't yet a recognised name to head up a brand new sitcom and eventually gave the role to James Bolam.

Yet they did cast him as a supporting character in the series which gained him the attention of television executives.

By 1969 George was ready to take on a major comedy role as an ITV sitcom came knocking. Being cast as medical student Paul Collier in *Doctor In The House* gave him his first identifiable role which made him a household name. Having been tipped off about the role by his good friend Christopher Timothy, George was so excited at the thought of a TV version of the legendary Dirk Bogart film that he rang the casting director to enquire about a part. The director informed him that they were just casting the students at the present moment and would concentrate on the teaching staff at a later date. At just twenty-seven and still exhibiting childlike features, this stunned the youthful George but he still secured a major role. Yet it wasn't just his acting skills which were being celebrated. He was also writing for the first series, under a pseudonym of Oliver Fry in collaboration with Jonathan Lynn. The most difficult thing about writing a show that you're also starring in is the natural worry that you're giving yourself all the good lines. Yet this didn't halt his passion for writing and deciding to drop the pseudonym after the first series. Ultimately, the character of Paul Collier was written out of the series in 1972 when George moved onto star in another cult sitcom of the day but he continued as part of the writing team until the series came to an end in 1977, with subsequent versions made for the Australian audience in 1980.

Back in 1972 however, George was cast as Bombardier 'Solly' Solomons in Perry and Croft's *It Ain't Half Hot Mum*. Being associated with the sitcom giants Jimmy Perry and David Croft was very important to the development of George's career and he was able to get to know Croft reasonably well, developing a friendship that lasted until Croft's death in 2011. As an actor, George has always been blessed with a great sense of foresight and has been able to determine the right time to leave a successful show. After just two series, George called time on Solly Solomons and *It Ain't Half Hot Mum* but still remembers this time with great affection and more than forty years on, he still delights when people identify him with such a special series.

Beyond acting, George is a celebrated children's author, writing his first collection of short, funny, bittersweet stories about growing up in the Fifties entitled *The Fib* in 1961 to national acclaim and it has since become part of the national school curriculum. The most of the his books, *The Balaclava Story* about a schoolboy called George who really wanted a balaclava to fit in with the rest of his peers. At the end of the school day, he finds a balaclava on the floor and is faced with a dilemma:, does he do the moral thing and hand it in to a teacher or does he keep it for himself? Such a simple idea was to hit home with classrooms full of children throughout the country and in 2006 these stories were collated into a special anniversary celebration of *The Fib* which meant a lot to him.

His writing credentials don't stop at books and sitcoms and in 1980 George created the BBC comedy drama series *Don't Wait Up* starring Nigel Havers and Tony Britton, dealing with life after divorce. Writing for someone of Havers' calibre was a dream for George as he knew instinctively what was expected and trusted his ability to take the words from the page to the screen. This formula proved successful and gave the BBC six popular series until 1990. The trials and tribulations of middle class life had only been portrayed through innocent do-gooders such as Tom and Barbara Good in *The Good Life*. Whereas *Don't Wait Up* was more of a gritty representation of love and marriage, was easily identifiable with its audience and was a contributing factor in the show winning countless awards. Almost forty years on, the show is still fondly remembered by an audience of thoughtful comedy lovers making this one of George's greatest achievements.

An elder statesmen of the Arts, George can now afford to be selective with the parts he secures and recent roles in BBC serials *Doctors* and *EastEnders* have been the fruits of this selectivity. At the time of our interview, George remained excited about future prospects in a career which has already delivered so much success. It was a great honour to meet and interview a figure who has contributed to a substantial body of television drama over the last half century. It seems a huge responsibility to be able to make a consistent contribution to the Arts and as an actor you are forced to cope with extra pressures with the risk of being typecast. Yet for over half a century, George Layton has remained at the forefront of popular culture, whether it's his portrayal of Solly Solomons in *It Ain't Half Hot Mum* or Paul Collier in *Doctor In The House*. In addition to those achievements, George Layton is a lovely man who remains a perfect example of this chapter's heading.

# Melvyn Hayes

In today's transient television culture, longevity is a concept which not many "performers" achieve. But for more than sixty-five years, Melvyn Hayes has been delighting audiences through a multiple of mediums, including film, television and theatre.

Living on the Isle of Wight is somewhat of a hurdle when it comes to finding stars on your doorstep. Surrounded by water, it's easy to conclude that the only celebrities on the island are those from the sailing fraternity. Yet it's also a popular destination for retirement and some of Britain's best loved stars have been known to come south to reap the benefits of island life. My first attempt to interview Melvyn Hayes was when I was writing my documentary on theatrical agents and became interested in hearing his side of the story. However it was bad timing as he was just about to undergo a substantial operation and was forced to decline my invitation to take part. We had previously met briefly at the book launch of a mutual friend on the island but I was too star struck to ask him anything. For some reason, I was in disbelief that the guy from *It Ain't Half Hot Mum* could attend a book launch on a rainy Tuesday night in Shanklin on the Isle of Wight, but his love for show business is so immense that he makes the most of the opportunity to be surrounded by it. It was only a few weeks into *Beyond The Title* that I thought about Melvyn and his promise that when he recovered he would do an interview. Unfortunately by this time my documentary was complete but I was thrilled when he accepted my request to be the third subject on *Beyond The Title*. He definitely helped me set the standard for all future interviews.

One of Melvyn's earliest roles was in the BBC television adaptation of *Billy Bunter of Greyfriars School* before taking the part of Frankie in BBC's influential 1955 science fiction series *Quatermass II*. Thankfully *Quatermass II* was among just a few shows that the BBC didn't wipe during the disposable era of the fifties and sixties and in 2005 it was released on DVD meaning that future generations are now able to enjoy Melvyn's early work. Just six years after Quatermass, the young actor would enjoy more success, securing a role in the 1961 comedy musical *The Young Ones* alongside Cliff Richard. Unbeknown to the cast and crew at the time, this film was able to capture the teenage angst of the day and reflected the social liberation which young people were enjoying. Suddenly rock and roll was becoming part of the British psyche and giving the youth of the country something to be excited about. Following the huge success of Elvis movies such as *Love Me Tender* and then later *Fun In Acapulco*, the British music scene had been crying out for a pop star who could make the seamless transition from Rock 'n' Roll to the big screen. The success of *The Young Ones* spawned a further two movies and Melvyn was delighted to play a leading role in this Cliff Richard movie trilogy.

So it was that two years later, the cast reunited for the 1963 Classic *Summer Holiday* where Hayes was tasked with driving the iconic bus to the edge of the cliff in his part as Cyril the bus driver. Having just half an hour training with a bus driving instructor before flying out to Athens to shoot the exterior scenes Melvyn found himself attempting to navigate the London bus along a narrow track next to a cliff. Under the guidance of director Peter Yates who would go on to create the 1968 mystery thriller *Bullet* starring Robert Vaughan and Steve McQueen, Hayes was forced to take his life in his own hands and trust that the director knew what he was doing. Luckily the apprehension paid off and Melvyn was able to create one of the most iconic scenes of 1960's cinema which he remains extremely proud of. As he says, "It wasn't *Annie, Get Your Gun* but we made an impression on young people's lives."

Returning to television in 1972, Hayes was cast as Gloria in the second hit comedy in the David Croft and Jimmy Perry franchise, *It Ain't Half Hot Mum* alongside Windsor Davies, Michael Bates and Don Estelle. Based on Perry and Croft's shared experiences of the entertainment corps during their separate postings to India during the Second World War, the series followed the Royal Artillery Concert Party based in Deolali, India as they attempted to raise morale for the deployed British troops. Forever theatrical and excitable, Gloria was far more at home on a stage entertaining the troops than he ever was on parade lead by the stern Sergeant Major Williams superbly played by Windsor Davies. The conservative, burly nature of the Sergeant Major was continually perplexed by the absurdity of Melvyn Hayes' Gloria which became one of the most loved aspects of the series. Irrespective of the obvious homosexual undertones, Melvyn remained adamant that Gloria was not gay, he was just theatrical and this became another element of the series which was never resolved. Instead the audience were left to make up their own minds on his sexual orientation and it was somewhat irrelevant to the series. This is the role which has probably defined Hayes' career but that hasn't stopped his love for the character of Gloria and his fellow actors in the show. At the time of our meeting, it had only been a matter of weeks since the tragic passing of the legendary Jimmy Perry, this brought an added emotional dimension to Hayes's responses as it was obvious that Perry's death remained extremely raw for him and the affection that he still holds for the late comedy writer was palpable. To the whole cast Perry was so much more than just a writer, ever-present at each stage of the show's development, his previous career as an actor made it easier for him to empathise with the cast and he often acted as a go-between with cast and crew.

At a time when satire and racism vicariously balanced on the fine line of decency, *It Ain't Half Hot Mum* remains the only sitcom to feature two languages. Actor Michael Bates was fluent in Urdu and so was able to bring a sense of realism to the series. Frequently criticised for its perceived racial stereotypes, *It Ain't Half Hot Mum* essentially celebrated the idiosyncrasies of two opposing cultures and charted the complex relationship between these two nations. The irony is that in every episode the Indians always got the upper hand while the English were always the butt of the jokes so in this case Perry and Croft were actually doing something that was considered revolutionary for its time. That truth of attempting to bring about racial harmony in such a politically volatile era is often overlooked.

Beyond *It Ain't Half Hot Mum*, Melvyn has built up a substantial career in the art of pantomime and live performance. From Mother Goose to Widow Twankey, the Dame has forever been the linchpin of panto and the great and the good of British television have all taken their turn at playing a cartoon version of the opposite sex. Over the years, it could be argued that the art of panto has in some way been trivialised by the influx of in-vogue reality television stars. As one of the 'elder statesman' of entertainment, it must prove increasingly frustrating when you get cast opposite a new reality star who can't sing, dance or be funny. This may be further evidence to suggest that the traditional pantomime could be in decline.

We then briefly returned to the subject of his repertoire of classic films as I had the desire to ask him about the 1985 festive blockbuster Santa Claus: The Movie, where he was cast alongside Dudley Moore and John Lithgow. To my amazement he confessed to have never watched the film himself. I didn't have the heart to reveal that in my family Santa Claus: The Movie is a Christmas institution. Yet it seems a little ironic that I may possess more affection for the film than he does!

In 2003 Melvyn starred alongside fellow sitcom greats including Mollie Sugden and Gorden Kaye for the cult sketch show Revolver in which a gallery of famous faces came together to star in a series of bizarre skits. As a fan of this show, I was interested to find out just how it was made and what it was like being reunited with former colleagues more than thirty years on from the sitcom boom of the 1970's. It was clear that Melvyn shared my love for the show and was bewildered as to why there haven't been more.

Outside show business, Melvyn enjoys a quiet life on the Isle of Wight with his wife and children. Over the last twenty years many local children have benefited from his support and loving nature through him and his wife being foster carers. You can see the joy in his heart when he talks about their many fostering success stories. Even at the age of 85 with a triple heart bypass just eighteen months prior to our interview, it was very easy to see that Melvyn remained a family man and despite vast professional success, his love for his family gets him through all of life's problems.

I thoroughly enjoyed my time with such a star of the big and small screen and was taken aback by his ability to recall situations which took place over half a century ago. If you met Melvyn without knowing anything about his glittering career in entertainment, you could be excused from thinking he was a retired dentist or perhaps a librarian, such is his humbleness about his accomplishments. It's only when he starts recalling the stories of his past that you realise you are in the presence of a British showbiz great. Irrespective of where Beyond The Title takes me in the future, I shall always be grateful for the moments spent him.

# Ray Galton OBE and Alan Simpson OBE

Legendary sitcom writers Ray Galton and Alan Simpson originally met in a sanatorium while recovering from TB and thus began a union which lasted over sixty years. In 1953 the pair joined friends Spike Milligan and Eric Sykes in the formation of Associated London Scripts – Britain's first scriptwriting agency. Such a creative hotbed of talent spurred a formidable output of work and it wasn't long before performers wanted to join this centre of talent. Mixing with the likes of Tony Hancock, Frankie Howerd and Peter Sellers, Ray and Alan were at the forefront of British comedy and it wasn't long before radio came calling. Just a year later, Galton and Simpson found themselves with a hit BBC Radio comedy on their hands in the form of the bittersweet *Hancock's Half Hour*. In 1956 *Hancock's Half Hour* made a successful move from radio to the relatively unknown medium of television and helped the British audience fall in love with the art of situation comedy.

The controversial decision for Galton and Simpson and Hancock to part company in 1961 was something which ultimately cost Tony Hancock his career as he failed to find anyone who knew the character of Anthony Aloysius Hancock better than the two people who created him. Yet the duo were already at work on another sitcom as part of the new BBC *Comedy Playhouse;* their own BBC Comedy series in which they penned six self-contained episodes starring some of the cream of British comedy. *Comedy Playhouse* went on to be a playground for both new and experienced writers to create pilots of potential series. One episode entitled "The Offer" surrounded the bittersweet relationship between father and son rag 'n' bone men; Albert and Harold Steptoe. The episode struck a chord with the public and a series was promptly commissioned. *Steptoe and Son* would survive in its many guises until 1974, despite the notoriously thwarted real-life relationship between actors Wilfred Brambell and Harry H Corbett and the genius of the writing elevated Ray Galton and Alan Simpson into comedy superstars.

Following the style of *Comedy Playhouse,* Ray & Alan were twice given their own single half hour series, in 1969 by London Weekend Television, *The Galton and Simpson Comedy* and in 1977 by Yorkshire Television, *The Galton and Simpson Playhouse,* always attracting a stellar line-up of cast members. In the mid-nineties, the pair teamed up with Paul Merton for two series which included some Hancock scripts thus paying tribute to the man with whom they started their glittering career.

In 2010 I had the absolute honour to interview Ray Galton and Alan Simpson about their unparalleled career in comedy and their dealings with various members of BBC management. The interview was part of research for a biographical drama script I was creating based on the life and work of Sir Bill Cotton. Yet being in the presence of two of the icons of British entertainment, it would have been a crime not to have touched upon their own glittering career. Over half an hour, the pair waxed lyrical about their life, career and professional partnership which I feel extremely fortunate to have witnessed. The stars they worked with, TV senior management who they worked under, they seemed to have a phenomenal photographic memory for everything. Stories about the early days of *Steptoe and Son* were fascinating to hear. I was in my element speaking to these two heroes of British comedy and hearing them bouncing off each other was really very special. The Bill Cotton theme suddenly became irrelevant because the opportunity to interview two of the greats of British comedy firmly overtook my ongoing research.

Sadly due to ill health, from this point Galton and Simpson decided to shy away from the spotlight with the exception of May 2016 when they emotionally accepted the BAFTA Fellowship via a pre-recorded acceptance speech. Tragically this was the last public appearance for Alan before his sad death in February 2017, followed by the passing of Ray just eighteen months later. I remain extremely grateful to have had a unique insight into the world of British comedy from this legendary writing partnership and for it to have been my first ever interview, I feel so blessed.

# Chapter Two – Television's coming of age

Following the generation of variety stars who had proved it possible for television to be part of everyday life, executives were desperate to see the new medium reach its fullest potential. This subtle change in the attitudes towards the art gave way to a new era in BBC senior management which ultimately resulted in a new generation of stars who were ready to push the medium to uncharted territory. Yet it would be some time before this cultural revolution came to fruition. In the meantime the new wave angst still managed to rock the very foundations of the showbiz establishment.

The first generation of televisual viewer was now approaching middle age and another demographic was putting heavy demands on entertainment. Throughout the early seventies, while the older generation were content on watching traditional variety shows of the day such as *The Morecambe and Wise Show* or *The Two Ronnies,* teenagers longed for Light Entertainment which represented their needs, desires and lifestyle. No longer was it appropriate for comics to recycle second hand mother-in-law jokes which had been doing the rounds for generations. This new, younger demographic were crying out to be comedically challenged like never before.

In contrast to the effect that punk was having on the British music scene, this invasion would have severe consequences for both the political and entertainment establishment. With the social unrest of the 1970's which began with the substantial rise in unemployment and resulted in the three day week, people were in desperate need of quality entertainment to provide a light interlude to the problems they were facing. To do this, television executives attempted to find entertainers who echoed this social change and placed them alongside recognised faces in a bid to offer something for everyone. This selection of entertainment was a novelty for the British audience and while the economic future looked bleak, television was arguably at its peak.

Paying homage to the transatlantic sense of humour, this group had ambitions of showing audiences something completely different. One liners were cast aside and in came the art of comedy storytelling which was proving popular on the American comedy circuit. The current doyen of BBC Light Entertainment, Dave Allen had since made a whole career of this relatively new art proving that the public liked this deviation on the ancient form. But now the new generation was determined to take this to heights which had never before been reached. Yet it would be a few more years before this style became the bedrock of BBC comedy but when it did, TV never looked back.

Working Men's clubs predominantly in the north of England surprisingly played an important role in the development of this new brand of entertainment and such acts could be found on the same bill as traditional front of cloth comics. This remains a fascinating era to study for its constant struggle with its own identity and on reflection the period somewhat stands alone as an example of when entertainment stood still. Indeed geography would play a vital part in the popularity of this new art form and just like old school entertainers, these people were forced to create a following in their specific area of the country. Over time the influx of such entertainers made its way onto television and offered something new. Theatrical variety was considered a dying art but it would be several years before the revolution of Alternative Comedy had taken hold. So in terms of comedy and Light Entertainment the late 1970's proved to be somewhat of a wilderness era. Yet it was still able to create iconic moments which would leave an indelible mark on popular culture.

Such a revolutionary attitude towards television carried itself forward into other genres and soon executives brushed aside their conservative values and made television which catered for a broad audience. For the first time television became "self-aware" and could boast a definite cultural heritage. Children's TV had long since been undervalued in its power to inform and educate, and efforts were made to update the genre to echo the social context of the time. In 1976 the BBC made the bold decision to devote the Saturday morning schedule to the children of Britain who had been televisually cast aside when it came to weekend programming. *Multi-coloured Swap Shop* was first broadcast on the 2nd October of that year and became an instant hit paving the way for Saturday morning television for the next thirty years. Just a year later, due to the show's undoubted success, ITV created a show to rival Noel and his team of future stars.

Suddenly Children's television had upped its game and no longer was it acceptable to make programmes which only parents would like. Such a radical ethos even extended to the BBC's flagship children's series *Blue Peter* which was considered quite twee compared to the outlandish output of the day. It was promptly decided that a new adventurous line-up was what the show needed to bring it in line with its exciting contemporaries...it was very clear that times were changing!

The 1970's was responsible for the start of an obvious shift in entertainment and the gradual awareness of the requirements of diversity and choice in our popular culture. Never had television been lumbered with so much responsibility in realising its true power to change the world. Therefore in many ways this "middle" generation had it harder than most but the enormous affection which the public had for the shows and presenters of then arguably remains unrivalled and the following examples are glowing testaments of this.

# Chris Tarrant OBE

It's difficult to overlook the vast contribution that Chris Tarrant has made to public service broadcasting over the last forty years, whether it's assisting with the development of regional television in the north of England in the early 1970's, pioneering the Saturday morning children's entertainment landscape of the late seventies or reinventing the primetime game show for modern Britain. You would think to interview someone of this calibre would take months and months of research to hone the knowledge in order to condense such an illustrious career into just ten questions. However, on receiving an email from his agent on a wet December afternoon with an offer of a phone interview with the great man the following morning, I only had an evening to perfect a list of questions for a broadcasting institution. Although I was obviously on a tight deadline, there was something enjoyable about going back over Tarrant's remarkable career and realising just how many television landmarks the broadcaster has spawned. A lot of the research felt like revisiting my own TV past and it was at this moment I realised just how significant Tarrant's contribution to popular culture has been. Whether it's *Tarrant On TV*, *Pop Quiz* or *Who Wants To Be a Millionaire?*, the broadcaster came to define my childhood and I just couldn't believe that he was now on the other end of the phone. In many ways his career has charted the changing face of television entertainment and how producers gradually exploited television to its full extent.

I started how I like to start each and every interview; at the very beginning. Starting his career as a newsreader for *ATV Today* in 1972 alongside Bob Warman and Anne Diamond, Tarrant quickly became comfortable in front of the camera and thrived upon the fast paced style of live television. This was the era when Breakfast television was still considered a new phenomenon and daytime TV was merely a pipe dream. Tasked with covering the more light hearted stories, Chris found himself traveling all over the country in the quest to get right to the heart of a story. For a young broadcaster this was an invaluable introduction to the world of television and gave Chris the basic tools and techniques for a life in British broadcasting.

Just two years later, the ATV Network launched *TISWAS*, the long awaited children's entertainment series which would attempt to rival the BBC's *Multi-coloured Swap Shop*. Originally hired as a producer on *TISWAS*, it wasn't long before Chris was promoted to presenter alongside Sally James and Lenny Henry. Being the only member of the team with broadcasting experience, it fell to Chris to anchor the programme. Yet it could be said that this was about as far removed from the serious nature of *ATV Today* as one could get, instead it was unorganised chaos and the only structure came when they were forced to adhere to the commercial break format. Going up against Noel and Swap Shop was an enjoyable experience for all the *TISWAS* team but they soon became conscious that there was a significant geographical divide between them. Generally, children from the south tended to favour Swap Shop while northern kids would opt for *TISWAS*. For over eight years Chris, Lenny and Sally welcomed the biggest stars in the world to join in on the fun which centred around allowing children to get one over on adults. Classic sketches including Lenny reading the news with Trevor McDonald have become part of the national psyche and despite his considerable accomplishments, *TISWAS* remains the first subject that people want to know about when meeting Tarrant. It's clear that this remains one of his greatest achievements in a long and glittering career.

Not content with conquering the art of television, Chris joined Capital Radio in 1984 initially chairing the Sunday luncheon programme before replacing David Jensen on weekday mornings. From March 1987 until April 2004 he presented the breakfast show to critical acclaim which frequently beat his major rivals; *Wake up to Wogan* and The *Radio 1 Breakfast Show*. To present a daily radio show for over fifteen years and consistently be in the running for the most listened to show in the country is no mean feat. This is testimony to Chris's talent as a broadcaster in breaking down the discourse of presenter and audience and make it feel extremely personal to each and every listener. As a Breakfast presenter, you have specific responsibilities which are unique to early morning radio such as traffic updates and newspaper reviews. Therefore it falls to the Breakfast presenter to make seamless transitions between each item and while others see this as an infringement on their individual style, Chris relished the opportunity to make his links as engaging as possible. Despite his vast television credentials, this remains one of Chris's greatest achievements.

Maintaining his television presence in 1991, Chris inherited Clive James' *On Television* and thus launched *Tarrant On TV* which celebrated the bizarre and wackiness of television around the world. Attempting to always find the fine line between gentle jostling and xenophobia, Chris saw his role as merely a reporter tasked with presiding over the footage. Any derogatory observations were completely created by the audience and for over ten years this was the winning formula of the series. This was one of the first programmes to explore alternative television from all over the world and gave an insight into how other countries tackled different types of entertainment. In an age before YouTube, *Tarrant On TV* became one of the only outlets for hilarious, outrageous videos and spawned a whole host of replica shows including the BBC's *Commercial Breakdown*, yet they failed to recreate the magic of Tarrant's original show. Maybe because of Chris's unique connection with the British public?

A switch to the BBC in 1994 to replace fellow DJ Mike Read for the early evening *Pop Quiz* was new territory for Chris as for the first time he wasn't part of the production team. Despite being surrounded by some of the biggest music stars in the world, taking over an already established show was something that Chris found difficult. For Chris to feel at home on a show, he's required to take charge over every aspect and being merely the new presenter, the dynamics didn't work. After just nine episodes, Chris decided to call it a day on *Pop Quiz* and promptly returned to ITV for the Saturday night game show *Man O' Man*. This was a dating show which was years before it's time with the same philosophy as Tinder but with a lot less anonymity. Each week ten eligible bachelors would stand beside a swimming pool hoping to impress the lucky girl. As merely an observer and commentator, Chris found it extraordinary to see how women behaved when coming face to face with the subject of their sexual desires. If they could conquer the final round and outdo model Kevin with a display of moving their muscles in time with the music then they would be in for winning the all-important star prize. So important that we've forgotten what it was! Despite its bizarre format, Chris loved doing *Man O' Man* and was sad when it came to an end in 1999.

Just a year before the final series of *Man O' Man*, Chris's producer at Capital, David Briggs came to him with an idea for a new game show. Fifteen multiple choice questions with four possible answers which led to a substantial jackpot giveaway. They had already played around with a similar format on the radio show but now were looking to launch it on a wider scale. *Who Wants To Be a Millionaire* was first broadcast on the 4th September 1998 to huge audiences as everyone sat intrigued as contestants chosen by who had the fastest finger, attempted to answer questions under a significant spotlight and tense music. Adhering to ITV's commercial break structure, Chris realised that he had the power to prolong the tension by going to a break when someone had just uttered those now immortal words "final answer". At first the producers were extremely apprehensive as to how easily the contestants would answer all fifteen questions. Yet when they were under pressure of being live on television in front of a studio audience, spotlights and music, it was so difficult to find the right answer.

Just five people went on to claim the jackpot, the first being Judith Keppel in 2000 who went on to be a successful television personality in her own right, appearing on BBC2's *Eggheads*. Yet it wasn't just the general public who thought they could win the jackpot. Over the years an array of stars from Alan Sugar, Carol Vorderman to Alex Ferguson and Paul McCartney had the chance to test their general knowledge and attempt to win a million pounds for their chosen charities. By the show's sign off in 2014, more than 1,840 members of the public sitting in the hotseat with prize money totalling almost £60,000,000.

In 2017 Chris found himself back on the road in Channel *Five's Extreme Railway Journeys*. For this he travels all over the world experiencing how other countries use railway systems. It was a great pleasure catching up with the one and only Chris Tarrant and I hope he continues to grace our airwaves for a long time.

## Jasper Carrott OBE

It could be said that the history of British Comedy is as diverse and wide ranging as the stars which it has spawned. The first era of post war comedy was dominated by Variety acts who had come up through the theatrical circuit and thrived upon playing to audiences with familiar routines which some comics stayed true to throughout their whole career. Yet by the early 1970's times were changing; Variety theatres closed, stars faded and gave way to a new brand of comedy. Working Men's clubs were now where people flocked when they wanted a laugh but it wasn't just comedy that was changing. The resurgence of Folk music became another catalyst for this minor revolution and if by chance you could attempt to mix the two, you were definitely the dish of the day. Nowadays it's impossible to imagine the obvious correlation between folk music and comedy but forty years ago it somehow became the norm.

Writer and comedian, but firstly a folk singer, Jasper Carrott was looking to do exactly that starting in his hometown of Birmingham. These were still the days when ITV was broken up into geographical areas around the UK and each region boasted their own brand of entertainment. With the exception of Granada, Jasper was lucky enough to secure a spot on each television region performing his early material which gained him a following and started to open many doors. Suddenly his stand-up routine became the most popular part of his act and he found himself headlining live comedy shows throughout Britain. Gradually he put an end to his music career as he started developing a cult following among working class audiences. He recalls on one specific occasion that his support act was none other than the late great Victoria Wood – something that seems almost implausible to imagine today when she is heralded as such an icon of comedy. This was testimony to Jasper's popularity and unbeknown to him, he was helping to create and champion a brand new generation of comedians.

So when I discovered that I had secured an interview with this comedy powerhouse I couldn't wait to ask him his thoughts on his pivotal contribution in changing the British comedy landscape. Following an unexpected invitation from his agent just days before, I met Mr Carrott at The Lighthouse Theatre in Poole where he was performing as part of the southern leg of his 2018 tour. I had received instructions to be there for 6pm when we could have a fifteen minute slot. So me and my PA Will made the familiar trip down to Poole meticulously looking at the digital clock on the dashboard of my car and saw the time edging ever closer to the designated appointment as we irritatingly became gridlocked in Friday afternoon rush hour traffic. As a nervous driver, I didn't want to add to Will's problems by keeping on mentioning the time as I knew there was very little that either he or I could do about it. Instead we both sat silently staring at the clock wondering if we would ever get there in time. Fortunately we drove up to the theatre with just minutes to spare but it had reduced our chances of getting more than a quarter of an hour with a comedy institution.

I was in absolutely no doubt that comedy gigs are notoriously extremely tight for time and once rehearsals, sound checks, refreshments are out the way, there can sometimes be little time for anything else, so it was very good of Jasper to make the time for me. When his agent arrived, he reinforced the fifteen minute time limit as they still had a lot to do before the show started so I knew that it would ultimately be up to me to prioritise my questions. When we eventually met, I was struck by how relaxed Jasper was about the whole thing and if we had met him without anything that went before, it would have been easy to think that he had all the time in the world. But of course he didn't and the stern face of his agent lurking in the corner was a stark reminder of this.

Normally when writing interviews, I order my questions in terms of putting my subject at ease while charting the landmarks of their career. Yet having been intrigued by this generation of comics for some time, I just had to go straight in and ask him his thoughts on where this period fitted into the story of British entertainment and how his generation bridged the gap between the variety era and alternative comedy. On hearing this, his eyes lit up as he licked his lips - clearly this was something that he was most passionate about. "Good question," he said as he took a sip of water and looked ponderous. It was here that he explained that his rise to fame coincided with the rise of comedy storytelling thanks to the talents of Billy Connolly and Mike Harding.

Such a minor revolution in Comedy was a substantial shock for performers and audiences alike. This generation had grown up on theatrical Variety but unlike their forefathers, they didn't need to go to the theatre to watch it because it was now a firm fixture of British television. Yet this formulaic, traditional style of comedy wasn't for everyone and those who required a far more edgy sense of humour were forced to look further afield for comedy which more represented them. Jasper was influenced by the great American comics including Bob Newhart and Tom Lehrer who would manage to create a dialogue with their audience instead of merely rattling off one liners. It was here that Jasper realised the direction in which he wanted to take his career.

Determined to set himself apart from the traditional stand-up comedy which was then dominated by jokes about mother-in-law's and Irishmen, Jasper always wanted to do something different. The socioeconomic outlook of the seventies offered little positivity for the youth and led to an uprising by this unheard demographic to rebel against the fixed social concepts which their forefathers merely accepted. This spilled over into television and suddenly audiences longed for something different. The sea change which Jimmy Tarbuck was referring to when I met him was obviously taking hold and while it proved problematic with Tarbuck's generation, Jasper was thriving upon creating a dialogue and highlighting shared experiences with an audience. This was a relatively new concept for British audiences and something that would have been considered a gamble in the mid-seventies. Yet with formidable figures including Jasper alongside fellow performers Connolly, Harding and Victoria Wood at the forefront, it was a sure sign of a success.

By 1978 Jasper had caught the attention of a number of influential television executives throughout the county as the comedy sea change continued to grow. Michael Grade, now Head of Light Entertainment at LWT had the desire to add him to the prestigious list of stars which became the subject of their own *An Audience With*. Usually reserved for established stars, this was the ultimate accolade and helped to catapult Jasper into the Light Entertainment mainstream. The show was seen by BBC executives who were quick to sign the young comic and offered him a prime time television vehicle. *Candid Carrott* was a sketch and stand-up show written and performed by Jasper, but it wasn't long before the show demanded bigger and better. A serial element was introduced to the format which offered it a different dimension in the same way that *The Two Ronnies* had The Phantom Raspberry Blower Of Old London Town and The Worm That Turned.

For this, Jasper penned a five minute spoof paying homage to famous cop shows of the 1970's. Such a dual protagonist sketch required an actor of a certain calibre to complement the comic timing of the star of the show. In the prep meeting with the producer, names of prominent actors were branded around until a producer uttered the immortal line "We need someone like Robert Powell". Instantly finding a telephone, Jasper had failed to disclose that Robert was a very good friend and made one phone call to secure the part. The sketch was so successful that the BBC brought two writers, Steven Wright and Mike Whitehill to transform this small sketch into a series of six sitcom episodes. Going on to run for four years on prime time BBC1, *The Detectives* starring Jasper alongside Robert Powell became a family favourite thanks in part to a fantastic supporting cast including George Sewell. The series followed the antics of "partners in crime" Bob Louis, played by Jasper and Powell's David Briggs as they attempted to solve ridiculous crimes.

Despite sitcom success, Jasper has always remained true to his stand-up roots and in 2018 was back on tour with a brand new show stand-up and Rock. Slowly becoming an elder statesman of comedy, Jasper exhibits no signs of slowing down and the flocks of people who queue up to see the great man do what he does best illustrates the great affection which the country still has for him. As an entertainment historian, it was fascinating to meet a figure with such a defining role in the evolution of British comedy and it may not have been the longest interview but the subjects covered were loaded with enough information to fill an entire book. Unfortunately I've only got room for one chapter but Mr Carrott certainly has a fascinating tale to tell. It was a great pleasure to meet one of the most interesting characters in comedy and I hope you'll agree that his story is just as dynamic and colourful as his comedy creations.

# Richard Digance

The 1970's remains a fascinating era for comedy historians as a result of the gentle deviation away from traditional front of cloth entertainment which the public had been bred on for generations. Suddenly audiences demanded something different as the baby boomers grew up with a totally new kind of taste in entertainment. The influx of underground folk music would have a dominant influence on the new showbiz landscape as Variety was slowly replaced by comedy storytelling. This revolution was quick to gather momentum and suddenly captivated every region of Britain. Pioneered by Billy Connolly in Scotland and Mike Harding and Jasper Carrott in the midlands, such a movement required a southern representative and by the mid-seventies they had one.

Writer and musician Richard Digance began his career as a singer/songwriter, performing comedy songs in and around the London area during the late 1960's. Before long he realised that the patter he created in between songs was going down well with his audiences. Popular with teenagers and students, this style of entertainment gathered momentum and in time would be the new Rock 'n' Roll. The rise of university review was vital to the development of Richard's career as he had a very definite audience who easily related to the messages in his songs. Such a following sustained his career throughout the 1970's as he toured around the UK and further afield, supporting some of the world's greatest artists.

My fascination with this era has always inspired the calibre of my subjects for *Beyond The Title* and when I discovered that the comedian was performing on the other side of the water in Southampton I realised that this was the perfect opportunity to attempt an interview with the versatile performer. I then promptly looked him up on Social Media and found his profile. Adding a celebrity on Facebook is always a gamble because, not knowing you from Adam, they have absolutely no reason to accept a request from you. Indeed I've also found myself declining many a random friend request, so it was a pleasant surprise when, within a few hours, Richard had accepted my request meaning that I would have an instant link to the man himself. Looking on his profile I saw he had a gig that coming Friday just across the water in Southampton and I promptly asked him for an interview prior to the show. I couldn't believe my luck when he confirmed our meeting and managed to free up some time prior to his gig for a quick interview…I was going to meet the great Richard Digance in person.

Just days later, my PA Ian and I found ourselves at an Arts centre on the outskirts of Southampton in preparation to interview the evergreen entertainer. On arrival it seemed that we had got the wrong place as there was something very spiritual about the theatre which had far more in common with a church than an entertainment venue. Meeting Richard Digance for the first time is a complete revelation as he's nothing like his on screen persona. Reserved, thoughtful and extremely humble, you would be excused for confusing him with a retired doctor or teacher for the simple fact that he remains a normal guy who obviously loves what he does.

It's difficult to convey to the TV audience of the 2020s just how big a star Richard Digance was during the eighties and nineties and sadly his contribution to Light Entertainment seems wrongly forgotten in today's transient TV culture. I remember him on various guest spots alongside the great Bob Monkhouse and although he didn't have a memorable TV vehicle, he would always feature on the top shows of the day. So my interest in Richard dates back to my early childhood and it was inconceivable to think that now he was sitting opposite me ready to answer my questions.

We recorded the interview in the small, intimate and rustic auditorium as Richard drank his tea and prepared for his show. Touring is in his blood and the anticipation to get on stage was almost palpable. There are some entertainers who avoid analysis of their industry and only live for the few moments they are on stage, while others love to fully explore the world in which they live in. Fortunately for the success of the interview, Richard falls into the latter category which was music to my ears. Like always, I had prepared a set of questions for Ian to deliver in his best Michael Parkinson voice. Yet I soon realised that the interview was about to deviate in fantastic fashion. Our shared love for some of the icons of British comedy gave the interview a natural flow and it felt like we had known each other for years.

The opportunity to support the comedian Steve Martin on an American stadium tour was too good to turn down. It was here that Digance learned the real disciplines of show business from this comedy giant who taught him the true meaning of humility. Martin's innate ability to switch between his on and off screen persona was something that really appealed to the Digance and the pair soon developed a rapport. Richard was in awe of his ability to create a larger than life persona for the screen which endeared him to millions while preserving his real life image of a shy, introverted individual. As a reserved soul himself, Richard was able to identify with this method and inherit a similar technique for himself.

Returning to the UK Richard secured appearances on the BBC's seminal late night music show *The Old Grey Whistle Test*. By this time, the comedic patter which had proved popular in the northern working men's clubs and also throughout the USA was a firm staple of his set. Being the only act on the show to offer such an interlude to straight music, Digance was invited to appear on a follow up episode presented by 'whispering' Bob Harris. This provided invaluable grounding for Richard to get comfortable with the medium which he would go on to make a formidable contribution to in the years to come.

Joining Thames Television in 1983 secured Richard his first TV special *A Dabble With Digance* featuring newsreader Carol Barnes. This was the springboard to TV success which resulted in him collaborating with names that included Jimmy Tarbuck, Cilla Black, Bob Monkhouse and Jim Davidson. His first BBC comedy appearance came on a 1987 episode of *The Ronnie Corbett Show* which meant a lot to the *Two Ronnies* fan and brought him to the attention of TV executives. A string of TV appearances followed Richard into the nineties where he became one of the biggest stars on the box. Yet a love of theatre and live performance always lured Richard back to his main love, the art of live performance and by 1996 he was ready for a change.

Casting television aside during the mid-nineties, Richard was back on the road with his trusted guitar doing what he does best. When he wasn't touring, he wrote a repertoire of books regaling stories from a life in entertainment. As a songwriter he has penned scores for TV theme tunes including the BBC's *Countryfile*. Over twenty albums of comedy songs sold worldwide, Digance has now a whole back catalogue of music which he regularly performs to live audiences throughout the UK. For him, the thrill of performing is to witness the joy in the audience's eyes brought on by either one of his quick one liners or a humorous ditty. This is what maintains his youth and even at the age of seventy, it was clear to see that the comedian was still hopelessly in love with what he does. It was an absolute honour to meet and interview Richard Digance and with a formidably fascinating career behind him, he has become one of the cult figures of comedy and his story rivals any showbiz icon.

# Peter Duncan

 British television is packed full of
nostalgic figures and moments which
viewers take ownership of and which
help to define a generation by
representing the fashion and fads of the
time. The presenters in such moments
take on a cult like status which never
really goes away, forever reminding
viewers of their innocent youth when life
was simpler. For a certain generation of
television fans, Peter Duncan shall forever symbolise the flagship BBC
children's entertainment series *Blue Peter*. Despite his and his colleagues
many accomplishments post children television, they will forever epitomise
the magic of kids TV. Sadly, I am *far* too young to remember Peter Duncan
at the peak of his *Blue Peter* supremacy but the manner in which this era
remains fondly remembered meant an opportunity to interview a figure of
this calibre was too good to turn down.

We met Peter at the Lighthouse Theatre in Poole where he spends the
majority of his time, directing and producing Christmas pantomimes. We
agreed to meet up around late morning as Poole is only forty-five minutes
from the ferry in Southampton and having lived in the Bournemouth area
for four years, I was familiar with the route. Yet on that specific day, traffic
wasn't on our side and we ended up getting to the theatre two hours later
than we originally expected. I really hate being late for my interviews

because I'm too aware that my subjects are some of the busiest people in the country and they have many commitments to fulfil, so time is at a premium. I asked my PA James to ring Peter and explain our situation, whereupon he completely understood and graciously agreed to meet us later in the day.

On first meeting Peter Duncan it's easy to forget that he is of a certain age as he still has the enthusiasm and zest for life of a twenty year old and this was evident just by the way he presented himself; youthful smile, modern attire and a constant presence on Social Media all are indicators of a guy who doesn't feel his age. When we finally sat down to get the interview started, Peter started asking questions about me and what I did. It was obvious that he wanted to know as much about me as I did about him. It was here I discovered that he had made a documentary with fellow *Blue Peter* star, Simon Groom surrounding the life of Joey Deacon, a sixty year old man with Cerebral Palsy back in 1980 following a *Horizon* programme on the same subject. This promptly led to a *Blue Peter* appeal which raised vital funds to build three adapted bungalows in the grounds of St Lawrence Hospital where Joey regularly attended.

Having explored that, we then began the interview proper and kicked-off with the fact that Peter had turned the *Blue Peter* role down two years prior to making his debut on the show in 1980 alongside Sarah Greene and Simon Groom. Attempting to recreate the magic of the memorable trio of John Noakes, Valerie Singleton and Peter Purves, the producers were looking to cast someone with a theatrical background to fulfil the variety element of the show. By this time Peter was almost a decade into a varied and successful acting career which brought him into contact with acting royalty including Sir Laurence Olivier.

Making his debut at fifteen, playing the part of Jim Hawkins in Treasure Island at the Mermaid Theatre in the heart of London's West End, Peter was quick to catch the acting bug. His parents had been involved in vaudeville entertainment ever since Peter was young and frequently held amateur pantomimes which united the whole community. It was here that Peter saw the effects that entertainment had in rallying support and enjoying shared laughter. Through panto his parents got to know some of the icons of Variety and he found himself surrounded by performers such as Danny La Rue who would have a lasting impact on him. Despite being in awe of Danny's style, Peter knew he wanted to do something different.

Peter then secured a two year stint at the National Theatre under the influence of Olivier. Despite enrolling at the Italia Conti Academy of Music several years previously, Peter admits that this period taught him the most about the business. It was here that he met his first girlfriend; the actress Lesley Manville (now better known for playing the starring role in the BBC Two sitcom *Mum*). Unknowingly attending the same school, the pair only met here and despite an amicable split, Peter and Lesley remain firm friends and are always on hand to celebrate each other's successes. He was delighted when Lesley was nominated for an Oscar at the 2018 event for her role in Paul Thomas-Anderson's period romantic drama Phantom Thread. It's clear that irrespective of his numerous achievements, Peter will forever be grateful to The National Theatre for making him into the all-round performer he is today.

Making his debut in the production of White Devil, Peter remained at The National performing alongside true giants of the stage including Derek Jacobi and Maggie Smith. In 1980 Peter was cast as a young tree man in the cult movie, Flash Gordon which gained him a new following of fans. Although his appearance was all too brief and resulted in the character's death, he remains synonymous with the film and over thirty five years later is astonished by the love still felt for the movie. This was also the year that Peter finally accepted the presenting role on *Blue Peter* and for four years defined a generation for eighties school children. Appearing on such a long running programme with so many loved presenters demands you to put your own stamp on it and together with Sarah Greene and Simon Groom, Peter set about doing exactly that. As an actor, Peter wasn't scared to go out of his comfort zone and so was able to embrace the challenges and trials which were put his way, making him the show's new 'action man', in the mould of John Noakes.

After *Blue Peter*, Peter starred in a series of travelogues for the BBC in which he took his family to a variety of locations around the world. *Travel Bug* which aired in 1999, followed the Duncan family on a six month vacation to some of the most desirable places on Earth. This was followed up with two further series for Channel Five and Sky and is one of Peter's proudest achievements. To capture your family at a specific moment in time is a very special thing and since Peter's family have all grown up and got lives of their own now, the show is a touching reminder of days gone by.

In recent years, Peter has returned to the stage and has even dabbled in producing and directing productions for Poole Lighthouse. Most recently writing, producing and directing his interpretation of Aladdin for Christmas 2017. At the time of our interview, he was still receiving accolades for his theatrical work yet still had dreams of securing that all important television drama role and only time will tell if he would achieve it. However, from his glittering career, even if a major role doesn't materialise, it's impossible to ignore Duncan's impact upon the Arts and his substantial legacy.

Like most evergreen stars, Peter remains both humble and modest regarding his many professional achievements and being in his company, you would never know what a versatile and talented artist he is. Yet for a generation, he encapsulated their dreams and aspirations of being an adult and remains a symbol of a carefree life. Irrespective of his vast accomplishments, Peter shall forever be part of an elite team who inspired and captured the imaginations of millions of children throughout the country and helped to define 1980's Britain. Although I'm sadly too young to be part of that era, I shall forever be honoured to have this insight into the workings of television from such an iconic figure. It was an absolute pleasure to meet Peter Duncan and I wish him continued success.

# Steve Nallon

The art of impressionism has been a popular pastime for centuries and whilst most people have the innate ability to imitate others, it takes a highly talented individual to take the recognisable character traits from another and project it onto a stage for maximum comedic effect. This ancient art form went from a casual "in-joke" which united a community to the bedrock of 1970's Light Entertainment as Britain's love affair with impersonation reached new levels. Finally, what had been a staple of theatrical variety was now slowly making the successful transition onto television and figures like Mike Yarwood and Stanley Baxter became household names.

Comic, puppeteer and impressionist Steve Nallon has been making Britain laugh for over three decades in theatre, radio and television. In his own words he is "a turn" and in an age where Variety is considered by many to be dead, he remains a shining example of an all-round entertainer. I met up with Steve in central London following connecting on Social Media and enjoying a friendly rapport on Facebook Messenger. This is the major benefit of being able to use my iPad independently of a third party as it's possible for me to forge connections with people by myself and they get a far better representation of me than if someone was to do it on my behalf. The ironic thing is that half of these people are unaware that I am actually writing messages with my nose and all of our correspondence is done through this technique. By the time we met though, Steve had done his research on me and therefore knew what he was letting himself in for which I believe led to a greater interview.

Upon meeting Mr Nallon, it was obvious that we were going to get on when we spent ten minutes before the interview talking about our favourite comedy. We realised that we had a great deal in common, most notably our love for the golden era of Light Entertainment. Steve was lucky enough to meet and even work with some of the icons from this period. It seemed a little bizarre that I had been watching him for years on various TV documentaries on the history of comedy and here I was enjoying lively conversation with the man himself. In terms of his own comedy Steve remains unique in an ability to straddle both sides of the comedy fraternity. Basically he is an old school comic who enrolled in the art of stand-up in the days when traditional comedy was under considerable scrutiny by new wave of Alternative Comedy. Throughout the eighties these two disciplines were able to co-exist side by side and frequently blended to create comedy magic and Nallon's substantial contribution to the satirical 1980's sketch show *Spitting Image* made him relevant for the rebellious era of Thatcher's Britain.

Growing up in the north of England during the 1970's, there were very few outlets for entertainers to hone their craft until working men's clubs throughout the country began to play host to live entertainment. It was on this circuit that Steve realised his comedic potential but it wasn't always a good experience and he would frequently have things thrown at him subject to the audience's opinion of his act. Yet as soon as his impressions of Hilda Baker and Frank Spencer were delivered, his success soared and he never looked back. He realised quickly enough that those few impressions were becoming the most popular part of his routine. It occurred to him that he wasn't a comedian at all, he was a comedy actor and was far more at home behind a character than he was as himself. In the same way as the great Ronnie Barker found it difficult to be himself in front of the camera, Steve felt vulnerable when forced to go on without a verbal mask. Working with the legendary Mike Yarwood in the eighties, he was instructed to walk out at the end of the show so that the audience would be able to see the man behind the voices. Yarwood himself would break out into a rendition of his familiar song *And This is Me* to end his shows. For Steve, this was totally alien as he wanted to remain invisible and anonymous from the public. It is a common misconception that all comedy performers have the innate ability to engage with an audience irrespective of the persona they are portraying. As an audience we struggle with determining those performers who are able to transcend the screen and talk directly to us. Not everyone is a Bruce Forsyth and if performers were allowed to stay in their own boxes maybe we wouldn't have lost so many to drink and drugs brought on by attempting to satisfy psychological demons.

In 1984 Nallon joined forces with the cream of British satire for the irreverent political puppet sketch show *Spitting Image*. The eighties was an extremely rich time for satire with three formidable figures in charge of the "West v East" Cold War world. Margaret Thatcher, Ronald Reagan and Mikhail Gorbachev provided extraordinary amounts of scope for potential comedy writers for the simple reason that they all possessed traits that were easy to exaggerate for comic effect. Growing up surrounded by strong matriarchs, Steve always found it easy to impersonate the opposite sex. In a strange way he felt that he understood what Margaret Thatcher represented and realised that when she believed in something, she would defend herself to the hilt. This provided a way in for Steve to perfect one of the most recognisable voices of the twentieth century.

When Thatcher resigned from office in 1990, it was not only the end of an era for Britain but political satire suffered greatly. The comedy world was changing and having seen his comedy idol Mike Yarwood struggle to adapt to the ever-changing comedy landscape, Steve Nallon didn't want the same thing happening to him. Yet Steve was not finished with the Iron Lady…in 1989 he wrote the satirical autobiography *I, Margaret* to critical acclaim. However, being synonymous with such an iconic figure has its complications and on Thatcher's death in 2013 Steve left her voice behind. He realised that there was something weird about impersonating a recently deceased high profile figure and promptly put his character of Thatcher 'to bed'.

Yet after a while, when The Iron Lady had passed into history so his caricature gained another dimension. In 2015 the writer and broadcaster Jonathan Maitland wrote a stage play surrounding the relationship between Thatcher and her chancellor of the exchequer Geoffrey Howe. Having portrayed her with so much accuracy during the 1980's, Steve was asked to reprise his role as the Iron Lady. This was the first time that Steve had played

Thatcher in a factual manner as opposed to playing it for laughs. It is testament to Steve's talent as a character actor that he was able to study Thatcher so intensely and create a three dimensional representation of such an iconic figure of the 20th century. Not often does impressionism develop into something so moving and such a process is truly remarkable.

Slowly turning into the elder statesman of impressionism, Nallon insists that it's a young man's game. Though this hasn't halted his creative output and he remains passionate about the arts. There is no doubt that the comedy landscape has changed from the satirical movement of the 1980's and comedy has become fractured and divided in the quest of appealing to so many demographics simultaneously. In a world where the public are increasingly the stars of reality shows, there doesn't seem to be the need for versatility in comedy which has led to the demise of variety and all round entertainment. Yet for a figure of Steve Nallon's calibre it is only a matter of time before producers are reminded of his great talents and I can't wait to see his next incarnation for the 21st century.

## Chapter Three – Broadcasters


The very concept of television denotes the presence of an authority figure to preside over events and present information to us in a clear and unbiased manner. The role of a broadcaster is as old as the medium itself and in TV's infancy, often doubled up as a continuity announcer who was usually on hand to preside over the beginning and end of a channel's nightly coverage. It seems impossible to imagine television without the constant presence of highly experienced presenters to guide us through the pictures we are witnessing. In over sixty years, broadcasters have been to war zones, reported on poverty, stood up to political leaders and so much more. Indeed it is difficult to sum up the full extent of a broadcaster's duties because it's heavily dependent upon the type of production which they are presiding over. Essentially they are the linchpin on which a programme depends and they take responsibility for the execution of the proceedings. In short, amongst the entertainment fraternity they are number one in the pecking order, feared and loved by both the audience and their subjects in equal measures.

From rolling news to live entertainment, these highly talented communicators always find a way to go beyond the camera and create a unique bond between themselves and the viewer. The feeling that despite broadcasting to millions, somehow these trusted figures are talking to you as an individual. Arguably television is the only medium to have this sensory power which makes broadcasting all the more potent. Both in times of crisis and celebration, these figures are forever present to analyse the action and capture a defining moment in history. As the medium itself has aged and evolved, these world changing moments have become part of modern British history and such recognisable figures have become vital in us understanding our own cultural identity. Teaching and making us constantly question the world around us, broadcasting has taken us to areas where we never otherwise go and is constantly shining a light on world affairs.

Beyond news and current affairs, broadcasters have another important role in the arts, to chart the changing face of entertainment. You may think this line seems somewhat familiar with what was discussed in the introduction and I would have to admit that I consider myself as a novice part of this group. As an interviewer, nothing satisfies me more than interviewing a figure from this 'broadcaster' category as they instinctively know the discourse of the interview and present themselves in a perfect manner. Unlike other disciplines, broadcasting isn't exclusive to one medium and with the influx of new technology anyone is able to create a channel of communication between presenter and audience. Consequently a revolution is currently taking place in each and every region of Britain where highly talented broadcasters are attempting to bring a glimmer of showbiz into the homes of local people. Over time this creates a social and historical artefact and is able to chart and celebrate the changing face of entertainment itself.

With utmost eloquence and perfect clarity, broadcasters aren't fazed by the prospect of live television and its many pitfalls. Instead they thrive on the spontaneity of the art and frequently love it when the show goes wrong. Fearless, confident and supremely intelligent, it's these figures who are looked upon to get TV out of embarrassing moments and time after time they always do. The following subjects are some of the most trusted presenters in the country who have helped to transform broadcasting into an art form.

# Krishnan Guru-Murthy

Following my success with obtaining interviews with stars from the world of Light Entertainment, I started to set my sights further afield in order to get an insight into the entertainment landscape from a broader selection of figures within television. I discovered that news presenters are increasingly accessible more so than other figures within the media as a result of how often they are on our screen. The very nature of the broadcaster is to create a sense of intimacy between themselves and the viewer and this has never been easier thanks to the steady rise of social media. Beyond this every news broadcaster has a responsibility to engage with their audience to break down the social discourse of television and create the illusion that they are both teacher and a member of the family.

So through my quest to find significant figures within the world of broadcasting who would be willing to be the subject of a "*Beyond The Title*" interview, I wrote to a whole host of agents asking them to put a good word in for me with their clients. What I failed to realise was that news broadcasters were all equipped with their own universal email addresses which were easily accessible, so that I didn't need to concern their individual agents and instead could cut out the 'middleman' and email them directly. I only realised this when I received an email directly from Krishan Guru-Murthy inviting me to ITN Studios to interview him in person.

Just a few weeks later, myself and my PA Ben found ourselves on Gray's Inn Road in central London preparing to enter the ITN studios. From the outside it remains impossible to realise that the building is host to hours and hours of television coverage per day and by merely observing it from afar you would think it was either a prestigious library or a crown court. As we sat waiting in reception, it was soon obvious from the amount of people coming in and out that this was the beating heart of ITN and despite it not having the glitz and glamour of BBC Broadcasting House, you were still aware that this was an important home of British broadcasting.

A few minutes later I spotted Krishnan Guru-Murthy as he made his way over to us and invited us to follow him. Meeting a famous person for the first time is always a strange feeling as it is totally out of context and it takes a few minutes to let the realisation kick in. As we jumped in the lift, myself and Ben attempted small talk with Krishnan and by the time we reached the right floor I felt ready to interview the broadcasting titan. Prior to the interview we were taken on a tour of the department and met the extensive team who finding the stories to cover. This included the iconic Channel 4 News studio which I had seen hundreds of times on my television, but now I was actually there. One of the most striking things about seeing it in real life is the size of it. On television the camera creates the illusion that it's a vast space, like a theatre or a football pitch when in reality it is merely a box room with a table and a chair facing an autocue. It was here that I realised the enormous power that television can have in creating a false representation of the setting which broadcasters are in and I found it fascinating to see the reality.

We made our way to a small office in the newsroom where we were able to assemble our sound equipment as Krishnan became interested in me and what I did. All of a sudden the great Jon Snow walked past and I instantly became star struck. Observing my reaction, Krishnan offered to introduce us which I immediately accepted making him go after his on-screen colleague. When they returned, it was great to witness the banter and chemistry between them both and it was obvious they were great friends off screen as well as on. After a while Jon bade farewell which meant it was time to get the interview underway as Krishnan sat back and waited for the first question.

Journalists and broadcasters are among my favourite subjects for interviews as they intrinsically understand what I am setting out to achieve and Krishnan didn't let me down. A stalwart of Channel Four nightly news since 1998, Krishnan Guru-Murthy turned down a career in medicine to become one of Britain's leading factual journalists of his generation. Making his broadcasting debut at a mere eighteen years old on BBC2's current affairs programme *Def II*, following auditioning for the corporation's alternative political series *Open To Question*. In 1991 Krishnan joined the flagship children's current affairs show *Newsround* and through its unique requirements learned how to present the biggest news stories of the day. To convey such topics to a younger audience the broadcaster is required to understand the full extent of the story. This was a vital grounding for a career in television journalism and on which he was able to build in the succeeding years.

By 1996 Krishnan had graduated from *Newsround* to become part of the BBC's live events team presiding over prolific national occasions. This included being a roving reporter on Election Night which is probably the most unpredictable job in television as you wait for the results from your chosen constituency. Fortunately for the '97 election Krishnan was tasked with getting instant reactions from MPs at Jeffrey Archer's election night party (that presumably was somewhat underwhelming due to labour's historic landslide victory) which was far more lavish than waiting in a cold town hall to see which local MP had won an individual seat. Therefore an event with the possibility of striking the fear of God into many broadcasters was a walk in the park for Krishnan.

The positivity of New Labour dissolved into national devastation a short three months later as the beloved Diana, Princess of Wales was killed in a car accident on a French motorway during the early hours of 31st August 1997. On his return from a scheduled trip to LA, Krishnan was dispatched to famous landmarks around London to gauge the public reaction to this heart-breaking story for BBC News. This was of course followed by the state funeral of Diana which saw Krishnan once again amongst the crowds outside Westminster Abbey to get the public reaction to a devastating but defining day for our nation. Such a small but pivotal role on such a defining moment in modern British history gave Krishnan invaluable experience of live events which he would build on throughout later years at Channel Four.

A year later, in 1998, Krishnan 'swapped sides' and joined the Channel Four division of ITN, to appear alongside the great Jon Snow. His on screen partnership with Snow has been a successful formula ever since and has been one of the main reasons why Channel Four News can offer more insight and analysis of the days major events. It was also apparent to Krishnan not just the place his former employer, the BBC, holds in the psyche of the nation but also the severe legal parameters that bind the corporation. ITN is independently governed and Channel Four News has the ability to ask the difficult questions that no other broadcaster can pose and is willing to take people to account for their actions. Having a slightly longer nightly news bulletin from the standard thirty minutes gives the journalists more time to delve into the stories that really matter.

Working at a small but trusted news organisation has its benefits when approaching hard hitting stories and Channel Four News has been lucky enough to scoop their fair share of world exclusives. As dual anchor Krishnan has reported and presented live from all four corners of the globe covering many disasters, conflicts and political movements, such as the Arab Spring in Egypt. In October 2016 he reported from Yemen for Channel Four's investigative documentary series *Unreported World* on the severe child malnutrition which had reached crisis point. Such a pressing and emotive issue was too important to save for a one-off feature documentary and it was decided that the story would go out in two instalments over consecutive nights on Channel Four News.

Having made his debut on the award winning *Unreported World* in 2011 investigating trouble in South Africa's townships, Krishnan has become synonymous with the programme and it goes some way to satisfying the frontline journalist in him. For Krishnan, it's refreshing to go somewhere and concentrate on the breadth of just one story throughout its entirety as opposed to presiding over general politics. In his eight years working on *Unreported World*, he's gone to Baghdad, USA, Yemen, Africa, India, Venezuela and Mexico to find the stories behind the news. It's obvious that despite being one of Britain's leading news broadcasters, investigative journalism remains his first love and *Unreported World* allows Krishnan the opportunity to do this.

Beyond news and current affairs, Krishnan also has the ability to rival *Beyond The Title* with his popular podcast series *Ways to Change the World* where he interviews significant figures from all walks of life and explores big ideas surrounding the way we think and live. This adds something different to an already extremely varied and versatile career. From *Newsround* to online podcasting, it seems that Krishnan Guru-Murthy has blazed many trails in the world of broadcasting and still at such a youthful age, it's exciting to see what awaits such a consummate professional. It was great to meet Krishnan and I wish him all the very best for the rest of his remarkable career.

# Jon Snow HonFRIBA

With the promise of an interview made when visiting ITN studios to interview Krishnan Guru-Murthy, I was adamant to arrange a meeting as soon as possible so I could interview another broadcasting legend. When I got home that evening I emailed Jon Snow with the hope of getting something in the diary. Unfortunately he was just about to take a deserved holiday and wouldn't be back into the swing of things for about a month. Normally when my subjects have high profile commitments to fulfil it is understandable that I have to remind them, when they accidentally forget about our arrangements. I am totally aware that I'm trying to interview some of the busiest people in the country with gruelling schedules full of professional engagements and events. However, Jon had no need to be reminded, sticking true to his word and within a few weeks myself and my PA Will found ourselves back at the ITN studios in preparation to interview a television institution.

This time, instead of attempting to record the interview in the crowded Channel 4 newsroom, Jon thought it would be better if we found a booth in the reception area where it would be quiet, away from the bustle of breaking news. I had my doubts as to the potential quality of the sound recording but as a consummate professional broadcaster, Jon assured me that it would still be of a high standard and frankly who was I to argue with such an expert. As we sat down to get the interview underway, I sensed that

Jon was excited about the thought of being interviewed and having someone to turn the tables on the man who has asked the difficult questions to politicians and dictators for decades. Despite being one of Britain's leading news anchors, there remains an ever present irreverent and unpredictable side to Jon which makes it fascinating to interview him as you never know what is about to emerge from his creative and intelligent mind. For an interviewer this is gold dust as instead of asking straight questions it's more like throwing subjects in the air for him to catch and turn to magic.

Journalist Jon Snow has become one of the most experienced and trusted broadcasters in Britain in a career spanning four decades which has seen him preside over some of the most defining events of the 20th and 21st centuries. Born in Ardingly, Sussex to parents George D'Oyly Snow, the Bishop of Whitby, and Joan, a pianist who studied at the Royal College of Music, Jon enjoyed a happy childhood at Ardingly College where his father was headmaster. After leaving St Edward's school in Oxford at the age of eighteen, Jon took the brave decision to spend a year as a teaching volunteer in Uganda, an experience which would completely change his life when he came face to face with the notorious dictator Idi Amin who had fallen asleep whilst his gun lay invitingly on the ground. This left Jon with an ethical dilemma; did he shoot this man, potentially saving the lives of hundreds of thousands of people? Or did he maintain self-control and not be arrested for murdering one of the most prolific dictators in political history? In hindsight the Ugandan prison service's loss was definitely British broadcasting's gain and promptly laid the foundations for Jon's life in politics and current affairs.

Joining ITN in 1976 was the first time Jon had appeared on television and he was very nervous as to how he would be received by the public. As a natural broadcaster, he had no problem in perfecting his delivery yet was constantly paranoid about his appearance through fear of an impromptu 'bogey hanging out of his nose' in the middle of a very serious and emotive piece to camera...fortunately this has yet to happen but the fear has never gone away. In November 1978 he was seconded to Vietnam to report on the plight of the boat people which gained him recognition within his field and brought him to the attention of senior management who liked what they saw.

By 1983 Jon had risen to be ITN's Washington correspondent and it was here that he learned the true meaning of Britain's 'special relationship' with the US. This was the era of Reagan and Thatcher and whilst on the outside it looked like the two leaders had an open and healthy understanding, the USA always had the power to flex its political muscle to make things work for them. So according to many journalists this special relationship may not be that special after all. America has forever been jealous of Britain's rich cultural heritage and this has become a strong incentive to keep us as their most prized ally. This understanding is still mutually beneficial for both nations but speculation remains as to just how 'special' the relationship actually is.

A born reporter and communicator, Jon never saw himself leaving the fast paced world of front line journalism. Yet in 1989 following persuasion from executives, he was lured into the safe confines of the television studio to present the new look *Channel Four News*. Still a relatively fresh news outlet, Jon was able to use his expertise as a reporter to hone his skills as a presenter in a relaxed and casual setting but still managing to convey the biggest stories of the day in a clear and unbiased manner. Learning from his journalistic predecessors including Alistair Burnett and Robin Day, Jon was quickly able to perfect his own style which has kept him at the very top of his profession for over three decades.

In 1992 Jon replaced his broadcasting mentor Alistair Burnett as the main anchor of ITN's election night coverage. Such a mammoth event requires an extensive production team along with countless reporters who periodically appear in the major constituencies as they await the results, spin experts who analyse the events as they unfold and studio guests who provide insight into the unfolding action. Therefore as anchor Jon was very glad of the unrivalled expertise of the people around him who helped the broadcast come together. As history tells us, the 1992 general election was won by John Major's Tory government with 336 seats, the first time a UK ruling party had won a fourth consecutive election in modern political history. Such a momentous night proved to be Snow's one and only occasion in the hot seat on election night but it was still a great experience in a career with so many highlights.

Having tackled election night, Jon returned to Channel Four News where he was now part of television establishment. An elder statesman of TV news he believed that the audience should see a more human side to his personality. He gave some thought as to how he would accomplish this without risking devaluing the content which he was presenting and finally decided upon wearing colourful ties to add some dynamism to proceedings. This is just the perfect amount of pizazz in order to find the perfect balance between serious and informal. Walking into the Channel Four News studio one is taken aback by just how small it is, yet Jon's authoritative tone naturally makes it feel like a palace.

In 2011 Jon launched the new look Channel Four Nightly News alongside former BBC reporter Krishnan Guru-Murthy as the programme updated from a solo anchor to a dual presenting team. This popularity has assisted Jon in obtaining cult status and got the attention of comedians and writers for his straight delivery. In 2005 Jon appeared on *The Big Fat Quiz of the Year* giving fake news stories based on song lyrics, with *"I Predict a Riot"* and *"Crazy Chick"*. Unbeknown to all concerned, including Jon, this would be the start of a long standing slot which would see him reading the lyrics to some of the year's biggest tunes. Most of the time Jon has no idea what he's reading but if it illustrates that the serious news broadcaster has a brighter side to his personality, this can only be a good thing.

In 2018 Jon volunteered to take a pay cut to help highlight the gender inequalities within the media. This was something he felt hugely passionate about as he doesn't see any difference in ability between male and female broadcasters and therefore sees absolutely no reason why men should be paid more. A man of strong principles, this was an issue which Jon felt needed highlighting and if that meant taking a pay cut then it was a worthwhile sacrifice. Such a gesture may be the perfect way to sum him up; an intelligent, principled broadcaster with a twinkle in his eye. Beyond the slight eccentricity and sharp wit is a born communicator who remains passionate about getting to the very heart of world news in order to present it in a relaxed way that the audience will trust and understand. Throughout my time as an interviewer for *Beyond The Title* I have met some remarkable people who are right at the top of their game. Yet very few occupy a firm place in the heart of our nation as he does and Jon Snow is one of the many aspects which go into making Britain great.

## Alastair Stewart OBE

The world of fine art is about as far removed from television and Light Entertainment as one could get when researching icons of popular culture. Yet during the summer of 2016 I received an email from an artist and photographer offering me the opportunity to take part in a project surrounding photographs of significant figures from the South of England. I was honoured to be considered as a subject for display at their grand opening at the Great Hall in Winchester and couldn't believe it when I attended the launch and found my portrait alongside icons of sport and entertainment including rugby star James Haskell, football legend Lawrie McMenemy and Dame Esther Rantzen. It was a strange feeling being at the launch surrounded by people looking at my photograph before approaching me as if I was famous...it was surreal. All of a sudden the crowd fell silent as Alastair Stewart walked on to stage and introduced the evening. Ever on the lookout for new subjects for *Beyond The Title*, a lightbulb came on inside my head and it became my mission to corner him and ask him for what I knew would be a fantastic interview. Luckily I didn't have to wait very long and when he walked off stage he immediately caught my eye and we were able to exchange contact details with the hope of arranging something in the near future.

The following day I emailed Alastair and to my surprise he instantly replied setting up a date where we would meet in a vestry room of a church just outside Waterloo Station straight after he had finished presenting the ITN lunchtime news. Ironically, this was the first and only time that I had paid for a venue to host an interview so I was really hoping it would be worth it. As soon as he arrived he made myself and my PA James feel at ease, I knew that this was probably one of the best £10 I had ever spent. By then I was just 8 months into *Beyond The Title* and so far the majority of my subjects had been comics and writers who frequently rebel against the fixed concept of the interview setting. However, I could tell that here was a figure who was absolutely comfortable with the pragmatics of the interview and excited to get started. Without discrediting previous *Beyond The Title* subjects, it was at this moment that I realised the potential that the podcast could have and with the right calibre of people who knew where it was able to go?

For over thirty five years, Alastair Stewart has been one of the most trusted and respected news broadcasters in the UK. Beginning his television career for Channel Four News, ITN promptly saw his potential as a news anchor and relocated him to the now familiar world of ITV News where he has since become an institution. Stewart began his distinguished career in news broadcasting surrounded by icons of the art including Alastair Burnet; a figure whom the young broadcaster had admired for a very long time. It was astonishing to think that Stewart was now co-anchoring the ITN News alongside his childhood hero. Working with Burnett taught the young broadcaster the many trials and tribulations of being a television news presenter and together the two Alastairs dominated the airwaves for over two decades and it was the perfect grounding for a life on air.

Having presided over so many events which have changed our world, it's impossible for Stewart to pinpoint one in particular which has remained with him and changed his outlook on life. Yet he states that the siege of a school in Beslan, South Ossetia on the first day of the school year was probably the most moving and poignant event he's been witness to. In the days of the ITV News Channel, Alastair was live on air for four hours to report on this emotionally moving story. With 334 fatalities, this was one of the most harrowing events Alastair has been forced to commentate on. The power of rolling news had never been so potent and they were able to remain live as the story unfolded, which Alastair saw as a huge responsibility. It is with stories like these that the public is reminded of the huge impact a newscaster has when reporting to the rest of the country. Prior to this story, not many people had even heard of South Ossetia on the Georgian Border, let alone the small village of Beslan. Yet overnight it went from obscurity to the centre of world media as broadcasters reported right from the heart of the conflict.

His relaxed but informative attitude to the art of news journalism made Alastair the perfect candidate to front GMTV's Sunday Programme from 1994 to 2001. In a crowded market of political programming, it's sometimes difficult to find an angle that sets you apart from the rest. However Alastair has always had the belief that politics should be accessible to everyone irrespective of their age, creed or background. Therefore this programme attempted to make politics relevant and stimulating for all. In turn, this set the benchmark for political programmes hereafter to reflect the opinions and desires of the man and woman in the street. The legacy of which still continues to this day with the array of Sunday politics programmes spread throughout the TV schedule. Beginning with Andrew Marr, followed by *The Politics Show* on BBC One and not forgetting Robert Peston on Sunday evening. It seems that this early attempt at reflecting weekend politics was something revolutionary for its time and together with the legendary David Frost, Alistair helped to set the standard for the presentation of politics to the masses.

As a lover of all things television, I am constantly fascinated by the many significant differences between ITV and the BBC and current affairs are probably one of the most obvious examples of this difference. Alastair was able to summarise this in a way which I had never heard before, stating that both networks were tasked with presenting the news in a non-biased, informative manner but with the benefit of ITV being able to be a little more "sassy" and relaxed about the stories that it wished to tell.

On the subject of news presentation, I was interested to know his views on the dual anchor team as opposed to the lone newscaster. As far as ITV are concerned, when it comes to news, predominantly two heads are better than one. As Alastair explained this is an invaluable technique for breaking news as while one anchor is presenting, the other is able to keep an ear to breaking stories which may be happening. A fascinating insight to the art of presentation.

Beyond the news, Alastair fronted the traffic fly-on-the-wall series *Police, Camera, Action* for ITV where he reported on the most outlandish incidents which happened on Britain's roads. In the days before real life cop shows, this was the first time television had gone undercover to expose dangerous automotive antics. Like most television formats, the show ran its course before being superseded by more reality based programmes. Yet *Police, Camera, Action* can rest safe in the knowledge that it created the formula for all other shows of this kind and its legacy still lives on.

Approaching his fourth decade in television, there seems to be no sign of Alastair Stewart slowing down and offers of TV work remain as rapid as ever. At the time of our interview in spring 2017, he was unsure of his next move but expressed an interest in the documentary world. Yet whatever is next for the man of the news, one thing is assured that he will do it in the same style and grace which the public has become accustomed to. It was an absolute pleasure to spend the afternoon with him and there's no doubt that when I grow up, I want to be Alastair Stewart!

# Alan Titchmarsh MBE, DL, HonFSE

My first recollection of Alan Titchmarsh was on the lunchtime entertainment series *Pebble Mill* which always provided distraction when off school with sickness. Although considered by many to be scheduled in the graveyard slot, *Pebble Mill* attracted the biggest names in entertainment to chat and perform in their studio. For me at such a tender age, I was in awe of how many big stars they could get and became familiar with the work of all the *Pebble Mill* presenters. Throughout the late nineties Alan Titchmarsh was hot property and became one of the biggest stars on television. Like so many I followed his career from BBC One lunchtime to the gardening phenomenon he is today.

In later years Alan purchased a holiday home on the Isle of Wight and was quick to understand the closeness of the community. It wouldn't be out of the ordinary to see him driving along Cowes High Street in his Mazda MX5 or bumping into him at a restaurant. Like some stars, Alan is happy to remain relatively anonymous when he's in his hometown and the whole community respect that. It wasn't until I started to take myself seriously as a writer that I realised the enormous benefit of having a figure like Alan on my doorstep and set about trying to make contact. In 2016 I organised an event to culminate in the completion of my radio documentary surrounding theatrical agents and asked him to present the event alongside my good friend John Hannam. Unfortunately due to a busy filming schedule, Alan was unable to offer his services but it would only be a few years before our paths met up again.

Ironically, this took place at the Isle of Wight Literary Festival 2018 when we were both the subject of presentation for our latest books. This was my first time at such an event and I was a little taken aback by the affection I received. At the formal dinner on the Friday evening, I remember meeting up with Alan who was experienced at this sort of function and his laid back attitude reassured me that I had every right to be there. A couple of days earlier we had enjoyed a fascinating telephone interview which was the perfect start to such a great weekend.

Since the 1980's Alan Titchmarsh has remained an ever-present face on our television screens and in the last twenty years has extended his repertoire to include novels and poetry. Beginning his television career in 1979 as the horticultural reporter for the BBC's early evening current affairs show *Nationwide*, Alan quickly became accustomed to the television studio and producers began to realise his natural flare in front of the camera. Such popularity coincided with the launch of daytime television in 1986 and Alan was put forward to present the entertainment series *Open Air* alongside relatively unknown presenters, including Eamonn Holmes, who was making the move from regional news presenter in Northern Ireland.

In 1987, following his success on *Open Air*, Alan secured a presenting spot on the lunchtime magazine programme *Daytime Live*, which had replaced the original 1972-era *Pebble Mill*. Eventually *Daytime Live* would become *Scene Today* and finally back full-circle to a relaunched *Pebble Mill* in October 1991 when Alan joined the presenting team. This was where his talents as a journalist and broadcaster really came to the fore as he was tasked with interviewing a diverse array of stars on live television. Sharing the scheduled daily episodes with showbiz reporter Ross King, TV presenters Judi Spiers and Sue Cook alongside TV Legend Gloria Hunniford, Alan was determined to put his own unique stamp on the show. This formula proved popular until, in 1996, the BBC sadly called time on *Pebble Mill*. Yet the experience of presenting a daily chat show would stand him in great stead for the latter part of his career.

Alan returned to television gardening in 1996 as anchor of BBC *Gardeners' World*, and in 1997 with the make-over series *Ground Force*, where he enjoyed huge success alongside his co-hosts Charlie Dimmock and Tommy Walsh. It took him a while to come to terms with the concept of the show, thinking that with just two days to renovate a garden from scratch, he couldn't see how this would be possible under such tight circumstances.

But *Ground Force* and the presenters managed to work their magic and averaging ten million viewers per episode at its peak, it became 'Appointment to View' television for the whole family and reflected the do-it-yourself revolution of the nineties. Adhering to the same structure as the BBC's interior design show *Changing Rooms,* the element of surprise became one of the biggest aspects of the show and raised the stakes for the team to get it right. For the best part of seven years Alan presided over some extraordinary feats of horticulture as the team successfully transformed typical backyards into inspiring gardens.

Although *Ground Force* ran for only eight years (Alan stepped down from presenting duties for the last series and Charlie Dimmock was promoted), it was to have a huge influence on the interior design shows of the early 21st century and helped to spawn many of the shows which still dominate the British television schedule. Popular shows such as *DIY SOS* owe much to the impact that *Ground Force* made two decades previously. *Yet Ground Force* wasn't the only horticultural show which Alan became associated with as in 1996 Alan replaced Geoff Hamilton on BBC2's long running gentle educational programme for people with green fingers, *Gardeners World.* This appointment was tinged with sadness after Hamilton's sudden death meaning Alan had to step into the breach earlier than had been planned. Not only had Geoff been a colleague with whom he shared many things, including contributing to his horticultural magazine, but he was also a long-standing friend. Alan presented *Gardeners World* for six years until 2002 when he handed over the series to Monty Don.

Such an association with all things green made Alan the perfect candidate to preside over the BBC's coverage of the annual Chelsea Flower Show. Originally a half-hour programme on BBC2 in 1979, the popularity of the event grew and it wasn't long before the BBC was broadcasting nightly programmes across the corporation. For over thirty years Alan anchored the event which combined his two great passions for horticulture and presenting live television.

A move to ITV in 2007 reunited Alan with the daytime chat show format. Over a decade after leaving the BBC's Pebble Mill, *The Alan Titchmarsh Show* reminded television audiences of his flair for live entertainment and chat. A glamorous array of celebrities from Hollywood stars, world-class musicians and politicians sat on his sofa for a conversation on every topic under the sun. Like all good broadcasters, Alan makes his guests feel as if they were in his lounge talking solely to him. This is something which looks easy on screen but is so difficult to perfect; only the best can pull it off. *The Alan Titchmarsh Show* ran for seven years and saw Alan get up close and personal with some of the cream of entertainment.

In 2016 ITV had the vision to update the gardening makeover show for modern audiences and launched *Love Your Garden* which followed a similar structure as *Ground Force* but with a bigger emotional element. With its mission being to transform gardens for those living challenging lives, *Love Your Garden* is a makeover show with a conscience and this may be the secret of its success.

Setting his gardening credentials aside, Alan has also published eleven novels about life and relationships. As someone who writes every day, prose and creative writing is something that comes second nature to him. His 2018 novel, The Scarlet Nightingale surrounds seventeen-year-old Rosamund Hanbury as she leaves behind the endless summers of her coastal Devonshire home for the fast pace of high society. Under the supervision of her aunt she is introduced to London Society in the glamorous 1930s. It is not enough for her. With the advent of the Second World War she joins the Special Operations Executive and is parachuted into occupied France.

At the time of the interview, Alan was embarking on a marketing campaign to promote the book and had been unveiled as a speaker at the 2018 Isle Of Wight Literary Festival along with yours truly which proved to be a roaring success. It was a great privilege to speak with Alan and I have no doubt he will continue to entertain us for many years to come.

# John Hannam

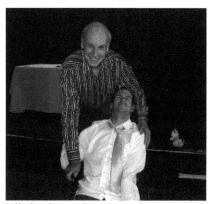

The art of conversation is something which the human race thrives on in order to go about our everyday lives and make sense of the complex world around us. When radio and then in the 1950s television began to gain momentum, producers were quick to realise that a large percentage of the audience didn't just want to be entertained. They also wanted to learn a little about the stars who entertained them. Early attempts at the chat show format included the BBC's *In Town Tonight* and *Face To Face* which irrespective of the formal pragmatics of the format, offered a personal insight into public figures for the very first time. But of course whatever the airwaves could do, print journalists knew they could do as well, if not better and more efficiently.

The success of national entertainment journalism spawned local press to incorporate entertainment into their newsrooms and suddenly all over Britain showbiz writers and journalists were heavily in demand in order to chart and celebrate the entertainment taking place in their area. Personally I feel that these figures are increasingly important to recording the changing face of the Arts as through their extensive interview archives they are able to identify the fashions within society at a precise time in history and can record the collective mood of the nation through these cultural figures.

Indeed the aim of my podcast was to achieve this exact purpose yet I was under no illusions that I was the first to have this vision. In fact recording and celebrating entertainment is almost as old as the art itself and has been thriving in areas and formats which many do not expect.

Local journalism is frequently overlooked when taking a glimpse at what the entertainment industry has to offer. It is extremely seldom that a high profile celebrity would select a local radio station to expose a world exclusive or to launch their latest project as a result of audience margin. You would never get a PR agent negotiating with the chief executive of a local radio station about attempting to get their client a window on their airwaves. In fact to some extent local radio works the other way round where showbiz journalist are forced to contact celebrities and their agents in the hope of getting a five minute interview to play on air. In this sense these highly talented people are forced to be extremely passionate about what they do in order to have the patience to do this.

Journalist and broadcaster John Hannam was born in East Cowes on the Isle of Wight and always had aspirations of following in the footsteps of his Variety heroes whom he'd grown up watching in the Theatre Royal, Portsmouth, where his parents would often take him as a boy. Here, he saw the likes of Benny Hill, Eartha Kitt and Tommy Trinder who each left a definite impression on young John and this made him realise where his true calling lay. After contributing articles to *The Stage* magazine, John looked a little closer to home for his next venture into entertainment. *The Isle Of Wight Evening Post* was looking for a showbiz reporter to write a weekly column entitled *'Stage Talk'* and with his connections to the world of entertainment, John became the perfect candidate.

John Hannam's *'Stage Talk'* got up close and personal with some of this country's favourite stars and consequently made John a local hero. But he knew he had so much more to offer. In 1990 the Isle of Wight secured the rights to create it's very first commercial radio station and John was selected to front a Sunday afternoon chat show simply entitled *John Hannam Meets*. Having written a column in the local paper since 1975, John had already interviewed the cream of entertainment and was in the middle of building an extensive archive of celebrity interviews. However now he had the opportunity to bring his chat show format to the airwaves and this was something which the people of the island seemed to like. The connections that he had made during his time as an entertainment writer proved vital to attracting a high calibre of celebrity onto his Sunday lunchtime series. For over a quarter of a century, many Isle of Wight residents associated John Hannam with roast beef and Yorkshire pudding for he provided the perfect accompaniment for Sunday lunch. Never afraid to move with the times, in summer 2016 John moved his successful radio show to an online podcast.

I first became aware of John's work when I was very young and my dad's best friend was invited onto his Sunday lunchtime show to celebrate a late local hero. At such a young age I didn't yet understand the difference between local and national radio, I just couldn't believe that Uncle Fred was on the radio and I even got a mention which resulted in John playing Take That's latest single *How Deep Is Your Love* which he dedicated to me. The next time that I would come into contact with John was in 1999 when I purchased a copy of his long awaited autobiography *I Was a Stage Door Johnny*. When I saw it in the book shop I was stunned by how many of my favourite stars were on the front cover and had to buy it. Who would have thought that twenty years later I would be writing my own book about the significant figures I've met!

The next time my path crossed with John's was in 2015 when I was conducting research for my documentary surrounding the relationship between theatrical agents and the stars of the fifties and sixties. I realised that I was in the company of a substantial authority of celebrity insights and his knowledge of agents and their charges were vast. When it came to organising the launch of my documentary *Following The Money* in 2016 there was only one man with the charisma and professionalism to pull it off and luckily John agreed. This was the start of a great friendship between me and the showbiz oracle.

Beyond broadcasting and interviews, John has written several books about his life in entertainment and has recently self-published three memoirs of his interviews with notable figures from the world of entertainment. Not just tales of some of the most prolific stars of the twentieth century but a tidy reminder of showbiz days gone by. Very few people in Britain have a more extensive interview archive than John, so consequently these books are a tiny slice of British cultural history. In subsequent years John has added to his literal repertoire with additional follow up books celebrating local people which I was honoured to feature in and it was really touching that he thought so much of our time together.

Over the last few years I'm delighted to say that John and I have developed a strong friendship and I have been lucky enough to get to know him reasonably well. I have witnessed first-hand his famous anecdotes surrounding some of the most prolific figures of the twentieth century and his great ability to tell a story. Whenever he embarks on an anecdote which starts with the words 'when I met…' you know that you're in for a treat.

From the mid 1970's to the post millennium era, John has recorded the changing face of entertainment and now has an unrivalled collection of perfectly polished interviews which will be able to be used as detailed time capsules for future generations to observe the popular culture of the time. I believe that this is John's greatest legacy and can only hope that I go on to enjoy my career in entertainment with the same passion and enthusiasm which still surrounds him today. I will be forever grateful to John for his involvement in the early stages of my career and long may he reign over our airwaves. Yet above all it makes me incredibly proud and privileged to be able to call the great John Hannam one of my dearest friends.

## Chapter Four - Comedy

What makes people want to be funny for money? For centuries comics have been a staple of any Variety bill originally hired to break up the various speciality acts and were known as jesters or clowns. Steadily growing in popularity and prominence, by the Second World War, comics became one of the most popular turns on a traditional variety bill and performers such as Max Miller and Charlie Chester became the first national comedy stars. When the comedy stars of theatres and Variety Halls eventually made their way to television, comedy as an art form never looked back.

Following on from the variety generation of the fifties and sixties came an era of comics who had been inspired by the punk invasion of the 1970's. The rise of Alternative Comedy during the latter part of the decade would shake the foundations of mainstream entertainment and give birth to anarchic comics who rebelled against the fixed concepts of 1970's Britain.

While Thatcher became a formidable figure who divided the nation, TV executives were tasked with the impossible job of maintaining a balance between the old school form of comedic television entertainment and the exciting new wave of comedy which was growing in popularity.

Just as this new brand of comedy was taking hold, there was a substantial renaissance of front of cloth comedy thanks to the popularity of British holiday camps Butlins and Pontins. These venues became a recognised avenue for the next generation of entertainers to gain a platform for their talent and attract the attention of TV executives who had the power to make them into nationwide stars. Television itself was changing and this generation benefited from the overhaul of senior management at both the

BBC and ITV. This lead to a new wave of television Variety, but not the sort that necessarily appealed to the conservative values of the older generation. This was music to the ears of Light Entertainment producers who were crying out for new stars to fill the family variety show void left by the stars from the golden era.

Irrespective of revolutions within the genre, the world of sitcom still had the power to unite the nation throughout the 1980's. The slow demise of traditional comedy variety shows gave way to situation comedy juggernauts which in some cases challenged the very structure of the art form, ranging as it could from the normal thirty minute slot to anything up to an hour, which proved extremely popular with the public. Despite new devices and new stars, the sitcom still relied upon a successful formula and writers, led by comedy powerhouse David Croft, could still add familiarity with their irreverent takes on everything from the French Revolution to the French occupation of WWII. The mainstay was lashings of innuendo and a saucy sense of humour.

As comedy grew up, new generations once again rebelled against the fixed concepts in which entertainment put them and suddenly comedians became masters of their own destiny. No longer was there a natural divide which separated disciplines and people were free to cross into other genres. The sitcom still remained a very important part of the comedy landscape but no longer needed the presence of a major star to add a sense of gravitas to the show. Instead the art employed unadulterated realism to reinvent sitcom and take it to uncharted territory as the format evolved quicker than ever before. Suddenly TV Comedy had the power to laugh at itself and satirise the fame obsessed world of post millennium Britain.

Such realism crossed the comedic border into comedy drama and accurately reflected the mood of the day. Bittersweet dramas such as *Cold Feet* and *This Life* tackled major issues facing nineties Britain finding the perfect balance between comedy and pathos which partially was influenced by David Renwick's seminal black sitcom *One Foot In The Grave*. Comedy was developing a harder edge and suddenly felt a responsibility to highlight issues facing 21st century folk. This social awareness has carried forward to the present day and comics such as Miles Jupp who constantly play on their own social pitfalls and use heightened experiences to illustrate their ineptness. It's this vulnerability which endears them to the audience and gets the crowd on their side.

It is fair to say that comedy has come a long way in the last sixty years from being the novelty act on variety bills to the multi-million pound generating machine of today. Comics are unique individuals who are often in a constant battle with their normal self and their stage persona. Yet the feeling of being the source of laughter can be a severe drain on their psyche which results in them seeking other devices to help them cope in the real world, with unfortunate results. This situation has robbed us of many of our best loved comics as time after time performers turn to drugs and alcohol to numb the pain of their own demons. Thankfully none of the following subjects have battled with this devastating syndrome but have learned from the harrowing experiences of their predecessors.

Today comedy is more self-aware than ever and isn't frightened to laugh or parody itself. As young comedians have grown up with the offerings of the previous generation, the art has become much more wide spread and self-aware, giving these performers more scope to extend into other genres. Therefore the comedy stars of today can double, treble or quadruple up as actors, presenters, singers or dancers. This aspect harks back to the tradition of Variety and vaudeville, and though the manner in which it's done is far more predetermined and less organic, the execution remains the same.

As a novice comedy historian, nothing gives me greater pleasure than unpicking and analysing the changing face of entertainment and the following subjects are fantastic examples of this change.

# Ben Elton

 Ben Elton is a comic who has long since divided public opinion with his comedic reputation surrounded by rumours and speculation of professional wrongdoing. Combining this with a career shift into musical theatre, the once prince of comedy has recently experienced the harsh side of the media as he continues to defend himself over issues surrounding the apparent Alternative Comedy divide amongst the showbiz elite. As a novice comedy historian, I've always found this particular subject to be one of the most fascinating in entertainment but never did it occur to me that one day I would have the opportunity to quiz the man himself about this very issue. This is just one of the many surreal experiences which I've been lucky enough to have during my time running *Beyond The Title*.

Some of my interviews take several months in the planning as we negotiate schedules, deadlines and diaries. Yet it's always quite refreshing when opportunities arise almost spontaneously and this is exactly what happened when I realised that Elton was performing at a local theatre on the Isle of Wight. I contacted the tour manager, already resigned to the fact that gigs on the island are often planned to the minute in order to compensate for the time and hassle it takes to get over and back from the mainland, but to my delight in this case, I was wrong. Just a few days before his Isle of Wight gig, I received an email from his agent informing me that Ben was willing to give me twenty minutes before the show on Saturday evening.

Over the days leading up to the interview I gave myself a lot of time to formulate and ponder the possible questions that I might ask. Here was a subject that I had seen interviewed many times yet I always felt that not even the legendary Michael Parkinson was able to ask the questions that the comedy world needed answering. Through no fault of his own, Ben had been the target of blame for the bizarre divide between mainstream and alternative comedy and with the prospect of interviewing him, I knew that I just had to ask him those all important questions.

Meeting Ben Elton was an absolute revelation and instantly changed my perspective of him, which had been created through the documentaries I watched together with what I had read around the subject. As we waited in the green room of the theatre I had no idea what to expect or what sort of person he would be. From the moment he walked into the room and shook my hand I realised that his reputation has been negatively tainted by the British media. As stated previously, it's always refreshing when my subject understands that its actually me directing the interview and treats me as an equal. Ben Elton was a perfect example of this and automatically directed all his answers to me, maintaining eye contact with me throughout. This awareness isn't surprising coming from the author of *Gridlock* a book with a central character who has Cerebral Palsy, mod Geoffrey Spasmo. This in turn gained Ben recognition from Cerebral Palsy charity Scope, of which he has since become a patron. So therefore he wasn't fazed by the way I communicated and was more than happy to give me time to execute everything I wanted to say, a fact which I shall always hold very dear. It meant a lot to me and I was quick to realise that this would be one of the best interviews I had ever conducted.

Exploding onto the comedy scene in March 1981 when he made his debut at the Comedy Store, writer and comedian Ben Elton went from budding comedian to one of the leading pioneers of British Alternative Comedy with political observations and a brash sense of humour. Having been bred on British comedy including Morecambe and Wise, The Goons and later Monty Python, the young Ben had the desire to emulate these heroes and set about making waves in the early eighties comedy landscape. Here is a man who is both in love with the art of comedy and the stars behind it. It's incredible that one interview could range from Aristotle to Shakespeare, Benny Hill to Ronnie Corbett before concluding with the songs of Queen and Rod Stewart. Yet such is the rich and diverse nature of Elton's mind, it's impossible to know where a conversation will end up.

Ben's rise to fame coincided with the steady development of Thatcher's Britain which notoriously divided the nation in an era of social unrest. Having such a forthright character for prime minister resulted in the rebirth of cutting political satire and Ben was one of the leading performers of this comedy revolution. Don Ward and Peter Rosengard opened The Comedy Store in March 1979 and made overnight stars of Alexi Sayle, Rik Mayall and Adrian Edmondson. Ben made his Comedy Store debut in 1981 to rave reviews, becoming an overnight comedy phenomenon with his quick witted repertoire of political angst. Reflecting the formidable backlash against The Iron Lady and the conservative values of eighties Britain, he was seen as a much needed rebellion for the downtrodden, forgotten youth and became synonymous with mocking the establishment. Irrespective of Thatcher's values, interestingly in hindsight Ben appreciates her commitment to what she believed in and thinks that forthright philosophy is somehow missing from today's political sphere.

In 1986, following a series of successful guest hosts including Lenny Henry, Ben secured a presenting role on Channel Four's *Saturday Live* and introduced future comedy heavyweights French and Saunders and Harry Enfield. Based on the variety formula of *Sunday Night At The Palladium*, *Saturday Live* challenged the foundations of traditional entertainment with satirical, anti-establishment values. At such a politically charged time, satire was arguably experiencing its biggest popularity surge and there was a growing requirement for comics to subvert the biggest stories of the day. As a young comedian, Ben took great delight in mocking the political establishment with his left wing observations. Yet while this material proved popular, he was adamant not to become a one trick pony and became aware of the need for the audience to witness the full extent of his comedy repertoire.

It was on an episode of *Saturday Live* that Ben was alleged to have made a joke about the late, great comedian, Benny Hill which prompted considerable backlash from the British media. The fact that Elton never even mentioned the comedy legend and would never criticise a figure of Benny Hill's calibre somehow was irrelevant as the press firmly grasped hold of the story and ran with it. As a huge fan of post-war entertainment, this left Ben mortified as the story escalated to the extent where he was personally held responsible for Hill's downfall. The extraordinary thing was that Ben was only 24 years old and had no weight within the TV fraternity but yet supposedly had the power to overthrow such a comedy icon. This is but one terrible example of injustice that has surrounded Elton's career, not only tainting future ventures but creating the illusion of a strong divide between him and his comedy heroes. Something which still upsets the comedian who has such love and passion for Britain's rich comedy heritage.

Beyond performing, Ben was also quick to master the art of screenwriting, penning the anarchic sitcom *The Young Ones* alongside co-writers Rik Mayall and Lise Mayer. Like Elton's stand-up, this series rebelled against the fixed concepts on which sitcom had been shaped. The show being the antithesis to what had gone before was seeming encapsulated and symbolised by Adrian Edmondson physically tearing down the opening titles of *The Good Life*. Surviving for just two series between 1982 and 1984, *The Young Ones* followed the frequently bizarre antics of four positively flawed students in a house share. Political activist Rik with a strange fascination for Cliff Richard, pyromaniac Vivian who often defied the laws of physics and would regularly sever part of his body only to magically fix it again. Then there was the hippie new age vegetarian Neil who would frequently set the kitchen alight when attempting to make what today would be considered a vegan dinner. Lastly Mike, the nominal 'leader' who was cool, laid back and a bit of a cockney wide-boy.

Following the enormous cult success of *The Young Ones,* Ben was considered the epitome of Britain's bright new creative talent and was promptly drafted in to assist *Black Adder* creator Richard Curtis on the writing of the second series of the historical based sitcom. On the subject of the writing process, Ben explains "Richard and I never wrote together. Our method was for each of us to work on a script and then swap and work on the other's writing. Our absolute rule was no looking back, if one or the other of us had cut something then it wasn't allowed to make an appeal, you had to lump it and move on. Of course you could always stick it back on the next draft swap! Mind you we rarely did because normally the line you least want to cut is the one you probably should.".

Ben Elton was now at the pinnacle of his TV success and in 1998 secured his own self-titled BBC1 stand-up series. *The Ben Elton Show* reunited the comedian with the format which had originally launched his career with the added bonus of a regular special guest. As a huge fan of the history of British comedy, it was a dream come true for Ben to welcome the legendary Ronnie Corbett to reprise his armchair monologues for nineties Britain. In addition Ben was fortunate enough to be able to write these sketches for one of his heroes, following in the footsteps of Corbett's former writers Spike Mullins and David Renwick. To think the comedian who supposedly had a strong angst against the older generation could feature such a comedy icon as Ronnie Corbett was simply implausible and proved to the sceptics that Ben Elton was an innocent party.

As the new millennium dawned, Ben decided to expand his reach and crossed an unlikely entertainment border into musical theatre. Directed by Christopher Renshaw and choreographed by Arlene Phillips, the original West End production of, *We Will Rock You* opened at the Dominion Theatre on 14 May 2002, with Tony Vincent, Hannah Jane Fox, Sharon D. Clarke and Kerry Ellis in principal roles. On the subject of musical theatre, Ben says, "Working on musicals hasn't really changed my perception of the arts. I have always loved musical theatre as an entertainment and a legitimate art form. I have never held with the snobbery (less commonly said these days) that musical theatre was 'for Grannies'. Musical theatre like any art can be bland and it can be cutting edge. Weill and Brecht's *The Threepenny Opera* is musical theatre. Rice and Lloyd Webber took an enormous risk when they created the first true rock musical and based it on the death of Christ! That's not to say that musicals need to be ground breaking to be brilliant, I think the musical I enjoy most is Grease."

In 2019 Ben Elton was back on the road with his first stand-up tour in fifteen years, playing to packed out theatres the length and breadth of the UK and around the world. Frustrated at the lack of trust in our political system brought on by issues surrounding Brexit, Ben has returned to the stage to vent his angst about the appalling goings on at Number 10. In a lot of ways, Ben feels more angst towards today's conservative cabinet, especially Boris Johnson, than he did towards Thatcher's Tory party of the 1980's. It seems that Ben's career has gone full circle and however many years have passed, live theatre will forever have an enormous pull for him. It was a great pleasure to meet a true pioneer of the alternative comedy scene.

# Arthur Smith

Through my own lack of cultural understanding, admittedly I was a slow convert to the art of radio comedy. Despite being aware of ground breaking juggernauts including *The Goon Show* and *Round The Horne,* radio had always escaped my entertainment radar and I didn't truly realise its pedigree or indeed, continuing potential. Yet when I was just thirteen, my PA introduced me to the diverse content on Radio 2 which was able to change my perception of the somewhat, in comparison to television, ancient medium. Saturday mornings were reserved for Jonathan Ross and his irreverent radio chat show which provided the inspiration for BBC One's *Friday Night with Jonathan Ross.* This was followed by thirty minutes of *The Smith Lectures* in which Arthur Smith presided over classic stand-up recordings from the BBC archives. As a fan of all things comedy, this was right up my street and encouraged me to follow Arthur's career to areas of the Arts that I had never been to before.

Over the succeeding years, I gradually realised that Arthur Smith somehow represented everything I loved about comedy, forever speaking so reverently about the stars I admired. Watching him on TV documentaries, Arthur seemingly shared my opinion on a whole host of different subjects surrounding the history of British comedy. So when devising the concept for *Beyond The Title* back in 2016, Arthur's name was always in contention for what I knew would be a fascinating interview. Yet as someone who likes to shy away from the showbiz spotlight, he was proving harder than most to pin down. After three years of *Beyond The Title,* I was determined to attempt a dialogue with the man himself and broach the possibility of interviewing someone I had admired for a very long time.

Several months went by without any contact and despite my best intentions, Arthur had somehow escaped my microphone. That was before I discovered his website with an email address and realised that this was my opportunity for a dream interview. To my delight, he responded with a very positive email and we started to arrange a meet up.

For some reason the prospect of interviewing Arthur filled me with both excitement and trepidation as essentially this was a figure whom I had admired for a very long time and frankly the thought of sitting opposite him asking him questions really blew my mind.

On the day of the interview, myself and my PA Ian made our way to our favourite financial company in London where we were able to secure a meeting room for the interview. This is always the source of great amusement for my family and friends as when it comes to finance I am totally useless and if you saw my bank balance you might agree. So for my interview subjects to perhaps think that I am in some way linked to the financial industry is an extremely hilarious concept. Yet if it provides the perfect ice-breaker then who am I to complain.

As soon as he walked into the meeting room, Arthur's bohemian laidback charm was enough to put Ian and I at ease and for a moment it felt like we were talking to someone we had known for years. Yet of course this wasn't any old man off the street and despite his remarkable humility, I was in no doubt that I was in the presence of a giant of comedy. With the niceties completed it was time to get the interview underway. I had done my research and knew that the following thirty minutes would be filled with great insights from one of the most fascinating characters in British comedy.

Making his Edinburgh Festival debut in 1978, writer and comedian Arthur Smith has been entertaining audiences for over forty years with his repertoire of quick fire gags and downtrodden persona. As a pioneer of Alternative Comedy, Smith honed his craft as a comedy MC and became resident compère of the Comedy Store during the mid-1980's mixing with the biggest comedy stars of the day including, French and Saunders, Ben Elton and Alexei Sayle.

By the mid-eighties Smith was one of the most influential figures in British comedy and it wasn't long before TV came calling. In 1985 together with his comedy partner Phil Nice, Arthur secured his own mockumentary series *Arthur and Phil Go Off* for the then relatively new network Channel Four. Surviving for two series between 1985 and 1987, *Arthur and Phil Go Off* proved to be the only TV vehicle for the short-lived double act. Despite a formidable comedy career, this was to be one of only a few TV opportunities that eventuated for him, which is surprising for a man with such an active role in the development of British comedy. Yet Arthur has always preferred live performance and the rest of his career epitomised that.

In 1991 Arthur teamed up with writer Chris England to write the critically acclaimed stage play *An Evening With Gary Lineker.* The popularity of the stage show caught the attention of TV producers and just three years later ITV adapted it into a TV drama starring Caroline Quentin, Clive Owen and Paul Merton. This coincided with the 1994 World Cup in the USA which famously England didn't reach. The drama takes place at the semi-final of Italia '90 between England and Germany as ardent fan Bill takes his wife Monica to revel in potential football glory. With brief cameos from John Motson and the man himself, *An Evening With Gary Lineker* proved a cult classic.

The Edinburgh Fringe was where Arthur found a loyal audience and began a lifelong love affair with the world's oldest arts festival. Over the years Arthur has used the parameters of the festival to its fullest potential in order to keep his shows both original and exciting for his audience. These have included hosting a gig on a touring bus and a live tribute to his late father. For Arthur as a comedian, Edinburgh is the only opportunity to network and socialise with other comics and thus the whole month of August becomes like one big comedy AGM. As a lover of live entertainment, Arthur relishes the opportunity to witness the best in emerging talent which is only possible in the confined space of a festival. With the added bonus of Edinburgh as a picturesque backdrop, Arthur struggles to think of a better way to spend each and every August.

His penchant for live comedy has made Arthur the perfect candidate to preside over comedy compilations from the archives and in 2000 he secured his own BBC Radio 2 series *The Smith Lectures.* As the self-proclaimed

"Night Mayor of Balham", Smith took the role of lecturer and teacher as he took listeners on a journey through the very best of stand-up featuring snippets from such comedy icons as Spike Milligan, Victoria Wood and Billy Connolly whilst also acknowledging the very best in new talent from all over the world. For over three years *The Smith Lectures* occupied the Saturday lunchtime slot on Radio 2 reserved for comedy vehicles. However, as a result of the overhaul of BBC management, by 2003 *The Smith Lectures* had disappeared from the schedules which was a sad moment for comedy fans.

Later in 2003 Arthur returned to Radio 2 for an eight part series celebrating 21 years of the Just For Laughs comedy festival in Montreal. As a first timer at the festival, he was able to offer his first impressions to the British audience and get up close and personal with some of the world's biggest comedy stars. The former Comedy Store MC was struck by just how many British comics attend the festival each year in the hope of extending their audience. The series became a definitive celebration of the thousands of comedians who have graced the Canadian festival and offered Arthur an insight into live comedy from all over the world.

Despite this transatlantic experience, Arthur has never lost touch with the comedy festival which helped to transform him into a star. Edinburgh shall forever hold a significant emotional pull for someone who has both performed and attended as an audience member magical nights at the festival. As an Edinburgh stalwart, it's extremely difficult for him to pinpoint his favourite show but he believes that the late Linda Smith remains a contender for the best live performance. Now a festival veteran, audiences still flock to Arthur's Edinburgh shows or to sit on the iconic Arthur's bench which has become a mainstay of the event. It's clear that Smith has become the unofficial king of Edinburgh and long may he reign over proceedings.

The most unlikely TV venture came to Arthur in 2003 when he teamed up with a host of stars including John Peel, Jeremy Clarkson and Rick Wakeman for BBC2's irreverent *Grumpy Old Men*. What was originally pitched to him as a filler in the schedules eventually became a runaway success. Yet the irony was that at just forty-eight years old, Arthur didn't class himself as either grumpy or old. Unbeknown to both cast and crew, *Grumpy Old Men* proved an enormous hit with the public and spawned spin-off series along with a live tour. What began as a brief TV interview had now become a middle aged phenomenon and over fifteen years later, Arthur remains synonymous with the programme.

As a performer, Arthur has always been content with his unique skillset and has never had the desire to expand his career to other areas. So when he secured a post as a reporter on *The One Show*, it was nothing like he had ever done before. Covering a variety of subjects from post boxes to literature, Arthur was tasked with bringing stories to life. Yet the lack of creativity and spontaneity allowed within these films made Arthur dissatisfied with his contributions to the show and he realised that TV broadcasting of this type wasn't for him.

Slowly becoming an elder statesmen of live performance, Arthur remains excited about the comedy fraternity and is proud to still be included within it. His enthusiasm and pride for the younger generation of comedians is almost palpable which may explain his lifelong love affair with the Edinburgh festival. Whether it's performing live comedy, writing TV drama or presiding over clip montages, comedy fans can all rest easy in the knowledge that Smith has always been and still remains an important part of the comedy dynasty. It was a special honour to meet and interview Arthur Smith and with such a varied career before him, he surely has earned the prestigious title of comedy legend.

## Larry Lamb

Each and every autumn, I start to get increasingly anxious that we have a notable Christmas guest on *Beyond The Title* as a fitting crescendo to the year. As the website has expanded, I realise the huge significance in being able to secure a big name to be our proverbial star on top of the *Beyond The Title* Christmas tree. By October 2018 I had still to secure such a star and was beginning to be concerned that we wouldn't have anyone to fill the seasonal gap. Just as I was beginning to give up hope, I came across an acting agent whom I'd never approached before. As I perused the website, there were a few familiar faces which I thought would be good 'potentials' but was still not convinced. Then I saw an image of Larry Lamb and instantly began to write an email. After dealing with management companies and agencies for the best part of a decade, I have grown increasingly accustomed to those contacts who are going to be helpful and those who will prove a waste of time. Normally, addressees which have an 'info@' prefix are usually not worth contemplating as it's reasonably accurate to presume that it's directed to an unchecked inbox where it will sit for eternity. Yet on this occasion, my pessimism was unfounded as within a few days I had received an email from Larry Lamb himself accepting my request for an interview. Christmas was solved!

We originally agreed to meet up at the Museum Of Comedy where I was already scheduled to be conducting another interview, but unfortunately due to unforeseen circumstances, Larry was forced to cancel which was a shame. He was extremely apologetic and promptly arranged to meet up the following month at the BFI Southbank. So it was on a cold November morning, myself and James wrapped up warm to brave the London winter air. When we arrived, I waited in the foyer while James went to enquire about our booked room. As I sat staring into space, I was tapped on the shoulder and looked round to see Larry Lamb dressed in full cycling attire as he unclicked his helmet. I managed to tell him that James was currently looking for him which briefly led to watching a scene from *Tom and Jerry*, but eventually they managed to find each other, we all found the room and I prepared for the interview.

Interviewing Larry Lamb isn't like doing a podcast with anyone else. He seems somewhat removed from the showbiz world in which he finds himself. He believes there was a considerable amount of luck attributed to his success and this has kept him grounded throughout his career. Therefore when asked to recollect, Larry remains extremely matter of fact about the whole thing. It's very clear that he takes everything in his stride and fame is something that doesn't bother him. So this was a very refreshing interview as instead of my subject waxing lyrical about their various accomplishments, Larry was unfazed by the whole experience.

Born in Edmonton, Middlesex in October 1947, Larry's upbringing was a million miles away from the East End persona of Archie Mitchell in the BBC serial drama. Yet in a career spanning forty years actor Larry Lamb has enjoyed a gradual rise to fame and his working class routes have been a great benefit to him and a major influence on the direction of his career.

Starting his acting career in North America, he took the advice of producers who told him to return to London which was then the bedrock of theatre and acting. His first role came in the 1980 television series *Fox* for Thames Television alongside Ray Winstone and Bernard Hill after being forced to turn down a role for the same production team just a few months previously. *Fox* followed the lives of five brothers who lived in Clapham in South London and had gangland connections. Written by Trevor Preston and produced by the legendary Verity Lambert, the series had all the elements for a success and forty years on remains a cult classic.

In 1981 Larry was cast as chief engineer Matt Taylor alongside the femme fatale Kate O'Mara for the BBC's North Sea serial drama *Triangle*, surrounding the domestic goings on of the crew and guests on the triangular crossing from Felixstowe to Gothenburg and Amsterdam. Created by Bill Sellers, the writer of *All Creatures Great and Small* and broadcast every Monday and Wednesday evening on BBC1, *Triangle* ran for three series between 1981 and 1983. Larry starred opposite stellar supporting cast members including Sandra Dickinson and George Baker and the premise of the show was promising, yet a lack of funding and low quality production sadly lead to the show's premature ending.

Larry's next major role came in 1988 when he was cast as the ring-leader Bruce Reynolds in the romantic crime comedy, *Buster* surrounding The Great Train Robbery. This wasn't his first brush with this subject as just three years previously he was approached by the BBC to star in a major new drama playing the part of the notorious Ronnie Biggs. The series was greatly anticipated by the drama department until political pressures from external sources halted the Corporation's enthusiasm. It was eventually demoted to an early afternoon play much to the irritation of the director and Larry himself. Therefore Buster has an extra significance for Larry as he was able to revisit the subject which he thought had so much scope. In fact, when he got the call to play another train robber, Larry couldn't believe his luck.

A surprise friendship arose from *Buster* between Larry and his real life character; Bruce Reynolds. This resulted in a bizarre phone conversation with Ronnie Biggs whilst he was laying low in Rio. Although Biggs was definitely less than complimentary about Larry's portrayal of him in the previous BBC drama, it did give Larry the unique opportunity to speak with the notorious figure. This criminal underworld is a fascinating area for Larry and in 2017 he returned to it when he starred in the British crime caper *The Hatton Garden Job*, based on the true story of four elderly men who burgled almost £200 million from the Hatton Garden Safe Deposit Company in London.

In 1996 Larry was offered a part in the BBC seminal drama *Our Friends In The North* alongside relatively unknown actors, Daniel Craig and Christopher Eccleston. For this he had to perfect a north east accent for the character of Alan Roe which he accomplished with style. Ironically on set during his two episodes, there was a northern actress playing a southern character so Larry was able to witness the obvious juxtaposition between the two. Larry remains glad to have been involved with such an iconic series that helped to define the nineties.

Eleven years later, Larry auditioned for a part in a new sitcom for BBC Three. He read for the part of Mick alongside writer Ruth Jones reading in for the other role in a two-hander scene. The crew loved it but the director wasn't convinced and sent Larry away not knowing his fate. A short while later he received a call from his agent informing him that the producers were unsure of his suitability and had invited him back to read the same scene with the already appointed, Alison Steadman reading the part of Pam. As soon as the scene started, it was obvious that he and Alison had unrivalled chemistry and the part was his. Not that at the time he, nor anyone else could have predicted just how *Gavin and Stacey* would change Larry's life forever. Synonymous with the twenty to thirty generation, the show hit on that undefinable something that captured the public's imagination and took sitcom to uncharted territory.

It was clear from the outset that this would be a different kind of sitcom to anything that had gone before and that extended to the making of the series. Filming predominantly took place in South Wales which meant both cast and crew were forced to stay in tight confines with each other for a few days per week for three months. The technique was used by the director Christine Gernon and writers Ruth Jones and James Corden for the ease of getting everyone in the right place at the right time, but of course it had other unlooked for benefits in that it brought the whole cast together and created a natural chemistry between all of them. Larry puts some of the show's success down to this unique process as in such a conducive environment it was hard not to become the character you were playing. So when he was in South Wales he wasn't Larry Lamb, he was Mick Shipman and this attitude was echoed throughout the whole cast, making *Gavin and Stacey* one of the best experiences of Larry's career. A decade and twenty episodes later, Larry is still synonymous with the character of Mick Shipman and it's the role he's most recognised for, something which he still holds so fondly.

For an actor, defining roles can be like buses; you wait for ages for one to come along and then two come at once. This was exactly what happened to Larry in 2008 when he was cast as the villainous Archie Mitchell in the heavyweight BBC serial drama, *EastEnders*. The controlling east end gangster with a dark past of abuse to daughters Ronnie and Roxy, Archie deservedly met his end when attempting a sexual assault on Stacey Slater. Although appearing in just 311 episodes, the character of Archie Mitchell played a dominant role in shaking up one of the most formidable families on Albert Square and was a great contrast with the lovable Mick Shipman in *Gavin and Stacey*.

These two shows helped to turn Larry Lamb from a jobbing actor into a household name. Yet it was still five years before he was offered another major television role replacing Dennis Waterman in the hugely popular *New Tricks*. This came at a price when it was announced that this would be the last series of the hit show. Such a blow for Larry encouraged him to ponder new horizons and a spot on *I'm a Celebrity… Get Me out Of Here 2016* cemented this. In recent years, Larry has united with the presenting talents of his son George for Channel Five's *Britain By Bike* where the pair cycle around all four corners of the UK which has extended his talents as a broadcaster.

Now into his seventh decade, Larry Lamb shows no signs of slowing down and at the time of our interview, he was getting excited about a possible brand new BBC1 drama. Yet within months of our meeting, it was revealed that there would be one more *Gavin and Stacey* Christmas Special for Christmas 2019 which would reunite the whole cast for what many believed would be the very last time. This would complete a significant chapter of his career and if only I had known I could have got a world exclusive for my Christmas *Beyond The Title*! However, whether he's playing Mick Shipman, Archie Mitchell or cycling the byways of Britain, he does it all with the same style and grace. It was fantastic to meet and interview Larry Lamb, a true gentleman.

# Miles Jupp

The following meeting with Miles Jupp wasn't any old meeting or interview. The writer and comedian Miles Jupp shall always hold a very significant place in the development of *Beyond The Title* for the simple reason that he was my first ever subject. Since having the original idea for the podcast I realised that one my biggest hurdles would be finding people who would be willing to take part in a short interview. By this time I was familiar with the discourse of the interview both from my research surrounding Sir Bill Cotton and my radio documentary. Therefore I had no problems with the content of the podcast, it was just finding a star who I could feature.

So when hunting for my first subject in the autumn of 2016, I remembered John Hannam's great technique of waiting at the stage door of a local theatre ready to attract the attention of a star. Yet of course with the invention of email and social media, it's increasingly easier to make contact with a performer and touring comics are probably among the most accessible just because they're forever attempting to look for platforms to plug their latest tour. Being quick to make the most of this opportunity, I researched on the internet to find out who was performing in my local area (yes, some celebrities do actually brave the water and make the dreaded crossing to the Isle of Wight!) and realised that the writer and comedian Miles Jupp was taking his one man show to the Medina Theatre. Again, with my experience of producing my radio documentary and my biographical drama, I was familiar with contacting and negotiating with agents and had no problem in creating email dialogue with them. I researched Miles Jupp's agent online and fired her a quick email. To my surprise and delight she was really enthusiastic about the project and it was agreed that Mr Jupp could offer me ten minutes before sound check to which I was so thankful for unbeknown to me, this was the start of something big! I was lucky enough to meet the man for a quick chat while he ate a baguette before taking to the stage.

Miles Jupp was now slowly becoming part of the British comedy elite thanks to his regular appearances on panel shows such as *'Have I Got News for You'*, *'Would I Lie to You'* and *'Cats Does Countdown'*. Starting his career on the stand-up circuit in the late nineties, Jupp was following in the footsteps of his comedy heroes Max Boyce, Arnold Brown and Tom Lehrer. In 2002 Jupp was cast as inventor Archie in the Children's BBC series, *Balamory*. For three years he starred alongside Julie Wilson, Nimmo and Kasia Haddad in the hit children's series. For a specific generation of children, irrespective of what heights his career reaches, he will forever be known as Archie, and he is more than happy with this. Children's TV bid *Balamory* farewell in 2005 but the way it's fondly remembered by the public, Archie is likely to live on for many years to come. It was here that Miles learned the discipline of TV drama which he was able to cultivate over the next decade. Being in the TV environment and learning basic television language including cutaways, two shots and single camera stood him in great stead for his later roles.

In June 2010 Miles secured one of many career defining roles when he was cast as lay-reader Nigel McCall in the cult BBC2 series *Rev* alongside Tom Hollander and Olivia Coleman. As is the case for most beloved sitcoms, *Rev* thrived upon pathos and created its fair share of touching and heart-warming moments. This was something which Miles enjoyed immensely and the character of Nigel was a dream to play. In an age where the traditional studio sitcom was arguably in decline, Rev was a shining example that there still remains a soaring appetite for the genre. The highly principled and extremely anal Nigel is essentially the yin to Reverend Adam Smallbone's yang and frequently became increasingly infuriated by the vicar's reckless behaviour. This chemistry became one of the most popular aspects of the show and for three series this formula proved successful making *Rev* one of the best sitcoms of the 2010's which in turn helped to put Miles Jupp on the comedy map.

In 2015 Miles entered the intrepid world of radio broadcasting when he replaced Sandi Toksvig for BBC Radio 4's satirical panel show *The News Quiz*. It was here he learned the pastoral responsibilities of being a chairman of a panel show and the duties which a host is forced to fulfil, needing to control the pace of the show while still allowing panellists the freedom to tangent, adhering to the loose concept of the game and of course awarding the points, which in any comedy panel shows are absolutely irrelevant. Despite the admin side of presenting *The News Quiz*, at the time of the interview, Jupp was a year into the role and thriving upon his new radio status. Four years later *The News Quiz* is still going strong with Jupp at the helm as he presides over some of the cream of British comedy as they take an irreverent look at the biggest news stories of the week. I hope his tenure on *The News Quiz* is a long and prosperous one.

In recent years Jupp has pursued his acting career, appearing as Humphrey in the Netflix period drama *The Crown* before a string of serious acting roles came calling, most notably ITV's *The Durrell's* and the BBC's most recent adaptation of *Watership Down*. This has given Jupp a brand new audience and it's exciting to see what he'll turn his hands to next.

Miles Jupp shall forever remain a very special interview for me as it was my first in podcast format and made me realise that such an idea could actually be successful. For him to give me his time on such a busy evening was incredible and obviously so generous of spirit. As we stopped recording, Miles advised me to keep persevering and be politely persistent with contacting my subjects to interview. In his words "persistence is the key". Such simple advice is something that I always keep in mind on the regular occasion when a subject declines an interview. Maybe this is the secret of his success: a quiet confidence about the many projects he conquers whilst not being frightened to take that big step to further his own career. It was an absolute pleasure to interview Mr Jupp on his life, career and beyond and I definitely couldn't ask any more of my first guest. All I hoped was that everyone could be as obliging and fascinating as he was!

## Vicki Michelle MBE

Unfortunately I'm far too young to have seen the original broadcasts of Vicki Michelle in her role as the passionate and lustful Yvette Carte-Blanche in Croft and Lloyd's wartime sitcom *Allo Allo*. Instead the first time I became aware of Vicki and her work was on the Saturday night entertainment series *Noel's House Party* where she played the part of Noel's randy next door neighbour. As I grew up, I became increasingly familiar with Vicki's work, most notably watching Sunday afternoon repeats of *Allo Allo* which were a firm staple of the BBC1 schedule. Unlike most actors, Vicki isn't fazed by being this parody of herself on screen which makes her the perfect guest for any Light Entertainment show. So throughout my childhood Vicki remained a constant face on my TV screen whether it was *Celebrity Squares* or *Noel's House Party* and as a result, I feel like I have grown up with her.

When I created *Beyond The Title* in 2016, there were so many names that went through my head of who I would love to interview and because of her constant televisual presence throughout my childhood, Vicki's name was near the top of that list. Combined with the fact that she works closely alongside one of my professional contacts led me to believe that it would be relatively simple to secure an interview with this sitcom icon. Yet with a gruelling schedule of work commitments and charity events, Vicki's spare time runs at a premium. However, our paths collided at the Museum Of Comedy in October 2017 when we both attended an *Allo Allo* themed show starring Sue Hodge aka Mimi Labonq. Waiting to go into the theatre to take our seats, I caught Vicki's eye as my PA Calum negotiated through the crowds in order to chat with her. It was here that I was able to brief her on what I did and ask her for the possibility of an interview for my podcast. To my delight she agreed and we swapped details.

Through a series of unfortunate events, arranging the interview proved to be more complicated than we once thought and as a result of her constant demand we were forced to put the idea on hold for the foreseeable future. It was only a few months later when I was perusing the website of my local theatre that I realised that Vicki was due to perform later that month and thought this was the perfect opportunity to finally interview the legendary actress.

Sure enough, when we met up again it was like meeting an old friend and despite her nationwide fame, Vicki remains extremely down to earth and humble about her vast achievements in showbiz. Being such a cultural figure, it would be easy for Vicki to be detached and a little nonchalant with her answers just as a result of how many times she has been asked the same question. Yet still being in love with the business, it's clear that Vicki enjoys talking about her glittering career and still has that zest for her work. So with the niceties out the way, Vicki was eager to get the interview underway as James pressed the red button on the sound recorder.

Making her screen debut on the cult 1960's serial drama Dixon of Dock Green, television and theatre actress Vicki Michelle has been entertaining the nation for over half a century becoming one of Britain's most recognisable TV faces. In 1972 Vicki enjoyed her first brush with the sitcom playing Terry Collier's (James Bolam) latest brazen girlfriend Madelyn in Clement and Le Frenais' sitcom revival Whatever Happened to the Likely Lads in an episode entitled The Ant and the Grasshopper which demanded Vicki to perfect her north east accent. The role was a success and Clement and Le Frenais invited her back for the feature length TV movie in 1976.

By 1978 Vicki was ready to take on her first major television role and auditioned for a part in Jeremy Lloyd and David Croft's new sci-fi sitcom Comeback Mrs Noah alongside her sister Ann. Luckily they were both able to secure parts and this gave Vicki her first professional encounter with the legendary David Croft who would go on to have a dominant influence in her later career. For Vicki, it was a great experience to share the screen with her sister who at the time was the more accomplished actress and this proved to be the perfect grounding for her. This forward thinking, space themed show was definitely ahead of its time and starred Mollie Sugden as Mrs Gertrude Noah, a 2050 housewife who wins a cookery competition to have a Britannia Seven, the UK's new Space Exploration Vehicle. Vicki played the French maid robot who aids Mrs Noah through her journey. For this she perfected her French accent which would prove vital for an upcoming role just a few years later. Come Back Mrs Noah survived for just one series but Vicki remains extremely proud of the way the show helped to move sitcom on and has very fond memories of working on such an original series.

Her next TV venture came just four years later when Vicki auditioned for another Croft and Lloyd production. David Croft had already enjoyed huge success with two sitcoms based on his experiences in the Second World War with Dad's Army and It Ain't Half Hot Mum but now with Jeremy Lloyd whom he had collaborated with in creating Are You Being Served, he was now ready to take on the French resistance. Knowing first hand David Croft's genius as a writer, Vicki felt compelled to audition and went for the parts of Michelle of the resistance (who was eventually played by Kirsten Cooke) and lustful waitress Yvette Carte-Blanche and the rest is history!

From the outset, both cast and crew of *Allo Allo* worked to a simple shorthand that the French were randy, the Germans were kinky and the English were stupid.

Therefore Croft, Lloyd nor the cast could never be accused of xenophobia because everyone was laughing at everyone and the general misunderstandings between the nations. This, combined with unexplained universal sexual interest in cafe owner René Artois added to the farcical aspect of the show and spawned Vicki's best known catchphrase "ooh, René!" This created the seductive throatal sound "ooh" which was enough to give any scene the preferred feeling of sexual desire. The late Gorden Kaye was the perfect linchpin for the sitcom and in his reliable hands *Allo Allo* became one of Britain's most successful sitcom exports and nearly forty years later it's still a staple of TV making *Allo Allo* one of Vicki's greatest achievements.

After *Allo Allo*, Vicki popped up on BBC1's Saturday night extravaganza Noel's House Party playing the part of his sexually frustrated neighbour who was deeply in love with Noel whilst everyone else around him thought he was a jumped up lord of the manor. Such a bizarre concept required an experienced actress to understand the parameters of the fictional world of Crinkley Bottom when everyone else was portraying themselves. It was here that Vicki learned Noel's incredible flare for comedic ad-lib and was in awe of how he effortlessly kept the live show together with constant mayhem surrounding him. Being a regular didn't make Vicki exempt from the dreaded Gotcha where she was invited to a restaurant in disguise to determine if celebrities received better treatment than the general public. This resulted in her supposed arrest, where, following her transportation to the local police station under escort, she failed to recognise her arresting officer as an actor from The Bill before finally being presented with her Gotcha by Noel also in disguise as a policeman. She always said that Edmonds would never get her but even a regular like Vicki was able to fall for the convoluted situation dreamed up by the unpredictable Saturday night host. Despite this, Noel's House Party was an absolute dream to be involved with and was a great Saturday night treat right up until the dawn of the new millennium.

As a performer, Vicki has always felt a huge responsibility to use her fame to help to highlight and support good causes. As patron of three national charities; Haven House Children's Hospice, Essex Women's Advisory Group and AA Dog Rescue, Vicki has witnessed first-hand the incredible selfless service of remarkable people all over Britain. Her great passion for looking after former servicemen and women has been the driving force behind her involvement since 2008 in the Bomber Command Association who acknowledges former members of the armed forces. To honour these great men and women who fought for our freedom is a great privilege and Vicki was immensely proud when the charity was recognised by the Queen. In doing this she was able to befriend a lot of the surviving Bomber Boys and hear their remarkable stories of survival and bravery. This is something very close to her heart and despite her involvement in a whole host of different charities and fundraisers, The Bomber Command Association shall forever occupy a special place in her heart as she feels it is increasingly important remember this generation of men and women who sacrificed their own lives for our freedom.

Returning to television in 2007, Vicki fulfilled a lifetime's ambition to star in a serial drama when she secured the role of matriarch Patricia Foster in ITV's Emmerdale. Doting mother of Jonny, Patricia arrives to give her blessing to his engagement to Paul. Making a surprise return on Jonny and Paul's wedding day, she is shocked to discover that the pair have already eloped but decided to properly marry again out of guilt. Unfortunately actors Richard Greive and Matthew Bose announced their departure from the show meaning that Vicki's portrayal of Patricia would be short lived. Yet Emmerdale was something that Vicki loved and satisfied her long time desire to star in a soap.

Never abandoning her love for the stage, at the time of our interview in early 2019, Vicki was enjoying being on a nationwide tour of the new comedy play Hormonal Housewives and delighted in playing a new venue each and every night. With her status as a national treasure assured, Vicki shows no signs of slowing down and was already looking ahead to the panto season of that year. It was a fantastic pleasure to meet and interview Vicki Michelle, and I wish her every success for the rest of her illustrious career.

# Sue Hodge

The life of a supporting actor can be extremely frustrating. The realisation that you're not the star of the show, the strain of obtaining significant roles and the overwhelming desire to be top of the bill can have a devastating effect upon an actors' self-confidence. However in recent years, co-stars of our favourite sitcoms have stepped out from the shadows of their leading counterparts and now find themselves in demand as live performances and panto have enjoyed a renaissance. Actress and entertainer Sue Hodge first came to public attention for her portrayal of pint-sized waitress Mimi Labonq in Croft and Lloyd's wartime sitcom *Allo Allo*. A role which has made her into one of Britain's most enduring and loved comedy performers.

*Allo Allo*'s constant presence on British television means that it has become a universal rite of passage for any avid comedy fan. Its popular repeated slot on the BBC on their Sunday afternoon schedule has introduced a new generation to the bizarre happenings at Cafe Artois. The first time I became aware of Sue and her position within the show was in 2007 when I sat down to watch the anniversary show *Allo Allo Again* celebrating a quarter of a century of the much loved series with a live special. It was here that I realised the magic of Mimi Labonq and her lustful relationship with cafe owner René Artois played by the late Gorden Kaye. Prior to this I had always associated the character of René with Vicki Michelle's throaty calling and Carmen Silvera's suspicious eye when spotting him with the opposite sex. Yet Sue Hodge and Gorden Kaye's on screen chemistry was so potent that it made me want to watch the entire series to observe this comedic 'sexual tension' between them.

In 2017, just a year into *Beyond The Title* I was looking at the autumn line up for the Museum of Comedy and realised that Sue Hodge was previewing her forthcoming tour *Allo Again: Mimi and Me* alongside her husband and pianist Keith 'Paddington' Richards. I thought this would be the perfect opportunity to interview the celebrated comedy actress and promptly located the details of her agent. To my delight I got an instant reply accepting my request. A few weeks later myself and my PA Calum found ourselves at the Museum of Comedy in preparation to see Sue Hodge's one woman show and of course to interview the woman herself. Upon arriving we discovered one minor problem; the lift was broken meaning that I would be forced to walk into the theatre aided by Calum. When I get excited my body goes into spasm and it's really hard for me to do anything. So when I was confronted by a room full of celebrities including the late Bella Emberg, Vicki Michelle and Sue Hodge herself I was almost taken off my feet and it was hard for Calum to control me. Thankfully when I returned to my wheelchair, Sue was ready to do the interview and all that Calum had to do was press record on the equipment.

Before we get into the essence of the interview, if you need a reminder as to the context of the podcast then here's a brief description: *Allo Allo* was first broadcasted on the 30th December 1982 and reigned over the television schedules for the next ten years making stars out of its cast members including Gorden Kaye, Carmen Silvera and Vicki Michelle. This was in the 'second incarnation' of writing duo David Croft and Jeremy Lloyd who had enjoyed unrivalled success during the 1970's with *Are You Being Served?* followed by the Sci-Fi sitcom *Come Back Mrs Noah*. Surviving for a decade from 1982 and 1992, *Allo Allo* was an instant hit with the British public and has been exported to over thirty-five countries to date.

Comedy actress Sue Hodge joined the show for the fourth series in 1987 as the pint sized blonde bombshell waitress, Mimi Labonq who was yet another sexually charged female to have her sights firmly set on the unlikely sex symbol of René François Artois played by Gorden Kaye. But of course,

René was "happily" married to the strong willed failed singer Madam Edith played by Carmen Silvera, who would regularly be on the warpath suspicious of her husband's potential sexual exploits with an array of waitresses. By the time Mimi Labonq entered René's cafe, the ensemble cast members were already established and the series was a big hit. So it seemed a big task for Sue to join a hugely popular show. Yet as soon as Mimi made her debut on the third episode of the fourth series, the public took her to their hearts and it wasn't long before she became a permanent fixture.

Sue's portrayal of Mimi Labonq was able to flourish right up until the final series in 1992 and her on screen relationship with Kaye grew ever stronger. For some reason, the watching nation became invested into the fallacy that this middle aged, overweight intolerant Frenchman could be the subject of so many women's sexual desires...he was no Brad Pitt! However, here was a man who could make even the strongest of women go weak at the knees and he often used this to his advantage. This was a great gift for the supporting cast as on occasions they didn't have to say anything to get a big laugh and Gorden Kaye would often play on it to hilarious consequences.

Like he and Jimmy Perry had captured so effortlessly in *It Ain't Half Hot Mum*, David Croft parodied the language barrier to a whole new level and played around with the art of language together with understandings in it. Having so many nationalities in one series gave Lloyd and Croft scope to explore the national stereotypes of each wartime country. The French were randy and clever, the Germans kinky and silly and the English were stupid. Officer Crabtree, played by Arthur Bostrom, perfectly epitomised this stupidity towards foreign languages displayed by the English when in a foreign country and his attempts to get to grips with the French language are now cultural mainstays. Most notably his and the show's best loved catchphrase, "Good Moaning" which was always certain to get a laugh whenever Crabtree entered a scene. Rivalling it in popularity came a catchphrase from Michelle Dubois of the Resistance (played by Kirsten Cook) as she would appear in the most unlikely places uttering the line, "listen very carefully, I shall say this only once".

*Allo Allo* was one of the most popular shows on television up until and beyond its final series in 1992 when the cast were forced to go their separate ways. Yet such a tight knit group wasn't going to cease getting together. They regularly met up at comedy conventions and television exhibitions

115

which celebrated the show's huge success and became like a long term family. By this time, Sue Hodge had returned to the stage with Gorden Kaye to do two national tours over two years of 'No Place Like A Home'. In 2002 Sue married Grantham rock musician Keith Maxon, better known by his stage name Keith 'Paddington' Richards.

In 2007 the cast of *Allo Allo* returned for a feature length anniversary edition of the show to celebrate twenty five years. For Sue, stepping back onto the set of the French cafe felt like coming home and when the characters were reunited on the studio floor, it was like they'd never been away. The success of the reunion forced Sue to realise that there still might be public appetite for the character of Mimi Labonq. With the help of Keith, Sue began to write a comedy stage play based on Mimi's tenure in that famous cafe.

Just a few months before Sue and I met, Britain lost a comedy great in Gorden Kaye and as one of his closest friends Sue was able to chart his tragic deterioration in the months leading up to his death in January 2017. I took this opportunity to ask Sue about her memories of what it was like to know the great man. It was obvious that Gorden meant a lot to her. Forever telling her that he didn't think he would make 70, the celebrated actor surpassed his own expectations and survived until he was 75 but a combination of the devastating effect of his major car accident in 1990 together with needing assistance with daily tasks lead to his sad decline and eventual passing. Yet by the way he is fondly remembered by the people who knew him it is obvious that Gorden was a star both on and off camera.

Still in demand as a live performer, Sue has now become synonymous with the art of pantomime and every Christmas you can be assured that the sitcom favourite will be appearing in a theatre somewhere round Britain to rave reviews. In addition 2016 saw the long awaited release of her book *"Allo 'Allo Mimi's Memoirs"*. This provided fans an opportunity to relive moments from the show alongside Sue's own insight into what happened to the characters since closing time at Café Artois. It's clear that over a quarter of a century on from the last episode of *Allo Allo,* there's still a great appetite for the series and Sue Hodge remains the perfect personification of the magic behind the Croft and Lloyd masterpieces. Beyond her vast theatrical success, Sue shall forever embody the cheeky, merriment of Mimi Labonq and for this she's extremely proud and I am extremely grateful for the time she spared me.

# Jeffrey Holland

When I was eight years old, I began my love affair with TV comedy and on one particular day my dad played me a video of a programme which he had recorded from the night before. Entitled *Oh Doctor Beeching,* it's not an exaggeration to say that this show was to change my life and made me realise my dream of one day being involved in the world of the Arts. I just loved the show and every time it was on I would fall silent with awe and wonder. It was like half an hour of pure heaven and I just couldn't get enough of it.

From researching around the show, I realised that *Oh Doctor Beeching* was the third instalment of a unique comedy franchise spanning two decades. Suddenly I had hours and hours of comedy to catch up on and I loved every second. It wasn't the most critically acclaimed series and 20 years on it's rarely cited as a comedy classic, yet there was something about the interaction between the cast which stirred something in me to follow these characters to areas I had never been before.

When I started *Beyond The Title,* the world of sitcom played a dominant role in my ideal interview line-up. Unfortunately, the late Paul Shane is no longer around to provide me with his side of the story but I was still adamant that I could interview Jeffrey Holland and Su Pollard. After spending months attempting to make contact with Jeffrey, I discovered that he was appearing at the Museum Of Comedy in London alongside the celebrated comedy historian Robert Ross in a live show entitled *Jeffrey Holland and Friends* where he recounted tales from his career in entertainment. I set about attempting to track down a good contact.

Embracing the steady influx of new technology, Jeffrey is extremely active on Social Media and I decided to tweet him. To my delight, he "followed" me and we were able to enjoy a successful dialogue which resulted in him accepting my offer of an interview at the Museum Of Comedy. By this time *Beyond The Title* had been running for two and a half years and I had met some of the most prolific figures of the twentieth century. But for some reason an interview with Jeffrey Holland filled me with both joy and trepidation because to me he is a comedy hero.

Arriving at the Museum Of Comedy is always a great feeling just because of how many great interviews I have enjoyed there. For some reason it felt different as I knew I was about to meet someone I'd admired for a very long time. On walking into the museum, myself and my PA Will made our way to the theatre area where Jeffrey caught my eye and instructed us to get set up while he finished up. We made our way to our favourite booth and as we were waiting, I was taken back to my eight-year old self avidly watching Jeffrey as the straight laced Cecil Parkin in *Oh Doctor Beeching*, but now he would be sitting opposite me answering questions which I had written.

In a career spanning half a century, star of stage and screen Jeffrey Holland went from supporting actor roles in television dramas to becoming one of Britain's best loved sitcom stars. Making his television debut in the serial drama *Crossroads* in 1964, Jeffrey made brief cameos in television dramas of the day before appearances in Perry and Croft's two greatest sitcom triumphs of the 1970's. Securing supporting roles in both *Dad's Army* and *It Ain't Half Hot Mum* respectively in 1977 and 1978, introduced the young actor to the writing duo who would help define the rest of his career.

By 1978 Jeffrey was starting to become a familiar face on TV and auditioned for the part of Jack Boot in the Christmas pantomime of Robinson Crusoe alongside Frankie Howerd. Yet unfortunately only a few days into the Christmas run, Howerd broke his leg forcing him to pull out of the production which automatically promoted Jeffrey to the top of the bill. Working with such a colourful character as Howerd meant that Jeffrey had been required to know both parts by rote to ensure the star of the show was kept on track. Therefore when asked to jump into the main role it was no problem for Jeffrey. Such an opportunity promptly put him literally centre stage and attracted attention from TV executives who could now consider him as a leading man.

Just a year previously, the young actor had taken part in a pilot sitcom episode written by Perry and Croft surrounding the bizarre goings on of a fictional holiday camp during the 1950's. The inspiration behind the show derived from Jimmy Perry's brief time as a redcoat at Butlins before going on to be a jobbing actor. Having delighted BBC executives with the pilot, it would be another two years before a full six part series was broadcast. *Hi-De-Hi* was an overnight hit and made stars of the major cast including Jeffrey, Paul Shane and Su Pollard. Jeffrey was cast as the holiday camp's comic, Spike Dixon who had decided to relinquish a career in income tax to follow his dream of becoming an entertainer. With the help of lifelong friend Ted Bovis (played by Paul Shane), he secures a job at Maplins which is currently under the new management of duck out of water Jeffrey Fairbrother played by the late Simon Cadell.

Over nine series and fifty three episodes, *Hi-De-Hi* followed the lives of the yellow coats at Maplins holiday camp as they welcomed guests with their unique brand of entertainment. Jeffrey had never met Paul Shane prior to their casting but as soon as they did, the pair knew they had obvious chemistry. Just as Ted and Spike seemed inseparable in the show, Jeffrey and Paul were quick to develop a great friendship off screen which had a very positive effect on their personas on screen. As camp entertainer, Spike usually became the butt of Ted's jokes which often resulted in him being picked up and thrown into the large swimming pool. Quintessentially a straight man, Perry and Croft used the character of Spike as a device that all other characters bounced off and in certain situations, he became the voice of reason to the madness that was unfolding.

*Hi-De-Hi* came to an end in 1988 but David Croft had already started working on another comedy masterpiece which would ultimately reunite the major cast members. An irreverent take on the British class structure of the 1920's it would pit stars of *Hi-De-Hi* alongside Michael Knowles and Donald Hewlett from *It Ain't Half Hot Mum* in an ensemble cast of best loved sitcom faces. *Dad's Army* stars Frank Williams and Bill Pertwee also joined the stellar cast as Lord Bishop Charles and Constable Wilson bringing a similar chemistry to the show as they displayed in their previous roles. First broadcast on the 29th December 1988, *You Rang M'Lord* toiled with the foundations of sitcom which had been in place for the last thirty years. Instead of relying on the standard thirty minute sitcom slot, Perry and Croft extended each episode to fifty minutes to capture the feel of a big budget period drama.

Jeffrey was cast as pompous footman James Twelvetrees who had illusions of grandeur that he should belong among the upper class elite and struggled with knowing his position as a servant. Forever being kept grounded by scheming butler Alf Stokes (played by Paul Shane), the pair enjoyed a love hate relationship throughout all four series and once again were able to hone their innate chemistry which transcended the screen. Over four series and twenty-six episodes spanning 1988 to 1993 *You Rang M'Lord* became a Sunday night teatime favourite which harped back to the golden years of British comedy and over a quarter of a century on, it's still being discovered by new audiences. Despite his other accomplishments Jeffrey remains extremely proud of *You Rang M'Lord,* although when it finished, he, Paul and Su still weren't done with sitcom...

In 1995 David Croft reunited the cast for one last time in his historical sitcom surrounding the railway strike of the 1960's in *Oh Doctor Beeching.* Jeffrey was cast as pompous station master Cecil Parkin brought in to save the failing station but is shocked to find his old flame May was now married to the station porter Jack Skinner, played by Paul Shane. This adds to the rivalrous tension between Jack and Cecil and formed the backbone of the series. There was always a mysterious black cloud over the identity of the father of May's daughter Gloria which was never answered and became yet another contentious issue between the two men. It was the first time that Jeffrey had played a figure of authority and thrived upon the newfound responsibility that it spawned. In the previous two sitcom outings, he had always been subservient to a higher authority but it was refreshing to play a character who was in charge.

*Oh Doctor Beeching* proved to be the last outing for David Croft's unique repertory company and ran for two series from 8th July 1996, with the last episode being broadcast on 28th September 1997. As always the traditional trio of Paul Shane, Su Pollard and Jeffrey Holland were joined by familiar sitcom faces including Stephen Lewis, Julia Deakin and Perry Benson who made up the stellar supporting cast which helped to make *Oh Doctor Beeching* a nineties family favourite. Surviving for just two series, the show possibly marked the end of an era for the traditional sitcom being the last ever David Croft production. Yet this repertory company was unique in delivering three separate sitcom triumphs with the same main cast. Something that Jeffrey remains extremely proud of.

Beyond sitcom success, Jeffrey's passions lay in the heroes of comedy itself which has dominated the latter part of his career. In 2001 he joined forces with Andrew Secombe and Jon Glover for a live broadcast of a very special stage show commemorating fifty years of *The Goon Show*. Performing those legendary scripts in front of a live celebrity packed studio audience was a very special achievement for Jeffrey and he was taken back by the fantastic reception it received. After the show Barry Cryer tapped him on the shoulder with the immortal words 'Spot on!' To have such approval from a comedy icon meant a lot to Jeffrey and it was at this point that he knew that they had pulled it off. For the great Spike Milligan to be alive long enough to hear a 21st century take on his 1950's masterpiece was a great feeling and witnessing Andrew Secombe getting overcome with emotion about stepping into his late father's shoes made it all the more meaningful. In short this was the best night that Jeffrey has ever spent in a theatre.

His other comedy hero is Stan Laurel. Jeffrey remembers being a boy and watching in the cinema Laurel, alongside his long term partner Oliver Hardy. It was here he realised the power of comedy and fell in love with the art. In 2013 Jeffrey fulfilled a lifetime's ambition when he wrote and performed a one man show entitled *And This is My Friend Mr Laurel* surrounding the relationship between Laurel and Hardy. He was able to play both parts to critical acclaim, this was his true passion and despite unparalleled sitcom success, he considers this his greatest achievement to date.

Jeffrey Holland shows no signs of slowing down and at the time of our interview was looking forward to embarking on a stage tour alongside his wife, actress Judy Buxton. This would be followed by reuniting with old friend Su Pollard for the 2019 production of Dick Whittington at the Grand Theatre in Wolverhampton. It was a great pleasure to meet and interview the legendary Jeffrey Holland and if you had told that nine year old boy that one day he would spend half an hour with the real life Cecil Parkin, I imagine it would have been enough to make him pass out. Yet that is one of the huge advantages of doing what I do and Jeffrey Holland is amongst the growing list of personal heroes that I have had the privilege to meet.

# Brian Conley

By the 1990's the popularity of new wave alternative comedy had started to wain and thanks to the talent of television stalwarts Cilla Black and Noel Edmonds, the magic of Saturday night was back and Light Entertainment once again ruled the airwaves. After so long in the television wilderness, this rebirth of the genre made overnight stars of people who would go on to dominate Light Entertainment for years to come. This generation of performers is very interesting to study as no longer did they have full on theatrical variety to fall back on like their forefathers and instead needed to have another string to their bow in order to survive the unpredictable glare of the spotlight.

Celebrating forty five years in show-business in 2018, comedian and entertainer Brian Conley was back on the road with his brand new show *The Greatest Entertainer in His Price Range*. Beginning his entertainment career as a warm up man for 1980's shows such as the BBC's *Wogan*, Conley was able to learn about the business from grassroots, something that he feels is missing in today's X Factor Generation. I was lucky enough to meet up with the evergreen entertainer on the set of the most southern leg of his tour at Shanklin Theatre on the Isle of Wight. Every time I go to interview someone in person, I always wonder what they are going to be like and how they will interact with me. After all, I imagine it's a little bit daunting when you have someone trying to interview you whilst you're in the middle of psyching yourself up to entertain a theatre full of people. Indeed, the last thing you may want is some jumped up journo wanting to ask you about something you did years ago. Yet what can I say, I'm persistent if nothing else!

When we got to the theatre we were guided into the auditorium where we waited for a short while before I heard the unmistakable voice of Brian Conley coming from the depths of the theatre before a door opened and out he walked. Instantly he made me feel at ease and was interested to know a little more about me and what I did so I left it to James to explain.

He quickly realised what I was all about and we struck up some banter before it was time to press record on the Tascam. Normally, my subjects sit pensively waiting for the first question, slightly apprehensive. Yet, this was Brian Conley and obviously he had other ideas. Of course he naturally wanted to get the first word in! I felt this was absolutely brilliant and made for a more interesting interview and if I was the butt of the joke so be it. He told the listeners I was sat naked in front of him which was putting him off (which was a lie! – At least on this occasion). Throughout the interview he kept making references to my ability to be quiet while James was delivering the questions which made the interview descend into chaos but it was what he did best. It is very rare that I am heard on my interviews as a result of my difficulty in communicating and for a podcast it's not ideal but his constant barrage of good-natured "abuse" aimed at me was too good not to include.

Toying with television throughout the 1980's, Brian struggled to find a vehicle which would showcase his talents as an all-round entertainer. Appearances on variety shows including *Live at Her Majesty's* helped to raise his profile and made him a recognisable face on television. Still being new to the small screen, Brian had yet to figure out which of his many talents he was going to bring to the forefront. He could sing, dance, act and be funny, all with the same confident enthusiasm which made him the perfect turn on the big budget variety shows of the day and it wasn't long before producers were snapping him up for his own television series. In an era when Variety and Light Entertainment seemed outdated and phoney, Brian Conley's cheeky chappie sense of humour would in time make shiny floor Saturday night entertainment relevant for nineties Britain.

In 1993 LWT launched *The Brian Conley Show* giving birth to a whole host of memorable comic creations including; Nick Frisbee and 'his old mate' Larry the Loafer, Septic Peg and Dangerous Brian. With one foot firmly in the era of traditional variety, this format showcased Brian's talent as an all-round entertainer. He could sing, dance (a little!) tell jokes and interact with the audience; the perfect formula for Saturday night entertainment. The *Brian Conley Show* survived for over a decade until August 2002 when talent shows began to dominate the airwaves, possibly marking the end of an era for family Light Entertainment. Despite this, Brian had created a plethora of lovable characters which are still fondly remembered two decades on.

Beyond television success, Brian has also enjoyed a varied theatrical career ever since his 1995 portrayal of Al Jolson in the musical of his namesake; a role which secured Conley a prestigious Olivier nomination for best actor. Relatively forgotten in today's society, due to the obvious racial undertones of his blackface act, Jolson was an extremely talented performer and it was great for Brian to pay tribute to one of Britain's first nationwide stars. This was the first major theatrical role in what would become a long list ranging from Edna Turnblad in *Hairspray* to Fagin in *Oliver* and it's obvious from how passionately he speaks of his theatrical career that Conley not only loves the format but that he isn't done with musicals yet…

In 2017 Brian Conley was back on Saturday night TV on BBC1's heavyweight extravaganza *Strictly Come Dancing*. Partnered by newcomer Amy Dowden, he survived the public vote and judges' comments until week five. This was somewhat of a disappointment for Brian who has been entertaining audiences for over forty years with sprinkles of dance ability. Yet he admits that it's primarily an entertainment show and every aspect is in place for entertainment purposes. Craig Revel-Horwood's on-screen persona is a character he plays for the duration of the show and he is completely different off screen. On the whole, Brian remains thankful for his *Strictly* experience.

In 2018 not only was Brian back on tour with his brand new show *The Greatest Entertainer…In His Price Range*, but he also returned to our television screens with the Channel Four game show *Buy It Now*. To see Brian on stage in full command of an audience is something to admire and his new live show is the epitome of this. Hysterically funny and partially unscripted, Brian has the ability to hold a theatre full of people in the palm of his hand for two hours. Like all great comics, he can make the audience part of his act, treading that line between making fun of them but without causing anyone to get offended… Well, almost. It was a great pleasure to meet the one and only Brian Conley and long may he keep Britain laughing for many years to come.

# Joe Pasquale

It is a well-known fact within the entertainment industry that comedians can be extremely difficult to interview. To get a real, in-depth insight into a comic's true take on the world can be compared to attempting to locate a small needle in a giant haystack…it's virtually impossible and only the elite interviewers have the know-how to tease it out of them. The secret of a successful interview with any comic is to know that whatever you do, you'll never be in full control of the situation and while you could attempt to regain power, it's often more entertaining for the listener to have the interview descend (or perhaps that should be ascend) into chaos while these jesters take full command. This is exactly what happened when I met Joe Pasquale in a little theatre on the Isle of Wight ahead of the southern leg of his 2017 stand-up tour.

I always like to be early for my interviews especially when grabbing five minutes with a star just before they go on stage. So me and my PA Ben arrived 10 minutes early and started to set up the equipment in a vestry room while waiting for the eccentric comic to make his entrance. Before long the recognisable squeaky voice was resonating down the bare corridor growing increasingly louder. One of the striking things about meeting

127

Pasquale for the first time is the sheer abundance of tattoos plastered all over his body which you wouldn't know by seeing him on television. This stems back to his great love for steampunk and the gothics of the 19th century, which he has just begun writing novels about. We realised that we had a mutual friend in the celebrated Colin Edmonds who is also a master of steampunk fiction which helped to break the ice and I guess it was good for him to realise that I was actually a media professional and not just a talented amateur. I later learned that Colin had in fact given Pasquale a little background about me so he knew what he was letting himself in for. This gave the interview more of a purity which is difficult to achieve when my subject has no prior knowledge of me. So I guess it helps to have friends in high places.

Pasquale has been making British audiences laugh for over thirty years since coming second on ITV's *New Faces* in 1986. Every talent show requires a "nasty" figure for the public to love to hate and in this series the sharp tongue of the writer and broadcaster *Nina Myskow* got the whole nation talking. Being on *The X Factor* of its day benefited Joe at such a young age as it gave him an insight into the workings of a television programme, an art which he would later hone as a comedy compère.

Joe made his debut at the *Royal Variety Performance* in 1993 and thus began a long association with the legendary show which has resulted in a host of memorable television moments. Who can forget the hilarious 1997 sketch with Des O'Connor and the mischievous llama who obviously wasn't house trained?

Joe's appearances on the show helped to transform him into a household name and made him synonymous with the *Royal Variety*. It was here that Britain fell in love with his unique brand of madcap humour, whether it's his spectacular failed magic tricks or a melody of irreverent songs including the now iconic "I know a song that'll get on your nerves" which interestingly he insists he hasn't sung for around two decades.

In 2005 Pasquale reigned victorious as King of the Jungle in *I'm a Celebrity…Get Me out Of Here*. One of the aspects which you don't consider as a viewer is the incredible boredom of each day. ITV only broadcasts a maximum of 45 minutes of footage per day plus the sister programme on ITV2 therefore there is a lot of time when absolutely nothing happens and for a natural entertainer like Joe, this would be enough to send you round the twist! Yet his laid back cheeky chappie persona eventually won him the series, cementing his popularity with the British public. This helped to extend Pasquale's audience and in 2006 he was put forward to reprise the legendary game show *The Price Is Right*. The show once presented by Leslie Crowther and Bruce Forsyth was back on our TV screens five nights per week in the slot now occupied by Bradley Walsh's *The Chase*. The revival was short-lived and even the Channel 4 sweetheart Alan Carr couldn't reinvent and reignite the game show for the late night audience.

Despite television success, Joe has never lost his passion for touring and his 2017 live show *The Devil in Disguise* epitomises this. Being in an elite pool of performers who can easily be at home in a large theatre or doing the late night stint at The Comedy Store, Pasquale has never been a one trick pony. In his words, "if it's funny then it's funny!" He regularly shares the same stage as "edgier" comics such as Joe Lycett and Romesh Ranganathan. So for him, there is no distinction between mainstream and alternative comedy – it shouldn't be analysed or quantified, it is what it is!

In 2018 Pasquale starred in the stage revival of the 1970's sitcom *Some Mothers Do 'ave 'em* playing the part of Frank Spencer. For this, he's found himself as a regular visitor to the Isle of Wight in discussions with the original writer of the sitcom Ray Allen. Joe was the perfect person to take this honour as he is among an elite group of comedians who have the ability to straddle both sides of the comedic sphere equally at home on the set of a gameshow or in a theatre packed full of punters. It may look simple to an audience who have grown accustomed to having multi-talented entertainers on demand but this discipline takes years to perfect and Joe has this in bucket loads. As I said, interviewing a comedian is a notoriously difficult thing to do, however to be able to quiz such a comedy powerhouse on his life and career was something very special and I just hope he enjoyed it half as much as I did.

# Paul Jackson

Being a novice comedy historian from a very young age, I have always been fascinated by big shows and the multi-talented stars who fronted them. Yet it wasn't long before I realised that behind such popular television, there always remains a highly talented, all seeing individual to oversee and control the quality of the show. Anyone who contributed to the development of Light Entertainment in its golden years has always been among those that I consider to be gods. These figures helped to create the very fabric of British entertainment which we still hold dear today and they were able to utilise television in a way that had never been done before. Personally I feel that these pioneers of television should be as celebrated as the stars they created and to have the opportunity to interview them is a real blessing.

After realising that a career in stand-up comedy wasn't for him, for over forty years, Paul Jackson has been integral to some of Britain's best loved television shows. Beginning his BBC career as part of Bill Cotton's Light Entertainment department during the early seventies, Jackson worked on a range of comedy programmes which brought him into contact with the biggest stars of the day. We met at London's BFI Southbank where I was lucky enough to interview him alongside a mutual friend; the TV consultant Dick Fiddy. This followed a chance meeting at the BBC Radio theatre where Paul was presenting a series for BBC Radio 4 Extra entitled *The Comedy Controllers* alongside Beryl Vertue, Jimmy Mulville and John Lloyd. However, this wasn't my first chance encounter with Paul as in 2010 he very kindly assisted me in my research for my major project screenplay based on the life and work of formidable TV executive Sir Bill Cotton by allowing me to interview him on the phone. As a former colleague and more importantly friend of Bill Cotton, the legendary former head of Light Entertainment, Paul was able to offer me an eye-witness account of what it was like to work in such a creative department at such a defining era for the corporation. Yet this further opportunity gave me the chance to ask more questions about his unparalleled career in television and I couldn't wait. Sometimes the people who spend their career behind the scenes have far better insight into the era than the figures who dominated it 'in the limelight' and Paul Jackson is a great example of this.

Of course television and Light Entertainment was nothing new for Paul whose late father, T. Leslie Jackson had been executive producer on shows of the fifties and sixties including *This Is Your Life*, *What's My Line* and *Call My Bluff*. As a result of this he recalls being shown around TV Centre visiting the sets of *That Was The Week That Was*, *Steptoe and Son* and *Dad's Army*. This offered the young Paul an insight into the business which would inform the rest of his life and he's never looked back. Unfortunately the Jackson dynasty within British television was a short one neither of Paul's daughters were interested in a career in the media. Yet this short-lived dynasty was able to chart the development of television from the experimental years of the 1950's to the multichannel landscape of post millennium Britain and this makes Paul rightly proud.

Finding himself at the centre of Bill Cotton's Light Entertainment department in the early seventies was invaluable experience for the young producer and was everything he ever dreamt of when he came to TV Centre as a boy. Securing the role as a Floor Manager for *The Two Ronnies*, Jackson was able to climb the ranks from Floor Manager to Executive Producer via roles as Vision Mixer, and developed a close working relationship with these two comedy titans. As he states, when you were working on *The Two Ronnies* you were essentially working for them and this was one of the only jobs in television where the producer and director were not the ones in charge.

Instead it was Jackson's job to make it possible for Barker and Corbett to do the things they wanted whilst maintaining BBC protocol, a combination which proved successful for the best part of twenty years until Ronnie Barker's shock retirement in 1987.

Paul was lucky enough to get to know both Corbett and Barker well and was able to develop a friendship which would outlive their BBC tenure. He was honoured to be invited to both of their memorial services at Westminster Abbey, where officials were granted special permission to carry four candles instead of two, a fitting acknowledgment to Barker and Corbett's place in British culture.

Towards the end of the 1970's, Britain was changing and with it arose a new brand of comedy which was slowly gaining a cult status within London's West End. The Comedy Store opened its doors on the 19th May 1979 and gave birth to a minor revolution soon to become known as Alternative Comedy. Television producers like Paul Jackson were slowly becoming aware of this comedy revolution and set about exploring how to transform it onto the small screen. This coincided with the introduction of Channel Four and the new network seemed like the perfect platform to air this new kind of show. *Saturday Live* hosted by comedian Ben Elton, who featured as a guest presenter for the first series, provided a variety show for eighties Britain, giving birth to home-grown stars such as: French and Saunders, Harry Enfield, Rick Mayall and Adrian Edmondson to name but a few. This provided a platform for Alternative Comedy to grow and by 1982 the BBC took their chance on the punk revolution in comedy as Ben Elton, Lise Mayer and Rik Mayall joined forces to break sitcom traditions with their anarchic flat-based series *The Young Ones*. It is very rare to encounter a figure who has straddled both disciplines between alternative comedy and mainstream variety but Paul Jackson became pivotal to both worlds.

Returning to mainstream Light Entertainment during the nineties, Paul Jackson was Producer on the Saturday night institution; *Blind Date*. By this time, the once unmissable show was beginning to go out of favour with the public. Forever in touch with her audience, Cilla had realised that the sun was slowly setting on the popular show and instead of going down with a sinking ship she wanted to be in full control of her own destiny. She chose a special live episode to make the announcement that having recorded the rest of the series, this would be the last time that the queen of British television would grace the *Blind Date* studio. Now Head of Entertainment at Granada, Paul felt he was required to enter the studio floor straight after recording in order to acknowledge such a landmark in the history of British television. As Paul states there are very few TV stars who manage to have a long and successful career on both the BBC and ITV and Cilla Black was among only a handful. There wasn't a dry eye in the house as both audience and crew said goodbye to the woman who helped define British Light Entertainment for generations.

Now into his fifth decade in entertainment, Paul Jackson has ditched his television management cap and now has the luxury of selecting the work he does. In 2017, he presented a series of programmes for BBC Radio 4 Extra entitled *The Comedy Controllers* and was just about to produce the latest series of *Benidorm* in absence of his late friend, Geoffrey Perkins. Although he was insistent he was slowing down and stepping away from the art which he loved, with the passion and enthusiasm he exhibits, you should never rule out Paul embarking on a new project.

Whenever I tell people what I do, it's usually only a few minutes before I'm asked about my favourite guest and it's a question which proves very difficult to answer. Yet simply because his career has spanned such a fascinating period in TV, I shall forever hold this interview as very special in the development of *Beyond The Title* and feel honoured to have interviewed such an integral figure in the history of British television.

# Chapter Five – Writers

So far, I have traced the story of entertainment mostly from the point of view of subjects who occupy hours of television coverage and dazzle in the spotlight of showbiz. Yet what hasn't been touched upon is the pivotal contribution of those behind the camera who create the very DNA of popular culture, the writers. These men and women are as far removed from the razzmatazz of entertainment as one could get, only having ownership of a project whilst it is in script form. Stereotypically we think of them as solitary, isolated souls spending sleepless nights drinking black coffee staring at a blank page, before taking everyday life and projecting it to a mammoth scale.

Unlike entertainers, writers don't tend to seek the limelight or have a heightened image of themselves. Instead they seem happy to maintain their anonymity which eliminates them from the trappings of fame. Yet on the rare occasions that individual writers do possess a certain level of celebrity, they invariably feel a responsibility to use it for positive means and raise awareness, and the profile, of screenwriters as a whole. Often in the past, these talented writers were destined for entertainment oblivion, forever upstaged by the characters and must-see moments they had created. This could be a source of bitter resentment between a writer and a performer as they both searched for a spotlight that only one of them could have.

Thankfully in today's entertainment climate, this scenario is considered a thing of the past and is not attributed to any of the following subjects. Instead they have achieved the remarkable status of celebrated figures in their own field and their work has received national acclaim. Yet the gap between writers and performers still looms large and rights for writers has become a hot topic on the entertainment agenda.

In recent years relationships between writer and performer have become entwined and the necessity for performers to write their own material has become a standard part of the entertainment landscape. This has had severe consequences for the role of the jobbing comedy writer as no longer is it a requirement for a comedian to have a team of highly talented joke creators surrounding them. Instead comics are a one man or woman band and this has forced these highly talented writers to carve out other routes for their unique talents.

Personally I feel a great affinity with these people as a result of my background in scriptwriting. I have first-hand experience of the painstaking process involved in breaking into the writing industry and realise the sheer dedication and stoicism attributed to the role of the jobbing writer. The piles of rejection letters, the constant criticism of your work and the general undervalued nature of writers in the industry are all contributing factors in the unpopular nature of the role. However if you possess a unique flair for echoing and subverting aspects of everyday life to the fullest dramatic effect then a lifetime of creativity awaits you.

Whether it's serial drama, sitcom or gag writing, the following masters of TV scripts all offered me their insight into life behind the camera and how they perceive their own contributions to the art of television. In a world where anyone can be a star, writers tend to shy away from the all-encompassing glare of the entertainment spotlight but instead create a formidable repertoire of work which frequently has the power to define a generation. To me, this is the true gift of a television scriptwriter and I hope you'll agree that the following subjects are fine examples of this.

# Tony Jordan

In the autumn of 2016 I was lucky enough to obtain a ticket to the London Screenwriters Festival in order to get insight and advice on how to go about getting my work noticed by the right commissioners and executives. At the time I was attempting to find an outlet for the radio documentary that I had recently created and had been recommended by an influential agent within the Arts to attend the three day event. So myself and my PA James found ourselves at a large London university with a thick itinerary as we attempted to decipher those sessions which would be worthwhile. Instantly I was drawn to one of the opening sessions; a question and answer seminar with the celebrated TV writer, Tony Jordan. It was here I realised the eloquence of the writer and how passionately he spoke about the Arts.

The seminar really captured my imagination and Tony's words stuck with me. I wanted to know more about his humble beginnings and how he managed to become one of Britain's leading television screenwriters. Having developed the concept for *Beyond The Title*, I thought it would be great to have Tony as one of my first subjects. I researched his production company *Red Planet Pictures* to establish whether he would allow me to interview him for my brand new website. To my delight, I received an email from Mr Jordan's PA inviting me to the headquarters of *Red Planet Pictures* to interview the man himself.

A few weeks later, my PA Will and I caught the train to Central London in preparation to interview the writing master. *Red Planet Pictures* is situated on the third floor of a high-rise building on Tottenham Court Road. From the outside it looks like any other commercial premises but as soon as you step foot through the door you realise that you're in a very special place where creativity thrives. Will and I made ourselves known to reception and waited to be shown to the appropriate room. Being guided around the office, it was easy to realise Jordan's substantial contribution to television drama over the past thirty years. Passing by floor to ceiling posters of *Death In Paradise, Life On Mars, Dickensian* and *Moving Wallpaper*, it became clear that this was a guy who remained proud of his accomplishments and so he should.

We entered a generously-sized boardroom where more giant posters of Tony's greatest successes adorned the walls. Soon Tony joined us, wearing a bright pink shirt and seeming both pleased to see me and impressed that we had made the trip up from the Isle of Wight just to talk to him. This is a common first topic of conversation between myself and my interviewees as it is a regular misconception that the Isle Of Wight is hundreds of miles away from London, yet in reality it's only an hour on the train but if it fulfils the perfect conversation starter, who am I to complain? From our opening conversation, it was clear that Tony and I were going to get on well. He not only was interested in my current work but wanted to know the things I had done leading up to the website and for a moment it felt like he had turned the tables. After a while I figured I better get Will to set the recording equipment up so we could get the real interview underway.

For over thirty years, Tony Jordan has been responsible for some of Britain's finest dramatic televisual moments taking him from serial drama to the latest in experimental television. The former east end market trader swapped selling stock for taking stock when he joined the BBC soap *EastEnders* in 1989 and consequently went on to become one of Britain's leading television screenwriters. Coming to scriptwriting at the relatively late age of 33, Jordan had already seen a lot of what life could offer which he believes has informed the majority of his repertoire. Being a market trader, he truly identified with the characters in Albert Square as he'd known those types of people and drank in pubs like *The Queen Vic*. Therefore this wasn't fiction for Jordan, it was basically the re-telling of the characters from his childhood.

As he states, if *EastEnders* is done right, it is quintessentially about "clans" and the connections between different families within a small tight-knit estate in the east end of London. This formula lends itself to the ability to play out classic tales ranging from Romeo and Juliet to The Canterbury Tales all inside 'Soapland'. This may be the closest we can get in discovering the secret behind *EastEnders* success.

Leaving the BBC soap in 2003, Tony established his own production company, *Red Planet Pictures*. Since then a plethora of hit television drama has risen from this creative hotbed including *Life on Mars, Moving Wallpaper* and *Death in Paradise*. Yet his passion definitely has to be the period drama *Dickensian*, the drama surrounding the nineteenth century author's most popular characters. The other aspect which sets this drama apart from its contemporaries is the episodic structure. Each episode is 30 minutes in length and the dramatic scenes that take place have a similar feel to a serial drama, but the obvious difference is the huge cultural and literary references which surround it, making it possible for there to be dramatic scenes between Scrooge and Oliver Twist….most writers idea of linguistic heaven!

Despite leaving the regular writing team on *EastEnders*, Jordan is often asked to return to the soap for the creation of special episodes surrounding loved characters. At the time of our interview he had just finished writing the thirty minute monologue which centred on Dot Cotton's grief following the death of husband Jim. To create such a touching and moving episode in monologue form for one of the most watched programmes on British television is no mean feat and takes an experienced writer like Tony to perfectly gauge the mood.

Jordan remains adamant that *Red Planet Pictures* shouldn't be all about Tony Jordan and is constantly on the lookout for fresh young writers to join this creative establishment. He is merely the figurehead of the company and allows his writers the freedom to explore their own concepts. At the time of our interview Tony was still writing and in his words is, "still trying to write that something that will get the whole world talking." Acknowledging that his longevity has gained him a substantial profile within the arts, Tony is quick to put his name to upcoming writers' projects in order to make their work more appealing to a potential producer. Now a well-regarded 'statesman' of TV drama, Jordan realises the significance of having someone of his calibre on board and is quick to lend a hand to the next generation of writers.

Adamant not to be grouped in the same category as such notable screenwriters such as Alan Bleasdale and Jimmy McGovern, Tony remains extremely modest about his considerable accomplishments and struggles to quantify his own success. Yet there is no doubt that here is a man who remains at the very top of his industry and deserves to be celebrated in the same vein as the aforementioned writing institutions. It felt so great to spend the afternoon with someone who obviously remains in love with what he does and if I can enjoy a fraction of his success, then surely I would have done something "write"!

## Laurence Marks & Maurice Gran

Growing up in the nineties, it was impossible to ignore the sitcom explosion of the time whether it was *The Brittas Empire, Men Behaving Badly* or the seminal *One Foot in the Grave*. Yet in our house it was *Birds of a Feather* and *Goodnight Sweetheart* that were family favourites. Unbeknown to me at the time, both these sitcoms were written and created by comedy writing partnership Laurence Marks and Maurice Gran. As I got older, I grew increasingly familiar with their work and realised that they were so much more than nineties sitcom powerhouses. Beginning their career submitting gags for popular comics of the 1970's, the pair ascended the television comedy ranks to become one of Britain's leading and most enduring writing partnerships.

Having been a member of the Writers' Guild of Great Britain for around five years, I receive the weekly newsletter featuring articles and news of events which may be of use to jobbing writers in the industry. Admittedly, I usually delete the email as soon as it pops into my inbox yet on this particular day I started to skim it and realised that Marks and Gran were appearing at a Writers Guild event at the Museum Of Comedy. A perfect opportunity to interview them about their career in entertainment.

After a bit of research I realised that the guys' agent was a figure whom I had many dealings with over the years. Peter Mansfield is the son of theatrical supremo Laurie Mansfield who has been responsible for the careers of so many icons of British entertainment including Cilla Black, Bob Monkhouse and Jimmy Tarbuck to name but a few. Peter and I have been in regular contact since 2010. Over the years, he has helped me with so many things in my career and now I came to him asking yet another favour. Luckily he didn't let me down and within a few weeks my PA Ben and I found ourselves at the Museum Of Comedy in preparation to meet two of the most successful writers in British TV comedy.

This particular interview was actually the first time I had ever visited the Museum Of Comedy, but straight away I knew this was somewhere I belonged. Artefacts of comedy legends lay all around the underground theatre which helped to create, for me, an air of spirituality, a perfect setting to interview such a formidable comedy partnership. This was also the first time I had interviewed two people at the same time and myself and Ben were unsure about how it would work. However, when we met Laurence Marks and Maurice Gran, we realised that they already had the interview setting absolutely nailed. They took it in turns to answer questions, taking one question each but obviously when the other one had something to offer on the subject they certainly contributed.

Almost everyone over the age of fifty in entertainment has their own unique story of working with the great Frankie Howerd. These experiences have become part of comedy folklore and add to the enigma surrounding him. But for Marks and Gran, writing for the master of the double entendre proved an extraordinary grounding in entertainment and the beginning of a successful career spanning four decades. *The Frankie Howerd Show* gave the writing partnership their first taste of television and when asked to write the material for his Royal Variety act that year, the pair were honoured to carry the mantle of so many writing giants before them and to be provided with a springboard to bigger and better things.

In 1979 ITV commissioned the first of many successful sitcoms from Marks and Gran, entitled *Holding the Fort* starring Peter Davison and Patricia Hodge alongside a young Matthew Kelly as they struggled with the trials and tribulations of bringing up a young family. Surprisingly, the inspiration for this did not arise from first-hand experience as neither Laurence nor Maurice had started a family but the conversations that occurred with their

141

respective wives spurred them into thinking about parental roles and responsibilities. At the time it was almost unheard of that a man should give up his career to bring up the family while the woman thrived in the professional world and this sitcom was able to raise questions about the very basic foundations of family life. Over three series, this formula proved a hit with the British public.

From sitcom, Marks and Gran plunged themselves into what was then considered to be relatively uncharted territory for comedy drama. ITV's *Shine on Harvey Moon* gave Marks and Gran their second hit TV series but more importantly it introduced them to the two actors who would dominate the rest of their career; Linda Robson and Pauline Quirke. Robson had played the part of Maggie Moon since the first episode and had asked best friend Pauline along to the rehearsals. As soon as Laurence and Maurice met Pauline they realised that she spoke their language and identified with the world that they were attempting to create. They cast her as Veronica; Maggie's best friend in the show and for the first time were able to witness the magic of the on screen relationship between Pauline Quirke and Linda Robson.

As good as *Shine On Harvey Moon* proved to be, Marks and Gran quickly realised that the chemistry between Pauline and Linda was so unique that it would be a shame not to exploit it. The two actresses were so close that they were seemingly able to know exactly what the other was thinking without saying a word. It was like the pair were in sync and instinctively knew what the other was going to do. In the same way as Morecambe and Wise possessed the innate ability to respond to whatever the other had said or done, Pauline and Linda naturally bounced off each other in a way that Laurence and Maurice had never seen before. Although they did have a few small differences in their personas. Backstage if Pauline was sitting on a sofa with her feet up, Linda would always come and sit next to her with a disapproving look followed by the stern line, "Feet!" forcing Pauline to put them back on the floor.

The prospect of having them work together again, gave Laurence and Maurice an idea for a sitcom about two sisters who were forced to move in together following their respective husbands being sentenced to prison. In Laurence's words, "Linda and Pauline just knew what to do and it was at that moment that we had found our Birds".

Like all great sitcom, the sense of entrapment is what gave *Birds of a Feather* its wings. Completing the trio of "the birds" was the middle aged vixen, Dorien Green played by Lesley Joseph. Originally a supporting character, Dorien slowly became a favourite with the public and was the perfect yin to Sharon and Tracey's yang. Her outrageous sex-centred behaviour provided great contrast with Sharon and Tracey's mundane life which offered the show an extra punch. As Laurence and Maurice explain, people sometimes thought it was the Dorien Green show which is possibly testament to Lesley Joseph's seamless portrayal of the "tart with a heart". *Birds of a Feather* reigned supreme over the BBC One schedules for almost a decade including eight Christmas specials. Hence why Laurence and Maurice both admit that Birds is their most famous show and one which gave them most acclaim.

The decision to revive the sitcom after fifteen years was swayed by talk of a touring stage show based on the series along with the original cast in 2012. This was a triumph and reminded the public of their great affection for the three women from Chigwell. It also gave Laurence and Maurice the idea to update the sitcom for post millennium Britain. At the time of our interview *Birds of a Feather* was back where it belonged on mainstream prime time and into its twelfth series but with one obvious difference; a channel shift from the BBC to ITV. *Birds of a Feather* continues to go from strength to strength and an enduring classic is assured for Marks and Gran. A sure sign that they have undoubtedly made it into the British comedy hall of fame.

In amongst *Birds of a Feather*, Marks and Gran also found time to pen Britain's first time-traveling sitcom *Goodnight Sweetheart* starring Nicholas Lyndhurst. Unlike *Birds of a Feather*, the writing duo were shocked by the show's success and were extremely thankful that they secured Nicholas Lyndhurst who was already a big star in Britain thanks in part to the heavyweight *Only Fools and Horses*. Another draw of the series was the semi-science fiction theme which was present throughout. This was a first for British sitcom and Laurence and Maurice were unsure if the BBC would take a chance on something so revolutionary for its time. *Goodnight Sweetheart* follows the life of Gary Sparrow who becomes caught in a parallel time vortex between World War Two and the present day and his two-timing marriages to Phoebe in 1945 and Yvonne in the present. In 2016 the sitcom returned for a special to commemorate the BBC's Sitcom Season and the pair haven't ruled out writing more, so watch this space!

After forty years in the business, Laurence Marks and Maurice Gran would be excused from taking life a little easier. Yet with a string of successful stage plays under their belt, they show no sign of slowing down, which for me as a fellow writer is excellent news as nothing gives me greater pleasure than seeing two great comedy writers keep on doing what they do best.

# David Quantick

One of the biggest draws which gave me the determination to become a writer was the unique ability to capture and chart the mood of the time through the cultural and socioeconomic factors which surrounds us. All writers are products of their time, responding to the events and experiences which define the era they live in. Whether its print, prose, script or gag form, writers have an unrequited responsibility to reflect the mood of the time and capture the fads and fashions which create popular culture. To do this through one writing discipline is an achievement, yet in a career spanning four decades, writer and journalist David Quantick has managed this success over a whole host of mediums.

Famously outspoken for his views on popular culture, I became familiar with the work of David Quantick on various BBC Four documentaries of the noughties. As a comedy writer and music journalist, he remains an obvious choice to contribute to any subject surrounding the music and television industry from the last forty years. As a fan of the history of entertainment, I avidly watched these programmes and as a consequence, grew increasingly familiar with Quantick's work. So when I was scouring Social Media and spotted his Facebook page, I knew we had to connect. Luckily he accepted my request and we got talking on Facebook messenger and quite soon I was on a train to Waterloo in preparation to meet him face-to-face.

We met in Central London at some financial offices which I had been given the use of by a friend. As I have mentioned before, that in itself is ironic because I know nothing about finance or the stock exchange so when David arrived he was slightly confused as to my choice of meeting room. The simple explanation is meeting rooms in London are few and far between (and expensive) so I was grateful that I had found a suitable venue. Sweeping the explanation to one side, it was time to get the interview underway and I knew that we were in for a fascinating trip through the world of entertainment.

Starting out as a music journalist for the NME around the time of the Punk revolution, Quantick quickly learned the fast paced world of music journalism alongside three of the most notable writers of his generation; Paul Morley, Danny Baker and Julie Burchill. Having such a focused youth demographic, David was quick to realise that his position at NME wouldn't last forever and recognised the need to spread his wings. The 1980's was a very rich time for political satire and David began writing sketches for the satirical puppet show *Spitting Image*. It was here that Quantick met Steve Coogan; a man who would be a dominant figure within Quantick's career.

Branching into radio comedy in 1990 for Radio 4's On The Hour introduced David to a group of writers and performers who he would be synonymous with for years to come. A defining show in the development of British Comedy, this series launched the careers of many of Britain's best loved performers and set the benchmark for the genre for the next twenty years. It proved the start of a working relationship between all four actors together with writer Armando Iannucci which would last for the next twenty years and beyond.

With only the one 1994 series of *The Day Today*, Quantick followed Chris Morris to Channel Four three years later for the controversial *Brass Eye*. This mostly involved enticing high profile celebrities to appear in promotional campaigns for made up charities including anti-paedophilia causes and the war against drugs. Who can forget Dr Fox claiming that paedophiles had more in common with crab DNA than humans? Or Claire Rayner telling Chris Morris that she could beat off more than one man at a time.

In 2002 David swapped political satire for the glamourised world of Light Entertainment in *Harry Hill's TV Burp*. This was different to anything

146

that he had ever done before and suddenly he found himself watching and arguing over twelve hours of television every day. Dissecting and analysing TV in fine detail was something extremely alien to David. Yet once Harry Hill had sprinkled his surreal, madcap humour over it, David could see that it would be a successful formula.

At the time of our interview David was into his fourth decade in entertainment, and showed no signs of slowing down. In fact he was adamant that writers should be able to enjoy the same level of fame as the performers who they write for. His appearances on documentaries surrounding popular culture help to raise his profile but they don't bridge the obvious gap between writers and performers. Maybe this is something which will be improved due to the rise of online content? It's clear that this is something that he feels extremely passionate about and believes that the industry needs to evolve to acknowledge the role of the jobbing writer. Yet in his own career, Quantick has risen to the very top of his profession and despite a perceived lack of plaudits from the modern entertainment fraternity, it's impossible to ignore his formidable repertoire of work and his pivotal contribution to British comedy.

It was a great pleasure to obtain a unique insight into the enigmatic world of David Quantick and in a world where there's so much selection, the writer and journalist stands out as a true maverick of his art. From all the interviews I have ever done, David remains one of the most surprisingly fascinating and I hope he continues to produce more of his outstanding writing.

## Colin Edmonds

Throughout the glory days of Light Entertainment from the 1940's to the 1980's, it was the norm for Britain's best loved comedians to employ a team of gag writers to assist with their ever-growing need for material. Everyone from Morecambe and Wise to Jimmy Tarbuck demanded the cream of UK writing talent to ensure their place within the annals of British comedy. Yet when comedians realised that they had the creative ability to produce their own material, the role of the traditional comedy writer became almost extinct and these talented individuals were required to find another outlet for their writing skills. Instead of begrudging the state of comedy and becoming bitter about the natural progression of the art, writer Colin Edmonds extended himself into another world of creativity.

Embracing the rediscovery of Steampunk, Colin has written a trilogy of books surrounding the mystical realm of Victorian music hall. *Steam, Smoke and Mirrors* was published in 2015 to rave reviews and the celebrated comedy writer can now add novelist to his impressive CV. This is just one aspect of a journey through entertainment which has spanned generations and has seen Colin become an integral part of the Light Entertainment landscape.

My friendship with Colin dates back to 2015 when I was creating my documentary on the history of theatrical agents and required a personal account of what it was like to be represented by legendary theatrical agent Peter Prichard. I got in touch with Colin to see if he would be willing to take part in a recorded interview about his friend and former agent. He immediately accepted and we arranged to meet at the headquarters of a media company in central London. On this specific day I had booked a room for three hours to interview three other contributors to this story and Colin happened to be my last of the day. My penultimate interview was the television executive Brian Tesler who produced the early televised episodes of *Sunday Night at the London Palladium* and is revered in the industry as one of the true icons of television. Ever organised, Colin was early for the interview and waited in the foyer as Tesler continued to wax lyrical about the early days of television variety. The interview with Brian Tesler reached its climax and as we said our goodbyes Edmonds and Tesler shared a friendly conversation as they crossed paths. I could see Colin was somewhat surprised to see such an icon of entertainment coming out from an interview with me, and I think it increased his expectations of both me and the interview itself.

Unbeknown to either of us, this would be the start of a great friendship between myself and Colin and I'm proud to have been able to get to witness first-hand his reserved sharp wit many times in the succeeding years. Over that time we have been able to celebrate each other's successes and experiences which has meant so much to me. It gives me so much pleasure to be able to call Colin a friend and I always look forward to our regular catch ups. It was obvious then, that in the first few months of *Beyond The Title*, I would ask Colin if it would be possible to interview him for the website and I was thrilled when he accepted.

We met at the Watford Colosseum where our mutual friend, the West End maestro, Mike Dixon was conducting a recording session of BBC Radio 2's *Friday Night Is Music Night*...which was strange because it was a Tuesday! Mike had recommended that we do the interview in the foyer of the colosseum, forgetting about the substantial air conditioning unit over the entrance which would let out a gigantic blowing and sucking noise every time the front door opened and shut. Therefore Colin was forced to keep his answers short and concise to avoid attempting to speak over the noise.

It felt like we were in our very own comedy sketch which in hindsight added to the authenticity of the interview.

Colin Edmonds began his illustrious career in comedy at the tender age of sixteen when he sold jokes to a whole host of comics including his hero Bob Monkhouse. Monkhouse was so impressed with the material that he persuaded his agent, the late Peter Prichard, to have him on his books. This prompted Colin to be considered as Monkhouse's lead gag writer and despite Peter Prichard not knowing much about the art of scriptwriting, he knew what material worked for Bob. This proved successful when negotiating deals with TV networks as more often than not Bob and Colin came as a package. So throughout the eighties and nineties, whether it was *Family Fortunes, Celebrity Squares, The National Lottery Live* or *Wipeout,* Colin would always be present to aid Bob with gags and has since inherited the truly legendary Bob Monkhouse joke book which notoriously went missing from BBC Television Centre in 1995. Of course providing material for such a master of comedy was a complete joy. Unlike many comics of the day Bob Monkhouse was an unrivalled wordsmith and always remained in full command of his own material. Therefore the writing process was more of a collaboration project between Bob and Colin as opposed to merely a supply and demand model for jokes. This understanding proved successful right up until Bob's death in 2003 and allowed Colin to get to know the comedy legend incredibly well.

His work with Monkhouse was to gain Colin acclaim among showbiz circles and it wasn't long before many comics and entertainers were lining up to have Colin write their material. In 1978 the BBC unveiled a new panel based game show entitled *Blankety Blank* originally presented by the late Sir Terry Wogan. Just like Monkhouse, here was a man in command of both his audience and the English language, so writing for Wogan was an absolute joy for Colin. Therefore, you can imagine Colin's delight when he found himself reunited with Terry for BBC *Proms in the Park* from the late 90's to the mid 2010's. Although Wogan often protested that he was not a comedian, it is obvious from the way Colin talks about him that writing material for the king of the TOGs (Terry's Old Geezers) was something he holds in very high regard.

Colin remained as lead writer on *Blankety Blank* for the best part of the eighties and saw the show through a change in presenter from Terry Wogan to Les Dawson. A natural intellect, Dawson felt more at home talking about nineteenth century literature and poetry than he did about comedy. In order to relate to him and his work, Colin was required to engage in a whole host of highbrow conversations ranging from ancient philosophy to romantic literature. It seems ironic that someone of such intellectual standing was lowering himself to compère a family game show and Dawson would regularly reinforce this sentiment to the director, Stanley Appel.

When comedy changed during the late eighties, writers slowly became redundant through the rise of 'The Superstar Comedians' who wrote all their own material. This left Colin unsure of his next career move. He still contributed material to BBC Radio 2's *Friday Night Is Music Night* but just lacked something he could get his teeth into. Then came the idea to write a steampunk crime comedy drama thriller featuring dual protagonists superintendent William Melville and his assistant Phoebe Le Breton. The follow up to *Steam, Smoke and Mirrors; The Lazarus Curiosity* received critical acclaim and the third instalment; *The Nostradamus Curiosity* provides the perfect climax to the steampunk trilogy.

It's extremely difficult to sum up the extensive repertoire of the great Colin Edmonds for the simple reason that his career has crossed so many disciplines, taking him to the very top of two separate worlds. As a gag writer and production consultant throughout the eighties and nineties, he provided material for some of Britain's best loved faces before becoming a pioneer of the continuing Steampunk phenomenon. Yet personally, I am extremely proud to call him a great friend and can honestly say that I know one of the nicest people in entertainment.

# Jonathan Maitland

The story of my interview with the writer and broadcaster Jonathan Maitland is one of mistaken identity brought on by my own stupidity and failure to carry out thorough research of my subject prior to securing an interview. So this chapter of my book starts with a grovelling apology.

When I was in the first year of my undergraduate course, I applied to appear on an ITV youth current affairs show surrounding the wants and desires of young people living on the South Coast of England. Luckily I made it through to the second round of auditions and received an email from the series producer Jonathan Maitland inviting me to ITV Studios to appear on the show. Unfortunately on that specific day, I had gone down with an awful cold and sadly was too unwell to attend.

Fast forward two years and Bournemouth University played host to a Royal Television Society event where professionals from the world of television featured in an exhibition where students had the opportunity to network. As soon as I saw Jonathan's name I made the connection between him and the TV show which I narrowly missed being a part of and figured it would be great to meet him at last. Thankfully I wasn't disappointed and he was a really lovely guy and gave me his contact information should I ever need to get in touch. A slightly mature gentleman, I figured that when I reached that point in my career where I may have required his advice, he might have already retired. Yet I knew that this was a huge sweeping generalisation and people in entertainment naturally have a longer shelf life than those in other professions...just look at Bruce Forsyth! So I lived in hope that our paths would cross again.

Almost a decade later, I was perusing Facebook and discovered someone who had the name Jonathan Maitland and wondered if it could be my contact from years previously. Upon close inspection of his brief bio, I realised that he worked for ITV Local just like my acquaintance and decided to add him as a friend, which he accepted. I messaged him to ask if he would be interested in doing a podcast interview with me for my website. To my delight he accepted and we agreed to meet at a church just around the corner from Waterloo Station. I started work on the interview with the man I thought I knew, detailing his whole career in news and current affairs before delving into his latter career as a satirist and playwright. This was a complete revelation to me as when we met at Bournemouth University no one had mentioned that he was the creator of so many stage plays and what with the university being home to one of the only scriptwriting degrees in the country I would have thought that someone would have made the obvious connection.

Of course what I had failed to realise was that there are two Jonathan Maitland's in ITV News and regional current affairs and I was about to interview the one who I'd never met. I only discovered this as he walked through the door of the vestry room of the church where we were holding the interview and I thought, 'Who are you?'

Despite my doubt I still went on to mention that we had met at Bournemouth University at which point he looked at me with a confused expression. He probably thought I was some crazed lunatic with early onset dementia or that my disability wasn't just physical! Fortunately my PA James is blessed with a certain amount of tact and was able to steer the interview in the right direction. I was left hoping upon hope that my pre-prepared questions would be in some way still applicable. Luckily, they were and luckier still, this Jonathan Maitland was a fascinating interviewee in his own right.

Jonathan started his career as a local journalist for regional TV where he got invaluable experience of the real world of breaking news. Getting up for work in the morning without a clue what you could be reporting on before promptly being witness to a world changing event is, I imagine, the thrill of news journalism. With regular appearances on ITV's *Tonight* current affairs programme, he has become a familiar face on our TV screens over the past two decades. Yet his expertise has been mostly nurtured behind the camera.

Jonathan remains relatively unique in being able to straddle both sides of the political scene in hard-hitting current affairs and hard-hitting satirical comedy. Being a celebrated playwright, Maitland is in a position to satirise those in government whom he was also interacting with in his role as a journalist. The association between Maitland and the comedy activist Chris Morris is a union which very few could imagine. Yet when you consider both of the gentlemen's fascinations with the power of politics, their careers' aren't that far apart. Jonathan's 2016 controversial stage play *Dead Sheep* was an irreverent take on the Tory cabinet of the 1980's and explores the complex relationship between Margaret Thatcher and senior members of the Conservative party. *Spitting Image's* Steve Nallon reprised his heightened interpretation of Thatcher for this satirical look at the goings on at Number 10 at such a pivotal time. In an age where popular satire is possibly considered old fashioned and formulaic, maybe this could be the future for this unique brand of comedy.

Despite comedic success, Jonathan's first love will always be News and Current Affairs and his varied journalistic CV epitomises this. Although in light of the current state which British television finds itself in, Maitland finds it increasingly difficult to find reasons to continue pursuing his journalistic career. Instead, he is concentrating his efforts on writing stage plays which offers him the creative freedom to hone his work in whatever direction he chooses. Never afraid to pass judgment on the state of the industry he loves, Maitland's outspoken beliefs makes him the perfect subject for an interview as his passionate honesty shines through everything he does. It was fascinating to meet 'this' Jonathan Maitland and to get such a raw take on an industry I thought I knew.

## Dick Fiddy

Ever since I can remember I have been fascinated not just by the development of television entertainment but also the production of it together with the social context which it finds itself in. History has never been so easy to chart and celebrate, and by analysing the evolution of British television it teaches us something about the way the nation has changed. The pioneers of early television have always had the power to interest me by the way they created something out of nothing and watching archive footage of those years, it's not difficult to see that it was very basic in its form. Technology was yet to catch up with the creative potential which executives saw in this new medium and they made a valiant effort with the tools they had at their disposal. I imagine not many of them would have thought that what they were doing would have such a dominant influence over future generations and it was such a shame that they had little time to record or preserve the programmes they were making.

It was only when television began to achieve its potential in the 1970's that people had the urge to look back over our television past to remember the fashion and fads which represented a particular time. It was also then when it was realised the BBC had wiped a large percentage of its early content. This coincided with social and political unrest and the television audience sought nostalgia and familiarity to get them through such testing times. However, there was little chance of being able to broadcast reruns of so much that had simply been deleted. For generations television has been closely regarded as the poor relation of film. Indeed, it could be argued that the disrespect which was shown by hours and hours of wiped television illustrates a historical lack of care by broadcasters for preserving Britain's cultural heritage. Then during the 1970's, vintage television began to garner interest from a wide section of the public and any footage that remained was regarded as being as precious as solid gold. It seems somewhat pertinent here to note that even throughout the seventies, programmes were still under threat of being cast aside. So it was that through the next few decades, it fell to TV historians and campaigners to somehow return any footage to its spiritual home.

In 1993 a joint campaign was launched between the BBC and BFI to appeal for lost TV and among the founders of the project was television consultant Dick Fiddy. A former television scriptwriter, Dick realised the significance in trying to trace the lost material and hopefully return it to its rightful place. Yet he did uphold one reservation in that the Corporation might have perceived the whole appeal as a witch hunt against them for erasing the tapes in the first place. But for Dick and the BFI, this was never the purpose of *Missing Believed Wiped* and they were just concerned with reuniting lost footage to its rightful owner and that's exactly what they've done. For over a quarter of a century, *Missing Believed Wiped* has gone from strength to strength and dozens of fans still gather each December to watch the results of their discoveries.

The first time that I became aware of Dick Fiddy and the *Missing Believed Wiped* campaign was on a 2002 documentary of the same name presented by the late comedy legend Terry Jones. In this programme he travelled all around the world unearthing pieces of film which unsuspecting members of the public had around their houses and followed the preservation process used by highly skilled archive engineers and technicians. It was amazing to see how they cleaned up such battered footage and were able to return it to its rightful place in the BBC archives. To me this is the epitome of what the license fee should be used for and I believe more exposure of this system should be celebrated on both TV and radio.

A year previously, Dick and the team had rescued two lost episodes of *Dad's Army (The Battle of Godfreys Cottage* and *Operation Kilt)* which the BBC broadcast as part of their Christmas line up. I distinctly remember watching this and the documentary surrounding the location of the lost tapes and was fascinated by the process. Later that evening the late and great Sir Terry Wogan presented an appeal for other lost footage missing from the BBC archives. It filled me with excitement and inspiration to think that someone out there had the answers to all these missing masterpieces and hopefully one day they will get it all back.

It would be several years before Dick Fiddy re-entered my consciousness as in my third year of university I decided to write my dissertation on a Freudian View of Women in 1970's Sitcom and for my reading list I decided to include *Missing Believed Wiped* by Dick Fiddy. On opening the book I realised that Dick's email was on the inside cover and decided to write to him to tell him what I was doing. Amazingly he replied not with a simple hello, but with a detailed account of sexism in sitcoms which I was able to use as evidence to support my theory. This was the start of a pivotal friendship which still survives today and when I embarked on my radio documentary surrounding the history of theatrical agents, Dick proved absolutely instrumental to the execution of the project. It was during that time that I was privileged to get to know the great man increasingly well. I was honoured when he agreed to play a significant role in the launch of my radio documentary in June 2016. I couldn't believe that a figure of his calibre would give up his time to appear at a local hall on the Isle of Wight just for me. It was a joy to know that Dick was not just someone I highly respected but also a good friend. Therefore when I developed *Beyond The Title* in the autumn of 2016, I knew he would be a fascinating subject for an interview.

We agreed to meet at the BFI which is our normal meeting place as this is where Dick is based for the majority for his time. In order to get the most out of my time I arranged to meet the producer Paul Jackson and quickly realised that he and Dick knew each other quite well. It was fascinating to hear the interplay between these two successful individuals and it forced me to realise that I was in the presence of two formidable authorities on British television. For a fan of the art of Light Entertainment, I was utterly in my element as I knew that there would be no question which they didn't have the answer to. On that specific day Paul Jackson was running a little late so we agreed that Dick would take the hotseat first while we waited for Paul to make his entrance. Sure enough it wasn't long before Paul silently crept in and sat listening intently to Dick's insight into his life and career. I remember being aware that Dick's story wasn't only fascinating to me but would also enthral fellow entertainment practitioners interested in hearing his analysis of entertainment.

Beyond *Missing Believed Wiped*, Dick remains one of the BFI's leading consultants and regularly chairs forums with the great and good of entertainment. In 2016 I attended a screening of the BBC's *Granada from the North* whereupon afterwards Dick chaired a discussion about the influence of the network alongside three esteemed panellists. His laid back approach to interviewing makes him the perfect compère for these events and although this was never his intended career path, there is no doubt that he is extremely good at what he does.

Since my time at university, Dick has always been extremely supportive of me and my many projects so it was nice to finally be able to turn the tables on him and interview someone who I'm lucky to class as a friend. Whatever Dick and the BFI decide to do next I'm sure will be a success.

# Chapter Six - The 90's

As a late eighties baby, the nineties was the period when I grew up and found my feet. As the embers of a divided Thatcher's Britain slowly dispersed, another cultural revolution started to take hold. Music and television arguably reflected the social and political climate like never before. Not since the 1960's had popular culture been so potent and the lower middle class came from the financial upheavals of the 1980's to take centre stage. Everyday folk were now able to take advantage of the financial boom of the upper middle classes but now everyone was benefiting from social mobility. These were halcyon days and if you were a teenager, there were big incentives to emerge from the darkness of the bedroom and potentially shine on a stage in front of millions.

The acid house scene of the late 80's had accidentally returned northern England back to the cultural capital of the world and irrespective of the negative connotation of drugs and alcohol, rock and roll became interesting again. A brand new sound swept the country as children of the 1970's finally came of age and fought back against a political system which had failed them. This was their time to express themselves and thus they created a whole era of soft rock melodies heralding a better life and how to achieve it. This bred a new found sense of positivity which was able to transcend the speakers and inspire a whole generation. Suddenly young people were making music for themselves which stood up and challenged the fixed concepts of a conservative government that they had grown up with.

If music could have the power to excite and inspire then television was forced to echo the anarchic feel of the decade. Riding on the coattails of cult experimental entertainment shows of the late 1980's and early 1990's including *The Word*, audiences grew accustomed to spontaneity and controversy within the Light Entertainment they consumed and it wasn't long before breakfast television adopted the structure and created something which had never been seen on British television.

This cultural change was also charted in the sitcoms of the decade and ancient love stories of boy meets girl were updated to echo this social revolution. No longer was sitcom necessarily for the whole family and the nine o'clock watershed was used to its full potential in order to bring the genre bang up to date. Audiences didn't want gentle comedy about slight observation between a man and a woman, or being fearful about meeting their future mother in law. This wasn't what the 90's were about, nor was it representative of the modern non-nuclear family dynamics.

The younger generation were starting to realise that they no longer had to put their elders on the untouchable pedestal and suddenly realised that the older generation were just as flawed and unfulfilled as themselves. They were taught to dream big and that's what they did even if it meant upsetting the political and social establishment or even worse their forefathers. This was the era when it seemed that anything could be possible and this message was reinforced both in the songs we listened to and the TV we watched.

However it was the later part of the decade which really cemented this definite social change and came to define the era. New Labour's landslide victory in May 1997 became the ultimate symbol that times were changing and a new sense of hope reinvigorated the nation as we prepared for the dawning of a new millennium. Television once again pushed the boundaries of production and had the financial power to celebrate and cover landmark events like never before. The influx of new technology helped the medium grow while still maintaining its potency within British life. So there was something for everyone to be excited about in such a pivotal decade and I believe the following subjects each contributed to making this era so defining.

## Leslie Ash

The first time I became aware of the actress Leslie Ash was when my Mum and Dad let me stay up to watch the nineties sitcom *Men Behaving Badly*. To me *Men Behaving Badly* came to define the nineties, echoing the lad culture of the day and Leslie Ash would in time play a dominant role in redressing the sexual divide which was considered a hot topic on the political agenda. I didn't realise at my tender age that Leslie was by then twenty years into a career that has seen her rise to the very top of her profession. She did then and has since always remained timeless in her appearance and is among only a few actresses to have been a sex symbol across three decades. It's difficult to think of many stars who have also been at the forefront of not one, but two social revolutions, yet this is exactly what Leslie has done in an unparalleled career in entertainment.

For a generation she represented the innocent freedom of youth as a result of her portrayal of Steph in the classic 1979 coming of age film Quadrophenia which attained her cult status among children of the seventies. Then in 1992 echoing the lad culture of the time, Leslie was cast as the long-suffering feisty Debs in Simon Nye's flat-based sitcom *Men Behaving Badly*. Being at the forefront of two defining eras of modern popular culture it would be easy to surmise that Leslie Ash's longevity was assured and her status as one of Britain's best loved stars would be irreversible. However, her story is anything but a showbiz fairy-tale.

Over the last decade Leslie sadly disappeared from our television screens following complications after contracting MRSA leaving her with severe mobility issues. When I contacted her agent, I ignorantly believed that Leslie had retired from the business, failing to acknowledge that this wasn't the case at all. The iconic actress in fact hadn't retired but was struggling to persuade producers to overlook her physical disability. As both a disabled person and a novice entertainment journalist, I found this utterly bemusing as to how such a star could be treated in this way and was intrigued to get Leslie's side of the story. We arranged to meet in a quiet wine bar close to where she lived in Fulham to record what I knew would be a great interview and I wasn't disappointed.

I'm always nervous when I meet significant figures who I have admired for a long time. I suppose part of me can't believe that I am here interviewing some of the people who I grew up watching and they are so willing to allow me such a fantastic opportunity. Therefore, waiting at a table in the empty wine bar was an anxious experience for both me and my PA James. Yet when Leslie arrived, her youthful persona and zestful outlook on life instantly put me at ease and with her bubbly personality, my nerves completely subsided and we were able to enjoy a relaxing, fruitful conversation.

Leslie made her television debut at age 4, in a 1964 commercial for Fairy Liquid asking, "Mummy, why are your hands so soft?" That one line was to change the course of her life and made Leslie a familiar face in Britain, but it would be a few more years before Leslie had another television credit to her name. As a teenager, she turned her hand to the world of modelling and became a cover-girl for teenage magazines Jackie and Pink. This brought the young Leslie into contact with iconic photographers of the time including David Bailey and Barry Lategan. Being a model, she had to allow herself to be entirely at the mercy of the photographer in charge of the shoot as they are the true artists and Leslie was lucky enough to work with some of the best in the business.

After taking a break from entertainment during the 1970's, Leslie returned to acting in 1978 when she appeared with her sister in the comedy film, *Rosie Dixon - Night Nurse*. However, just a year later, Leslie was cast in the first of many career defining roles as Steph in the big screen smash

Quadrophenia alongside the young Phil Daniels. This British drama loosely based on The Who's 1973 album, tells the story of unrequited love between Leslie's character Steph and Phil Daniel's Jimmy on the backdrop of a mod rally from London to Brighton. The cult classic struck a chord with a very definite section of the British public and transformed Leslie into a star.

At the time of release the film enjoyed moderate success but it wasn't until the early nineties when it got rediscovered by a new generation who identified with the social freedom that the film celebrated. The image of Leslie Ash and Phil Daniels riding off into the sunset on the famous motorbike appealed to the young rock stars of the day and helped to form the basis of nineties mod culture. Bands such as Blur and Oasis modelled their look on the mod image of the 1960's and heralded the film as an inspiration. Suddenly Leslie Ash wasn't just a celebrated actress but a cultural icon for modern Britain. Even now rock superstars like Kasabian are quick to site Leslie as one of the original hipster chicks and she has always remained on the cutting edge of popular culture. Today Leslie is always amused when stars from the new generation reveal that she was their first crush but it is also a great feeling to know that the film had such a vast impact on future generations and still has the ability to inform an audience.

A string of comedy cameos followed Leslie into the eighties with possibly the most famous being her 1983 portrayal of the damsel in distress Melissa Winthrop in *The Two Ronnies* spoof *Raiders of the Lost Auk* written by David Renwick. Ronnie Corbett was cast as the heroic Indiana Jones which became ironic to Leslie when they were climbing a plank and the pint sized comedy legend turned to her and revealed that he was scared of heights. This epitomised the joyous experience of working with such Light Entertainment heavyweights and gave the young actress the perfect grounding in the genre. Very few people of her generation can boast to have worked with the legendary Corbett and Barker and this is an experience that she will always cherish.

Throughout the 1980's Leslie was able to secure small parts in television comedies of the day and then in 1983 appeared opposite Nicky Henson as Nancy in the ITV situation comedy *The Happy Apple* before popping up for a cameo role as the hopeful applicant cleaner in the ITV sitcom *Home to Roost* alongside the late John Thaw. In the mid-eighties she also secured a regular role in the detective show *C.A.T.S Eyes*, then in 1992 Leslie secured probably her most celebrated role as Debs in Simon Nye's seminal sitcom

*Men Behaving Badly*. The first series took the form of a light-hearted ITV early evening comedy predominantly starring Harry Enfield and Martin Clunes with Leslie and Caroline Quentin playing the two, almot peripheral, love interests. Yet when the show transferred to the BBC after just one series, the characters of Debs and Dorothy became increasingly integral to the show's success. This wasn't the only difference in the switch to the BBC as Harry Enfield's character Dermot was replaced with the lovable oaf Tony played by Neil Morrissey.

Throughout the succeeding series of *Men Behaving Badly*, the will they, won't they relationship between Tony and Debs became one of the most popular themes in the show. The enduring sitcom decided to end on a high at Christmas 1998 which saw the hapless Gary and Tony finally committing to Dorothy and Debs. Like any classic situation comedy, *Men Behaving Badly* reflected and celebrated the mood of the time whilst keeping one eye on the zeitgeist. The nineties was a pivotal decade for British culture; the rise of Lad Mags, Ladettes, Britpop, New Labour each impacted on the way Britain saw itself and *Men Behaving Badly* was able to satirise this. This not only made the sitcom one of the most successful programmes of its generation, but in turn reignited Leslie's popularity in the public eye.

After *Men Behaving Badly*, Leslie took the leading role in ITV's heartwarming Sunday night drama *Where the Heart Is* alongside Lesley Dunlop and Philip Middlemiss. Having known Lesley Dunlop for many years, this was an absolute joy for Leslie and was able to secure her very first title role. Replacing the outgoing Pam Ferris who had played the lead in the series from the start would have been a daunting prospect for someone unfamiliar with the cast and surroundings. Yet having such connections made the transition easier for Leslie which made her time on *Where the Heart Is* so enjoyable. Filming took place in Yorkshire where Leslie had spent much of her time during the nineties when her husband, Lee Chapman played for Premiership football side Leeds United, so having such fond memories of the place it was great to return.

During 2003-2004 Leslie had also starred in the BBC's police drama *Merseybeat* and not long after these roles in 2009 Leslie began a year's stint as Vanessa Lyton in the BBC's medical drama *Holby City*. This was Leslie's last credited performance due to a series of ill health episodes. In 2004 Leslie contracted a rare, near fatal form of MRSA which confined her to a wheelchair for over two years. Since then, she has re-taught herself how to walk and can now walk without the aid of sticks.

In contrast to popular belief, Leslie hasn't discarded show business for good and is often found on a range of chat shows discussing her remarkable career. However, she is not frightened to go on the record with her belief that there doesn't seem to be the opportunities for disabled people in her business. Even with a distinguished career in entertainment, she still feels invisible within the industry that made her a star. In today's supposedly inclusive society, such an issue remains somewhat of an indictment on an industry that prides itself on its inclusive attitude towards diversity. This is a situation which hopefully will improve due to high profile figures such as Leslie highlighting this issue.

It was a great pleasure to spend the morning with Leslie and with such a diverse career in entertainment, it's impossible to know where it will take her next. Yet we can rest easy to know that thanks to her iconic roles in film and television, Leslie Ash has always and will always occupy a very special place in the hearts of the nation.

# Gaby Roslin

Continuing to celebrate those figures who helped define the decade when I first became aware of the enigmatic world of entertainment, for me no one sums up the nineties better than the evergreen Gaby Roslin. I started school in 1992 and as an early riser in my youth, I would always be up and ready hours before I needed to be. To keep me occupied, my mum would switch the TV on and allow me to watch suitable shows which were on at that time of the morning. On one particular day, Mum happened to turn it over to Channel Four where they were preparing to launch a brand new early morning entertainment show. Even though I was young, I clearly remember acknowledging that this was a special event and from then on I fell in love with the magic of *The Big Breakfast*. It generated great interest in presenters Chris Evans and Gaby Roslin and opened my eyes to an unlimited choice of entertainment.

When I started *Beyond The Title* in 2016 the former breakfast presenters were two of my most desirable subjects. Obviously Chris Evans has reached a level of fame where it's almost impossible to have any sort of contact with him and despite attempting several times, I always hit a brick wall (I did in fact meet Evans back in his Radio 1 days but obviously it was at a time when podcasts had yet to be developed and *Beyond The Title* was a mere twinkle in my eye). Yet access to a PR database extended the pool of stars I could contact and perusing the website, my eyes were drawn to an image of Gaby Roslin and I knew I had to contact her. Within an hour, I had received an email from Gaby's agent offering me a telephone interview later that day. This was music to my ears and I instantly set to work on a list of questions celebrating her remarkable career in TV. Normally, interviews take a considerable amount of time researching my subjects but I was confident that I knew a great deal about Gaby and so the preparation took me no time at all.

For over thirty years writer and broadcaster Gaby Roslin has been one of Britain's favourite television hosts. Beginning her career in 1986 on the children's series *Hippo* on Sky's Superchannel before going on to appear in the ITV Saturday morning entertainment series *Motormouth* alongside Neil Buchanan and Andy Crane. *Motormouth* ran from 1989 to 1992 and was ITV's competition to the hugely popular *Going Live* on BBC1.

In 1992 Gaby secured one of her career defining roles when she starred alongside Chris Evans for Channel Four's *The Big Breakfast*. This was the first show which echoed and satirised the biggest stories of the day interspersed with big stars and unpredictable events. Two hours of live television five days per week is no mean feat and as a broadcaster it's vital that the chemistry between the two main presenters is natural to make the show look seamless. Luckily Gaby and Chris had this magic formula and instinctively knew the breathing patterns of the other. The early days of *The Big Breakfast* survived with no script and very limited direction meaning that when the red light was on, Gaby and Chris had free reign over the show. This was a dream for Gaby and made her four years on the show some of the most enjoyable times in her career.

Sadly, just two years into *The Big Breakfast* Chris Evans left for BBC Radio 1 and over the next two years a plethora of television faces would partner Gaby on the famous yellow chairs. One of the most popular presenters was the veteran television broadcaster Keith Chegwin who began life on the show as a roaming reporter knocking on the doors of unsuspecting members of the public. Yet it was only when he came into the safe confines of the studio that Gaby witnessed his true talent as a broadcaster. Tragically our interview was just a few days after the news broke of his untimely death and Gaby spoke fondly of her experiences working with such a TV hero. As a co-presenter, he was so generous and his professionalism made the whole crew relax as they realised that he was a safe pair of hands and a natural broadcaster. You could hear from the way she spoke about him that Gaby highly respected Keith Chegwin and his loss was felt keenly.

In 1995 Gaby joined the presenting team on *BBC Children In Need* alongside Sue Cook and Terry Wogan. Just a year later, Sue Cook left the show and Gaby then developed a long association with the incomparable Terry Wogan which in time would transcend the seven hour telethon as TV executives realised the chemistry this unlikely duo created. This prompted Gaby's former TV 'husband' Chris Evans to devise a daily magazine show which would showcase the magic in the *The Terry and Gaby Show*. First broadcast on Channel Five on the 2nd June 2003, it ran until the 26th March 2004 and featured some of the biggest names in entertainment gracing the studio sofa. It was everything that Gaby thrives on; live TV and celebrity chat in the presence of a broadcasting master and her dear friend, the much missed Sir Terry Wogan.

Throughout the late nineties, Gaby was one of the most recognisable faces on the box thanks in part to her Saturday night BBC1 series *Whatever You Want* making her the first female television presenter to host her own Saturday night show. This prompted her to be put forward as part of the presenting team for the BBC's coverage of the celebrations surrounding the arrival of the new millennium. Together with Michael Parkinson, Michael Buerk and Jamie Theakston, Gaby was on air for a staggering twenty eight hours as she presided over the turning of the New Year in each country in the world and brought us unmissable entertainment including *The Two Ronnies, Black Adder* and *Parkinson*. This was a real thrill for Gaby who loves the buzz of live television and instead of becoming tired at working continuously for well over a full day, for Gaby it was a dream come true.

In January 2010 Gaby replaced Joanne Good as the co-presenter of the breakfast show on BBC Radio London alongside former Big Breakfast colleague Paul Ross. For almost three years, the pair were live each morning discussing the days' hottest topics. Gaby is the first one to admit that she's not a journalist and her talent is more about making people feel good and letting them forget about the troubles of the world instead of debating them. So when she landed her Sunday afternoon show in 2013 she was determined to make it a sanctuary of light hearted fun and her loyal audience seems to share her philosophy.

Now into her fourth decade in entertainment, Gaby showed no sign of slowing down and her 2018 Radio 4 panel show *Gaby's Talking Pictures* epitomised her capacity to grow and adapt as a performer. Gaby kindly invited me along to a recording of the show alongside comedians John

Thompson and Ellie Taylor which I quickly accepted for the chance to see the lady doing what she does best. Recorded at the London headquarters of RADA, the show celebrated famous movie quotes as performed by impressionists Alistair McGowan and Ronni Ancona. It was amazing to see Gaby's off air interactions with the guests and her gentle patter with the audience. Recording two episodes back to back is a gruelling process and as the chair, it is very difficult to maintain order. However, as a consummate professional, Gaby made it look effortless. In short, her natural persona which resonates through the airwaves equips her with the ability to transcend years and genres. It was a great pleasure to speak with Gaby Roslin and a delight to watch her work in a live environment.

## Phill Jupitus

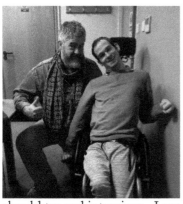

It's a funny experience being a podcaster. Trying to obtain interviews from household names is like trying to crack the Da Vinci Code. When you tell people that you do interviews with figures from the world of entertainment they normally respond with a tenuous link to knowing someone who either worked for someone famous or have a relation who once was a runner on a low budget TV movie who I should try and interview... I am always left wondering, why? In what sort of universe would people listen to an interview with someone who one day worked with a Hollywood star or once shined the shoes of a B lister? Yet occasionally a friend can indeed be very well connected.

So it is with my friend and former university tutor, Jo Tyler who enjoyed a very successful career in radio working for BBC Radio 1 during the late nineties before helping to launch 6Music in 2002. When we met at Bournemouth University in 2009 she was Head of Radio Production and Cross Platform. We realised that we had a lot in common, most notably our love for vintage entertainment. It was back then that she told me that I would really get on with her friend Phill, but it took her six years to tell me that her friend Phill was the celebrated writer and comedian Phill Jupitus. As soon I discovered the true identity of "my friend Phill" it then became my mission to get her to arrange what I knew would be a fantastic interview.

Phill and I met up at Bournemouth University where he was leading a radio comedy lecture and I managed to wangle an invite. It was a strange feeling being back in the same lecture theatre where I had spent so many hours listening to various people wax lyrical about a whole range of various subjects. Yet this time was most definitely different. This was a subject I felt passionate about and I was fascinated by the man and his career. After the lecture, we were escorted to a radio studio where a technician set up the interview to be recorded in studio quality. This was a luxury for both me and my PA James who were used to recording interviews just about anywhere from a noisy corridor to an echoey theatre but this one was guaranteed to be flawless. Such professional surroundings encouraged me just to sit back and enjoy the interview and Phill's fascinating story didn't let me down.

Beginning his career as a cartoonist for a local music magazine, writer and comedian Phill Jupitus has enjoyed a varied career spanning three decades. Honing his skills as a poet, the young Phill frequently performed his growing collection of poems in 'underground' pubs and clubs around London. This was the 1980's and Phill's raw poetry captured the youth angst of the day which had more in common with Johnny Rotten than Edgar Allen Poe. Soon enough he found himself on tour with some of the biggest music acts of the day including Billy Bragg and The Housemartins. Even now it seems incredible that poetry could be used as a supporting act for the biggest pop acts in Britain and its popularity still remains a mystery to Phill himself. Before too long, Phill began to feel comfortable on stage and developed a patter with the audience in between his poems. Just like the majority of the comedians I've interviewed, he came to the realisation that his chatty conversation was proving more popular than the poems themselves which prompted him to contemplate the art of stand-up comedy.

In my short time as an interviewer most of the comedians who I have met have fallen into comedy as a by-product of another talent which helped them break into entertainment. In the same way that Jasper Carrott and Richard Digance had originally set out on the folk music circuit before realising that comedy was a viable option, Phill did a similar thing with poetry. To me, this remains a strange concept as comedy is a notoriously difficult discipline and one which many find it almost impossible to break into. So the very fact that comedy came as a secondary profession is testament to Phill's unique flair for the art.

This was the era of alternative comedy and political satire was the popular dish of the day. Traditional styled jokes were considered old fashioned and something that would make your parents laugh certainly wasn't cool. Instead younger audiences demanded something which reflected the world they lived in. Whereas Jasper Carrott and Richard Digance found themselves in the difficult generation which bridged the gap between traditional variety and alternative comedy, by the time Phill began his career, the punk revolution of comedy was in full swing. Venues including Don Ward's Comedy Store provided such entertainment and in turn gave birth to a whole new generation of comedians.

Phill was quick to develop an unconventional way of creating material by doing minimal writing and flying by the seat of his pants. This technique has been successful throughout his career as he finds it very difficult to make himself write. He's far more comfortable when a show comes to him naturally. Such a definite comic style does not mix well with the inevitable influx of hecklers. After thirty years in comedy, Phill has little patience with audience members who feel obliged to shout out random utterances to spoil the comedian's set. Why should one person ruin the show for everyone else?

Television came calling in 1996 when Jupitus became a team captain alongside comedian Eddie Large on the second series of the comedy panel show *Gagtag*. Unbeknown to him, the panel show was a genre which Phill would become synonymous with for the next twenty years, yet sadly *Gagtag* was cancelled after this series but it did bring Phill into contact with the great Bob Monkhouse, someone whom he admired greatly. Throughout the 1980's Bob Monkhouse had suffered from misrepresentation by both the British media and pioneers of alternative comedy who frequently used him as a symbol of the outdated traditional entertainment which was considered as being out of touch with new audiences. The public and some performing artists had temporarily forgotten the extensive encyclopaedic knowledge which Monkhouse possessed and that unlike many of his generation, he wasn't content with dragging the same material out year after year and had always looked to update himself to stay abreast of the time. For this, Bob began to develop a cult status amongst the new comedians of the day and was always present in the audience of a comedy club to see a new and exciting performer. A meticulous student of comedy, Bob also remembered individual jokes and it was always a good feeling when Bob praised Phill on the calibre of his material. Unknown to Phill at the time, Bob would frequently arrive at comedy clubs in disguise and inconspicuously watch gigs from the fire exit to avoid getting noticed. A testament to the high regard in which Bob held him.

In 1996 Phill united with the comic talents of Mark Lamarr and the late Sean Hughes for BBC2's music panel show *Never Mind the Buzzcocks*. A panel show surrounding pop culture was something that had never been attempted before and with it came the threat of unpredictable and sometimes controversial behaviour from popstars which the three thrived upon.

Over the course of eighteen years, Phill remained a constant face on *Never Mind the Buzzcocks* missing just one episode when he was replaced by Frankie Boyle. Sean Hughes was replaced by Bill Bailey in 2002, someone whom Phill had known previously from years of working on the circuit and the pair already had chemistry. Having this connection, they were able to play off each other for comic effect which gave the show more of a sense of fun. More changes were on the way in 2005 as host Mark Lamarr left, leaving a huge void. A full series of guest presenters gave Phill the opportunity to bounce off different celebrities and like all great comics, he's at his very best when he's completely unscripted. Together with Bill Bailey, they often ran rings around an array of famous faces and when Simon Amstall was hired as the new presenter, the madness continued and became a major factor in the show's longevity.

Beyond panel show success, Phill has never lost his love for music. In 2002 he was selected to launch the BBC's digital radio station 6music where he fronted the weekday breakfast show for five years. His extensive musical knowledge also made him the perfect candidate to join the BBC's presenting team at the Glastonbury Festival alongside Jo Whiley and Lauren Laverne. To broadcast live to the nation for hours at a time and with the added responsibility of ensuring that you introduce the right acts at the right moment is no easy feat. Just another string to a very large bow!

Phill works to a mantra of giving everything a go once. He's made one sitcom, chaired one panel show and presented one live breakfast show. In 2007 he put himself out of his comfort zone yet again when he auditioned for a major role in a West End musical. Originally interested in the part of Wilbur Turnblad in *Hairspray*, Phill was then offered to read for the drag act

Edna replacing the outgoing Michael Ball. He instantly loved the role and so did the producers and for the best part of two years Phill was Edna and got the West End bug. Since *Hairspray* Phill has starred in a string of theatrical triumphs including *The Producers* alongside fellow comic Jason Manford. It's clear that Phill is an extremely versatile performer who has grown to love the thrill of the stage lights.

When I met up with Phill in the summer of 2018 he was back on the road with a brand new stand-up tour *Juplicity*, and showing no sign of slowing down. His popularity amongst students and pensioners alike is as potent as ever. This interview will always stick out in my mind because it was in a professional setting in terms of recording quality and was absolutely perfect. In such a setting what better subject to have than a mastermind of comedy. Equally at home in a radio studio or theatre or television studio, there is no limit to the entertainment outlets he is able to put his hand to. It was great to meet Phill Jupitus and I can't wait to see what's next for this man of many talents.

# Mathew Priest from Dodgy

Ever since the beginnings of modern popular culture, each generation has laid claim to the sights and sounds which defined that specific era. It was Teddy Boys in the fifties, psychedelia in the sixties, Glam Rock in the seventies and New Romantics in the eighties. Yet by the nineties, music stars had learned from what had gone before and longed for less constraints and more freedom. The catalyst for such change came in 1993 when the controller of BBC Radio 1 Johnny Beerling was fired and the fresh faced Matthew Bannister was recruited in his place. Bannister wasn't afraid to make big changes in order to regain the desired Radio 1 audience of 16-24 year olds. Out went old fashioned DJs like Simon Bates and Dave Lee Travis and in came bright, young and enthusiastic broadcasters such as Jo Whiley, Chris Evans and Zoe Ball. With this overhaul came the new sound of Radio 1 with the entire playlist rewritten.

A few years earlier, best friends Nigel Clark and Mathew Priest formed a musical duo. Calling themselves *Purple* they uprooted from their respective homes in Bromsgrove and Redditch and headed for London on the search for success. There they met bass guitarist, Frederic Collier who agreed to join the band. Yet success eluded them and they were all forced to go out and get "real" jobs. Nigel was recruited as a factory worker for Austin Rover and quickly found himself in a mundane 9-5 job surrounded by colleagues who had been doing the same job for a lifetime. This prompted him to realise that there must be another way to live life, away from the tight confines of the rat race. Such a feeling inspired him to write a song which resulted in the Britpop anthem; *Staying out for the summer*, which allowed all of them to escape the mundane rat race for good and form the band known as Dodgy.

This song quickly gathered momentum and promptly found itself on the prestigious playlist which made up 'The New Sound of Radio 1'. Dodgy were in good company on the playlist and were happy sharing the airwaves with other likeminded groups, Blur, Oasis, Supergrass, Ocean Colour Scene, Shed Seven and many more. Suddenly music had something to say again and perfectly echoed the mood of the times. The nineties were rooted in unashamed optimism and the music reflected it. These were the days when the UK Top 40 mattered and it was a great honour to appear on Top Of the Pops.

Dodgy's third album *Free Peace Sweet* helped to define the nineties with a string of hits including *In a Room* and the festival anthem *Good Enough* which reached number 4 in the UK singles charts but this song became so much bigger than the original chart billing. The easy melodic tones of this track makes the song easily identifiable after the first few bars and has contributed to it becoming a sing-a-long classic evolving into something even bigger than the band even imagined. The simple reason for this, as Mathew states, is the song repeats the chorus over and over again. Essentially it's just a great happy song and people feel good whenever they hear it.

Dodgy's connections with my hometown on the Isle of Wight date back to 1996 when they opened the Newport branch of HMV. Unfortunately I was too young to attend but the gig has gone down in Isle of Wight as one of the defining events in the history of the county. Just a few years later, they returned to the Island to headline an evening of live music to launch the start of the famous Cowes Week and this time my best friend and I were old enough to experience it for ourselves as we sang the night away to their timeless nineties anthems. This would be the first of my many interactions with the veterans of Britpop.

In the summer of 2007, the band announced a reunion tour, featuring the original line up and have been together ever since. As Mathew highlights, Dodgy have been together longer this second time around than back in the nineties and still seem to thrive on life on the road. In the coming years they hope to increase their performance fee and have their sights set on playing bigger venues. Yet the thrill of performing for all four guys remains as potent as it ever did in 1995 and as soon as they step on a stage, they have the energy and showmanship of their twenty year old selves.

Over a decade since seeing Dodgy on Cowes Yacht Haven, the guys returned on the most southerly leg of their nationwide tour and I just had to buy a ticket. At this time I was several months into *Beyond The Title* and thought it would be great to attempt to interview them at the gig. I promptly looked them up on Twitter and sent them a short message about who I am and what my intentions were. Within half an hour I received a message giving me an email address to use to arrange an interview with drummer Mathew Priest prior to him taking to the stage at the Medina Theatre.

I've always been fascinated by the socioeconomic factors which contributed to making the nineties such a culturally rich decade and always had the desire to interview a figure who represented this. Therefore as soon as I had secured the interview with Mathew I knew that this would be the perfect opportunity to ask these sorts of questions. As someone who was right at the centre of such a social revolution, I thought he would be the perfect candidate to give me an insight into what it was like to live through such a defining period for popular culture. When James posed him the question, he was a little taken aback, I don't think he expected to be asked these types of questions by a spasming man in a wheelchair! This has to be up there with one of the best reactions to a question as he sat back in his chair and took a long while to ponder it. Eventually he explained that at that time there was plenty of disposable income which people could benefit from and this had a substantial impact on the music industry. Combined with the new sound of Radio 1, it proved to be a pivotal time for music and Dodgy were lucky enough to be an integral part in this social revolution.

Since our interview, Mathew and I have kept in touch and I've been lucky enough to see Dodgy perform on numerous occasions. Over a quarter of a century since they enjoyed their first taste of success, the guys still thrive upon the ecstasy of live performance. Their gigs are always full of unadulterated nostalgia and if they can maintain that energy, they'll be "good enough" for many years to come. It was a great pleasure to meet Mathew Priest and I hope he and Dodgy continue performing for years to come.

# Fay Ripley

In 2016 ITV reunited audiences with Mike Bullen's cult bittersweet comedy drama *Cold Feet* to rave reviews which spurred subsequent series to follow due to popular demand. For actress Fay Ripley, who played the part of Jenny Gifford, this was yet another successful turning point in a career spanning three decades. I was lucky enough to interview Fay to coincide with the finale of the 2018 series when I learned the fantastic news that there would be plenty more *Cold Feet* to come.

Up until this point I had been relying upon thorough research and a certain amount of luck to secure me interviews with some of the best loved figures in Britain and I guess it had worked. Yet I realised that in order to continue the calibre of my subjects I would need to lean on other services to offer me a helping hand. When I registered with the aforementioned online PR catalogue, it was to expand my pool of figures who I could approach. Personally I always prefer to obtain my interviews organically as opposed to relying on a third party to do the leg work for me as I get huge satisfaction knowing that I have been responsible for every stage of development. However, I received an email informing me that the website was offering a considerable discount and I figured it was worth a go.

My team and I then spent two full weeks scouring the website and making the most of having an endless list of contacts, emailing agents, communicating with management companies and sifting through the vast array of celebrities who were listed. Within a few hours, responses started to flood in, mostly with negative tones which didn't fill me with much hope. However, a few days later I received an email from Fay Ripley's agent informing me of the great news that she had accepted my invitation and wanted to do it on the phone the following morning. Not having much time to prep, I set to work researching the major highlights of her career as I understood what would usually take me a few days was now reduced to a few hours. You would think this to be a painstaking process but having grown up with Fay's work, I got an extraordinary amount of enjoyment looking back over a career which I knew so well.

Phone interviews aren't great for me as I realise that from a technical point of view I won't be able to have such an active role in the interview than if I meet them in person. It's difficult to convey on the phone that I'm actually the one who is in control of the interview even though they never talk to me. But as soon as me and my PA Ben picked up the phone to Fay, I knew that she understood my situation and her laid back manner perfectly complimented the gentle style of the interview. It quickly became natural and felt like we were just nattering to a friend as Fay's relaxed persona was able to transcend the telephone line and put us all at ease.

After leaving school, Fay Ripley joined the London School of Music and Drama in 1990, much to the disapproval of her father who always thought that she should have a "proper job". For this, he resulted to drastic lengths to discourage her from following her dream including enrolling her on a napkin folding course. Yet the napkin industry's loss was definitely television's gain as Fay always knew that her true calling lay in drama and while other wannabe actors opted for traditional drama schools or good old fashioned rep, Fay opted for this relatively new form of training which put her on the path to success. Making her professional debut in *Around the World in Eighty Days* at the Liverpool Playhouse in 1990, Fay got a taste of performing to a live audience for the first time. Unlike most actors, for Fay, the theatre doesn't have the same excitement as television which she thrives upon and so is more at home on a television set.

In 1995 Fay made the surprising move to horror in the cult movie *Mute Witness*. For an actor, there's a fine line between comedy and horror as it all stems from people's reactions and impulses. So it doesn't matter whether you're confronted by Frankenstein or a naked James Nesbitt because the facial expression is still the same. It seems that every part that she plays, Fay's attitude is paramount to find the warmth behind the character simply because she is a warm and fun-loving person. This amiable nature has allowed her to conquer the difficult transition between actor to television presenter. Fronting Christmas cookery items on ITV's *Lorraine* in 2017, Fay is equally at home as herself or in character and her effortless television persona epitomises this.

Probably one of the most daunting things for a television actor is to resurrect a popular series from the past. This was exactly what Fay signed up for when she was cast alongside Martin Clunes for the 2009 return of *Reggie Perrin*. With scripts written by the late David Nobbs, the programme managed to maintain its bizarre and bittersweet undertones but unfortunately ran for only one series in light of Nobbs' untimely death in 2015. Playing the part of Nicola, the long suffering wife of Perrin, was a joyful experience for Fay as being supporting cast meant she could hide behind the star of the show. As an actress, Fay remains extremely generous and gracious to those around her and despite undoubtedly being at the top of her profession, she's not precious about holding top billing. Another example of her wonderful humility as a human being.

Despite her vast acting credentials, Fay's proudest achievement is her series of cookery books. In 2012 she launched the first book entitled *What's For Dinner?* Followed by *Fay Makes It Easy: 100 Recipes To Impress With No Stress*. This was a passion project for Fay and she feels a wonderful sense of pride when she is stopped in the street by someone who tells her that these books have changed their lives. As a working mother of two, Fay has first-hand experience of juggling a career with raising a family so these books are a helpful guide to making mealtimes interesting without having to spend hours and hours slaving over an oven. Raising such an issue with her, it's not difficult to see that this has huge significance within Fay's life. Far more than just a project, it's a labour of love and something that she remains extremely passionate about.

But of course, Fay's most celebrated role came in 1997 when she was cast as Jenny Gifford in ITV's cult Comedy drama *Cold Feet*. Originally auditioned for the part of Rachael (eventually given to Helen Baxendale), the producers saw something different in her and offered her the part of Jenny Gifford alongside John Thompson's Pete. Not as glamorous as the character of Rachel it nonetheless did give Fay the opportunity to play more of a comic role alongside someone whom she had known previously. The pair naturally had a great deal of on-screen chemistry and made a perfect pairing which became one of most enduring parts to the series.

The experimental camera angles and cutaways were considered revolutionary for its time and the original way in which a scene was written meant that the audience only got to the action either one second before or after a dramatic moment had taken place. This makes the show different from any other and possibly the key factor to its longevity. *Cold Feet* originally ran for five series on ITV and followed the lives of three couples coping with the strains of modern life: David and Karen Marsden – the dysfunctional career driven married couple who use alcohol to hide their problems, Rachel and Adam – childhood sweethearts who are torn apart by tragedy and Pete and Jenny – the couple who are always up for a laugh. Yet in 2004 the show came to an end following the death of Rachel. In one of the most dramatic scenes in television drama her car tragically collided with a lorry on a busy junction while she placed a cassette in the car's player. Typical of *Cold Feet's* fast paced style, they didn't dwell on the horrific nature of the accident. Instead they centred the action upon how each character dealt with the sad news. For the cast and crew this was the end of an era as the country said goodbye to six good friends for what appeared to be the very last time…but it wasn't.

In 2015 the cast and crew of *Cold Feet* were summoned for a meeting in Manchester. This was the first time that they had reunited in over a decade and Fay had severe reservations regarding bringing it back. She really didn't want to go and was praying that she would be involved in a minor accident just to prevent her from attending. Yet when she arrived unscathed, it was like they had never been away and their unique chemistry was still there. Perhaps this is testament to the show's appeal that no matter how much time has passed its still well received by the audience.

So whether it's her critically acclaimed portrayal of the loveable Jenny Gifford in *Cold Feet* or her natural gift for live television, Fay Ripley has been a constant face on our screens for over twenty years and long may she continue to be on British television.

# Gordon Kennedy

The 1990's was an explosive era for entertainment and the Arts, brought on by the social economic turmoil of the previous decade. Suddenly Britain was on the up and the concept of money had never been so important. Radio and television benefited from the financial boom and suddenly performers were able to think big to create timeless comedy. Since I sat down to watch the launch of the National Lottery in 1994, Gordon Kennedy had been a familiar face on my entertainment radar and was one of the people who I followed. Although I was far too young to appreciate his comedy pedigree, his presence on nineties television was something that I never forgot and ever since I've been very interested in where his career took him.

I got in touch with Gordon through Social Media where I was able to tell him all about me and my podcast to which he had the fantastic idea to arrange an interview to coincide with the launch of the new series of BBC Radio 4's sketch show *The Absolutely Radio Show* based on the early nineties Channel Four series. We met at BFI Southbank where I had done so many great interviews and I knew that this one would be no different. We waited in the foyer in order to show him to our allocated room and as soon as I saw him I knew we were about to spend an hour with a thoroughly nice fellow. Dressed in casual attire he introduced himself to my PA Will and me, but no introduction was necessary as I felt like I had known him for most of my life.

Technology always plays a dominant role in the success of an interview and I have to admit that on this particular day, it wasn't on our side as halfway through, the sound recorder decided to stop working. This is one of my biggest pet hates as my subject could be offering some unique insight into their life and work, but if they're not being recorded it's somewhat irrelevant. Yet thankfully Gordon had the time to re-record the interview which was an absolute godsend. This time everything worked and I could relax and listen to tales from a remarkable career. When meeting one of my subjects, it's always difficult to know whether they are comfortable with the interview setting. Yet as a natural raconteur, I knew that we were in safe hands with Gordon.

Gordon Kennedy's rise to fame reads like the synopsis of a feel good action comedy. A group of Edinburgh school boys have a dream of one day entertaining the nation with comedy sketches which they write in their bedrooms and through a series of events, their dreams come true. This is exactly what happened when Gordon teamed up with lifelong friends; Moray Hunter, Jack Docherty and Pete Baikie to create a comedy quartet who made their debut at the Edinburgh Festival in 1980 under the name, The Bodgers. This act proved successful for five consecutive festivals and successive Perrier Comedy Award nominations meant that London beckoned. Once there they were introduced to fellow performers Morwenna Banks and John Sparkes and the team expanded. This led to the radio sketch show *Bodgers, Banks and Sparkes* in 1986 which saw all the members of what would become *The Absolutely Radio Show* unite for the first time. Soon after, they decided to create their own production company Absolutely Productions which still survives today and provides content for major Radio and TV broadcasters.

Together this comedy group would go on to write and star in the cult anarchic Channel Four series *Absolutely* which rebelled against the satirical comedy landscape of the time. In the age of Alternative Comedy which thrived on a political agenda, *Absolutely* took an anarchic, irreverent view of the world with its roots firmly set in the Goon and Python traditions. Sketches such as Stoneybridge Town Council, the Little Girl, Denzil and Gwynedd, Calum Gilhooley and Frank Hovis captured listeners' imaginations and offered something completely different to the fast paced satirical arena of the time. First broadcast on Channel Four in May 1989, *Absolutely* ran for four series over four years until 1993 and provided an ideal vehicle for the team.

In early 1994 Gordon received a mysterious phone call from the BBC inviting him for a highly confidential meeting at TV Centre. Intrigued by the secretive manner of the offer, Gordon agreed and assumed it would be a part in a forthcoming drama series or similar. As the meeting progressed he got increasingly baffled as to what this offer could be. Eventually it became evident that the BBC had secured the rights to broadcast the brand new National Lottery from Camelot and they were looking to assemble a presenting team to front the live Saturday night extravaganza including the draw. Yet as a television actor, Gordon was perplexed as to the relevance of his inclusion in such a project until a TV executive told him that they had a desire for him to co-present the show alongside Anthea Turner. His initial response was to fold into fits of laughter before declining it three times. Yet the BBC were persistent and eventually it was too good of an opportunity to turn down.

For eight months Gordon and Anthea took the three Lottery machines around the country as they reached over 22 million viewers on a Saturday night, introduced the biggest stars to perform and generally kept things on track while the audience waited on the draw and to see if they had become millionaires. Astrologer Mystic Meg was on hand and Carol Vorderman regularly used mathematics to help work out the identity of the lucky winner. All of these elements together with the all-important draw normally took place in a fifteen minute programme and so timing was key. For a presenter on this type of show, the job is extremely easy because there's always a team around you ensuring that everything goes smoothly and all you have to do is say the right words at the right time. This formula proved successful and was a contributing factor in the National Lottery regularly featuring in the week's top five watched television shows. More than twenty years on, Gordon remains proud to have contributed to this important slice of TV history.

By a slice of 'Lottery luck' Gordon was now one of the most popular broadcasters in Britain and it was only a matter of time before another presenting role came calling. This time he teamed up with Cheryl Baker for the Sunday morning series *The Eleventh Hour* which was broadcast live from

BBC Television Centre and surrounded different hobbies and pastimes. With a production crew made up of many individuals who were alien to the art of live television, *The Eleventh Hour* rewrote the rule book by ignoring basic production principles such as the time it takes a presenter to walk between items. This frequently meant that Gordon was forced to run from one side of the BBC studios to another within seconds to maintain camera continuity. Such a rustic feel set the series apart from other entertainment programmes of the day and being under the umbrella of the educational department meant that the show fulfilled all aspects of the BBC trinity to 'inform, educate and entertain'. So for two years Gordon presided over the most wacky stunts and activities although even today he still remains unsure as to what the series was actually about.

After live broadcasting, Gordon returned to the relatively safe ground of acting in 2003 for the military based BBC1 drama *Red Cap* alongside EastEnders star Tamzin Outhwaithe. Cast as Sgt. Bruce Hornsby who was tasked with investigating the mysterious disappearance of stolen duty free alcohol from a paratrooper's lover in the first episode, Gordon finally had a recurring acting role in a mainstream television drama. *Red Cap* reigned for two series on BBC1 and gave early cameos to young actors who would go on to play a dominant role in the growth of TV drama including Chris O'Dowd, Joanne Froggatt and Nigel Harman. The series came to its climax in 2004 after just thirteen episodes and Gordon was left seeking yet another venture.

Just three years later, he was cast in another BBC1 drama which was definitely poles apart from the military world of *Red Cap*. The BBC wanted to update the story of Robin Hood and make it relevant for a post millennium audience. Gordon was cast as Little John, the merriest of Robin's Merry Men who was ever loyal to the protagonist throughout the series. Created as a mid-Saturday evening drama to cater for the late teenage demographic, *Robin Hood* joined an elite list of similar popular dramas to occupy this time slot including *Merlin*, *Atlantis* and the juggernaut *Doctor Who*. These shows were originally designed to run back to back throughout the year and fulfil this forgotten demographic, giving teenagers something that was carefully crafted for them. The series was cancelled by the BBC after the third series following complications with the shooting locations together with the departure of multiple characters, including the lead actor.

In 2012 The Comedy Unit in Glasgow approached the cast of *The Absolutely Radio Show* to reform for a one-off radio special reviving and celebrating their classic sketches. Astonishingly, almost the entire original cast agreed and reunited for the first time in nearly two decades. Whilst rehearsing, they got an overwhelming urge to update the sketches to see what the characters were up to twenty years later. This resulted in Stoneybridge Town Council bemoaning the fact that London was chosen to host the Olympic Games over their sleepy town. They soon realised that this content would be far too much for just a short special and began to ponder whether a new series could work. The *Absolutely Sketchorama Special* aired on BBC Radio 4 in September 2015 to rave reviews by the radio firmament and a BBC Audio Drama Award, which has led to three further series to date.

Now into his fourth decade in the business Gordon Kennedy remains as in demand as ever. At the time of our interview, the versatile performer was looking forward to starring in the period drama *Harlots* for the US Network Hulu alongside Lesley Manville and Samantha Morton in a story dealing with 18th century prostitution. It's very clear that Gordon is always up for a challenge and his extensive body of work illustrates this. It was a great pleasure to meet and interview Gordon Kennedy and I am sure he will continue to have a remarkable career.

# Mike Dixon

The British Light Entertainment scene is believed to be unique in encompassing endless outlets of talent under one umbrella. Yet the role that music plays in the popularity and longevity of such an art is sometimes forgotten or overlooked by the dominance of Comedy and Variety within the public's eye line. However, for almost forty years, musical director Mike Dixon has been honing his craft behind the camera working with the cream of UK talent. Although not a household name, his journey through entertainment spans generations and the roll call of stars who have dazzled thanks to his unique talent is truly remarkable making him just as fascinating as the figures he has supported.

After graduating from the Trinity College of Music and Drama in 1979, Mike landed a production role on the nationwide tour of Andrew Lloyd Webber's *Joseph and His Amazing Technicolour Dreamcoat*, before working on a long line of West End triumphs during the 1980's. Then in 1989 Mike was approached to become musical director for an Andrew Lloyd Webber medley for the Royal Variety Performance. This began a long association between Mike and the Royal Variety and in 1993 he was promoted to MD for the whole show. In doing this, Mike has worked with the cream of global entertainment including such true greats as Diana Ross, Cilla Black and of course, The Muppets. In his own words, "Where else would you be able to work with so many different stars and so many different styles of music?" At the 2005 Royal Variety, Mike met the legendary Dame Shirley Bassey and thus began a very successful five year stint as her Musical Director and Conductor, the pinnacle of which came when they headlined Sunday afternoon at Glastonbury 2007.

My association with the West End maestro dates back to 2015 when I was deep into my research for my radio documentary surrounding the history of theatrical agents. For research I watched again the 2006 ITV3 series *The Best of The Royal Variety* and was so fascinated by Mike's telling of the technical malfunction in the midst of Shirley Bassey's 2005 top of the bill performance that I instantly reached for my iPad, typed his name into Google and found his website. I noticed his email address at the bottom of the screen and saw this as a great opportunity for me to contact the man himself. This resulted in Mike playing a dominant role in the execution of my documentary and I was honoured when he agreed to be a speaker at the launch of my documentary in June 2016.

This was the start of a friendship which would continue to blossom over the succeeding years and when I created *Beyond The Title*, I always thought that Mike would be an incredible subject. His career has taken him to the very top of his industry, working with showbiz royalty alongside actual royalty and I've regularly been able to hear such anecdotes about his work with some of the greats of entertainment. It was clear this interview would contain some of the biggest name drops *Beyond The Title* had ever heard and I couldn't wait to get started.

I met up with Mike along with the celebrated comedy writer Colin Edmonds at the Watford Colosseum in between rehearsals for BBC Radio 2's *Friday Night is Music Night;* a programme which he's had the pleasure to work on since 1999. To see Mike in full command of an orchestra is something to admire and it's quite clear why he's in such high demand by the cream of UK Light Entertainment. Working on such a varied show can be quite refreshing for an MD as no two shows are ever the same and most surround a definite theme. His favourite subjects covered include The Battle of Britain, D-Day and the career of songwriter Leslie Bricusse. In an age when Variety is almost extinct, it's good to know that live performance is alive and well and Mike is the perfect advocate for this art.

On returning home, disaster struck as we realised that the severe background noise overshadowed the recording and in turn deemed the interview obsolete. Fortunately having known Mike for a number of years, I was able to message him explaining what had happened and he was more than willing to repeat the interview at a later date. This time we met at offices in Central London where we were able to re-record the interview in perfect acoustic surroundings.

It's always an absolute pleasure for me to spend time with Mike and I wish him all the best for whatever comes next in such a glittering career in entertainment.

## Chapter Seven - The New Age of Television

As the carefree nineties gave way to the new millennium, a cloud of uncertainty swept the world as we all held our collective breath and awaited the impending technological cataclysm that was the millennium bug. The threat was that the year 2000 was going to mark the beginning of a technological slowdown. Yet no disaster manifested and the truth was the noughties saw information technology grow to become a vital part of everyday life.

If technology was going through a rapid escalation of capability, then television would be forced to update and reinvent to make way for new formats and more importantly new stars. Audiences no longer were interested in merely passively staring at two dimensional pictures on a screen but now had a burning desire to become the stars themselves. The birth of Reality Television offered such an opportunity and it wasn't long before the public were the stars. For producers this was the ultimate dream as they could make popular entertainment on a shoestring budget without the need for big star wages or expensive studio time. We became fascinated by having power to decide the imminent fate of the protagonists within the programmes we were watching and thrived on the attorney it offered. This formula proved so popular that celebrities suddenly became enticed into this world of created reality and fully embraced the new fame game of the 21st century.

This phenomenon of watching ordinary people become stars crossed the television border and entered all aspects of the entertainment landscape as suddenly it became our mission to find out more about ourselves. In the stressful world of post millennium Britain, unexpected strains on modern life separated the classes in a way that hadn't been seen since the political unrest of the 1980's. Now thanks to inspiration from our American cousins, the lower middle class had a platform to air their views about their own situation and could take advantage of professional help in exchange for exploring their issues on daytime television. Loved by students and housewives but berated by TV critics, the 'reality' talk show format continues to divide the nation with scepticism surrounding the psychological support of contestants and recent high profile controversy hasn't helped to improve this image.

Over half a century from the birth of *Opportunity Knocks,* talent shows once again offered the public an opportunity to shine. Now with the added dimension of an instant telephone public vote, the audience felt like they had complete control over who would be a star and figures like Simon Cowell and Nigel Lythgoe had the power to create such an illusion. The talent show format was firmly back on the television map and once again dominated the Saturday night schedule and it wasn't long before the BBC wanted in on the action. For this they relied on an old format with an even older star at the helm to bring the sparkle of ballroom dancing back to Saturday night, resulting in the birth of a new breed of entertainer. Dancing became en vogue and reinvented and raised the profile of anyone who graced the floor.

The political world desired to maintain the superstar revolution of the 1990's yet pressure from the Middle East would in time ruin New Labour's dream. Meanwhile a new wave of politics was starting to take hold which ultimately became the new phenomenon of Britain and would create new stars and a whole lot of surprises along the way. This new brand of politics inevitably made its way to television and thanks to satirical shows combined with our constant fascination with celebrity culture, these figures became an integral part of our television landscape.

It's clear that the 21st century entertainment culture seems somewhat removed from the showbiz climate of the past. In bridging the once enormous gap between performers and audiences, television has never been more accessible which has made the job of its stars all the more difficult. Yet the appetite for entertainment remains as vital as it has ever been and the following subjects have all been shining examples that the art of television is still alive and well.

# Jeremy Kyle

When we met in 2018, writer and broadcaster Jeremy Kyle was still riding high in the ITV daytime schedule and despite being under constant scrutiny his 'tabloid talk' show was a hit for the network. Yet the show would be officially cancelled in a wave of negative PR for both the programme and the presenter on 15 May 2019, after the death of a guest, whose appearance had been filmed the week before but not aired.

I had met up with Jeremy at his resident golf club for an intimate interview and knew I was extremely lucky as he is renowned for resisting any form of interview on either television or radio. I can only think of one other interview that I have seen him undertake and that was with Jonathan Ross back in 2013, so I knew that there was a certain amount of exclusivity surrounding an interview with one of the most recognisable faces on British television.

When we arrived at the golf club, myself and my PA James were shown to a large boardroom with a heavy oak door. I imagined it would have suited a James bond villain well as a room in which to plot the overthrow of the world. A little of me figured it would be ideal for the upcoming meeting, yet as soon as I met with Mr Kyle I realised he was anything but a caricature nemesis. Forever on the receiving end of negative exposure from the British media, Jeremy was rightfully a little wary of me and my agenda and I suppose you couldn't blame him. However, when I reassured him that it was my aim to celebrate and encapsulate his life work, he began to relax. In fact, this interview was a great example of the process which an interviewee goes through when they are the subject of questions which they have no former warning of. As soon as he realised that he and I shared the same television hero in Sir Michael Parkinson, he instantly became more invested in the concept and I knew at that moment I was in for a great interview. You can always rely on Parky to lighten any mood!

In a career spanning two decades, Jeremy Kyle went from presenting a late night sports show on commercial radio to fronting Britain's leading public talk show for over fourteen years. Yet the clientele of *The Jeremy Kyle Show* seemed a million miles away from his own upper middle class upbringing where his father was a personal secretary to the late Queen Mother. Unlike his father, Jeremy held no alliances with the establishment and whilst undoubtedly respecting his father's loyalty to the Royal Family he knew that his talents lay elsewhere.

Beginning his career as a salesman, Jeremy was quick to make the move to broadcasting. Self-confessed as "the worst musical DJ ever," he discovered the ability to find subjects which stirred a reaction from his audience. In the era before social media, Jeremy was quick to realise the importance of creating a response from his audience and making them feel part of the show. In 2002 Kyle secured a late night phone in show on Virgin Radio entitled *Jezza's Virgin Confessions* which ran for four hours each weekday evening. It was here that Jeremy realised his talent for helping people with their problems and finding the perfect balance between care and intrusiveness. Just a year later, Jeremy was promoted to the 9am until 1pm weekday slot as his appeal continued to grow. This was the era when Chris Evans became a major shareholder in the station and sadly Jeremy became the collateral damage in Evans' downfall.

Now dismissed from Virgin, in 2006 ITV made Jeremy a surprise proposal for a weekday morning talk show. Drawing inspiration from American styled talk shows like *The Jerry Springer Show* and *Oprah*, *The Jeremy Kyle Show* adhered to the conflict/resolution structure but with the added element of providing aftercare led by Graham and his team of highly experienced therapists and counsellors. Jeremy and the production team took their job very seriously and understood that people, in some circumstances were entrusting them with their lives. This is something that was never taken for granted and Jeremy feels an enormous sense of responsibility to help people with real problems.

The array of people who queued up to appear on the show was what made *Jeremy Kyle* unique. More than a television programme, it offered members of the public who may not be in a financially stable situation the opportunity to be counselled by a highly skilled team. Whether it's a suspicious father seeking a DNA test or a whole family being reunited, Jeremy always tackles thought provoking stories which require emotional investment from the audience. To use this to its fullest potential, Jeremy was demanded to be as opinionated as possible in order to act as the unmistakable moral voice of the audience. It was testimony to his ability as a broadcaster that he was able to find the balance between impartiality and sympathy.

Apart from domestic disputes, the show shone a light on inspirational children going through the toughest of times. In partnership with the *Make a Wish Foundation*, Jeremy met some of the bravest children in Britain and rewarded them with life changing experiences. He remains adamant that this was a very important aspect of the show and although these specials were often too few and far between, they still went some way to giving both the series and indeed Jeremy himself a sense of perspective. At the risk of devaluing the validity of the regular issues that were raised in the show; on encountering children with fatal conditions and families coping with awful circumstances, suddenly people cheating on their partners, parents who won't go to work and rehabilitated drug addicts melts into insignificance. It's also evidence that *The Jeremy Kyle Show* wasn't afraid to shy away from the hard hitting stories which grip the nation. This is when his talent as a broadcaster comes to the forefront and suddenly it was no longer a talk show, more vital lessons in life. Maybe this was the real objective of the show?

More recently, Jeremy has joined the team on ITV's *Good Morning Britain* where he presides over the biggest stories of the day alongside a presenting team including Kate Garraway, Susannah Reid and Charlotte Hawkins. It is obvious that Jeremy feels just at home debating the biggest political stories as he does presiding over people's personal problems and treats both with equal respect. This is possibly the reason why ITV chose him to front a series of investigation programmes similar to the seminal *Cook Report*. Over five series, *The Kyle Files* investigated some of the biggest stories affecting Britain today. From knife crime and legal highs to underage drinking and drug culture, if it's got Britain talking, Jeremy and the team will cover it. In the time slot previously occupied by *Tonight with Trevor McDonald* in between the double bill of *Coronation Street*, *The Kyle Files* has become appointment to view television for anyone who wants to learn more about the world around them.

It was very interesting to note that even at the time of our interview, Jeremy was very quick to take nothing for granted. He absolutely loves what he does but, "when the Grim Reaper of television" comes knocking he won't fight to maintain his fame as family always comes first. Jeremy's adoration for his family is something that beams from him in all that he does and says and is an incredibly endearing quality that I don't experience too often when doing these interviews. With that being said, being such a successful and consummate broadcaster, there will always be a calling for Jeremy's unique relationship with the British public. It was a great pleasure to meet Jeremy Kyle and learn more about a man who receives such mixed publicity.

# Stanley Johnson

It's very clear that 2019 was a pivotal year in the extraordinary life of the Johnson family who have gradually risen to national prominence since the phenomenon of Boris first appeared on the scene. An inspired booking on the BBC's flagship satirical panel show *Have I Got News For You* catapulted the former journalist to national stardom and suddenly the public demanded to know more about the eccentric politician. Being submerged into the celebrity obsessed culture of post millennium Britain, the public couldn't get enough of such an original character in politics and suddenly it wasn't just Boris who became a star. Writer, politician and former member of the European Parliament, Stanley Johnson has enjoyed a varied career in public service and has now become an unlikely reality star thanks to appearances in *I'm a Celebrity... Get Me Out Of Here* and BBC One's *The Real Marigold Hotel*. Yet before this newfound television fame, Stanley led a full and active career in politics, something which it seems has been passed down in the Johnson genes. A Conservative MEP for Wight and Hampshire East from 1979 to 1984, Stanley became accustomed to the way of life on the Isle of Wight and gradually became aware of the importance of its relationship with the rest of Great Britain. Winning a 95% landslide victory at the 1979 election meant a great deal to him and added to the incentive to serve the people of the island to the very best of his ability.

Not forgetting his connections to the Isle of Wight, in 2018 Stanley was among the headlining speakers at the Isle Of Wight Literary Festival to promote his new book *Kompromat* released just a year previously. Recently releasing my autobiography, I found myself on the same festival line-up and was hoping to use my newfound author status to secure an interview with him. I googled him, found his website containing details of his email and sent him a message. Renowned for embracing new technology, I knew he was active on Social Media and constantly remains on the cutting edge of entertainment. Sure enough within minutes, I received a reply from Mr Johnson accepting my request and we eventually arranged to meet straight after his talk on the Sunday morning.

Waiting outside the allotted room for Stanley to finish his talk, I was struck by just how many people were listening to his presentation. I was overwhelmed by how well turned out my session had been, but this was on a different scale. It was here I realised the true power of this new wave of politics which made me all the more determined to learn the background behind such a phenomenon. Luckily the festival had allowed us to use the staff area to record the interview and we agreed to meet Stanley there after he had met his adoring public.

It is well documented that Stanley is never without his phone either texting, tweeting or on Instagram and as he walked into the room his hand was attached to his phone similar to someone a quarter of his age. We promptly enjoyed a selfie which he instantly posted on Instagram, something which has become second nature to the most unlikely reality star. Within moments my phone started vibrating in the back of my wheelchair and I assumed that it was someone urgently attempting to get hold of me. Yet on closer inspection I realised that Stanley had just tagged me in a post which was already getting a lot of attention on my frankly sparse Instagram account. After such excitement it was time to get the interview underway as Stanley sat intently waiting for the first question.

Politics is in Stanley's heritage which may have been an influential factor in determining the eventual careers of his offspring. His paternal grandfather, Ali Kemal Bey was one of the last interior ministers of the Ottoman Empire and was tragically assassinated during the Turkish war of independence in 1922. This devastating experience was to have a lasting effect on Stanley's family and helped him to form his personal view on politics which has been vital to his career.

Beyond domestic politics, Stanley also had a significant interest in the international concern of population growth. This has informed many of his written works including his 2009 book *World Population and the United Nations: Challenge and Response* and is something which he feels immensely passionate about. To him, this issue should be right at the top of the international political agenda and something that should not be taken lightly. According to statistics, by 2050 the world population is set to be around 9.5 billion and Stanley is calling for population stability at the earliest possible date to prevent a worldwide epidemic in the coming years.

As a writer, Stanley has published a whole host of books on a variety of subjects but in 2017 he stepped into satirical literature when he released *Kompromat:* an irreverent take on the events within the world of politics in the last few years. This discussed everything from Trump to Britain's decision to leave the EU in a slightly humorous and satirical way illustrating that Stanley isn't scared to tackle the big issues facing Britain today - think *Private Eye* in literature form! This has extended his audience as a writer and now he can boast of being a master in both fiction and nonfiction. Today, over forty years after his first book, *Life Without Birth: A Journey Through the Third World in Search of the Population Explosion,* Stanley is still producing formidable bodies of work and has hordes of intrigued fans queuing up for his talks at various festivals.

Obviously having much more of a vested interest in national politics has made the novel all the more revealing and gives it a sense of gravity which arguably other writers would lack. Being the father to one of the most influential politicians of our time, Stanley has enjoyed watching Boris's rise to prominence and is extremely proud of his son as a writer, politician and personality. He believes that Boris's stance on the handling of Brexit was the right one and at the time of the interview, was adamant that Theresa May's government would soon realise that Boris's projected ideologies would prove successful. It was quite prophetic, given that just nine months after our interview this became a reality as Prime Minister Boris moved into Number 10. Stanley remains extremely proud of all four of his children and is quick to celebrate all their successes; the journalist and television presenter Rachel, the politician Jo and environmentalist Leo.

In recent years, Stanley has developed something of a career in television, first in 2017's *I'm a Celebrity... Get Me Out Of Here* before checking into 2018's BBC One's *The Real Marigold Hotel*. Whilst in the jungle he made an unlikely friendship with *Made In Chelsea's* Georgia Toffolo, better known as Toff. This union kept Britain entertained for three weeks in December 2017 as the pair slowly discovered how much they had in common despite the substantial age gap. They've both kept in touch and when Stanley was looking for a quote to promote his most recent book, Toff was quick to oblige. Stanley returned the favour by appearing as a cameo in various episodes of *Made In Chelsea* which I imagine was something that he never thought he would be doing before entering the jungle!

Stanley's other television contribution took him back to India after sixty years for *The Real Marigold Hotel* alongside eight other well-known pensioners including Stephanie Beecham, The Krankies, Bob Champion, Syd Little, Susan George, Peter Dean and Selina Scott. Being the only senior citizen in the group to have previously experienced the Indian way of life, Stanley was able to make obvious comparisons between modern India and how the country was over half a century ago. On the subject of old age, Stanley confessed that this experience didn't alter his perception of the ageing process at all but he still enjoyed learning what India had to offer those in the autumn of their lives.

At the time of our interview he was the sprightly age of seventy-eight, and remained as sharp and active as ever . It was a pleasure to meet and interview the multi-talented, interesting and erudite Stanley Johnson and I can but wish him many more years of adventures.

# Lee Ridley

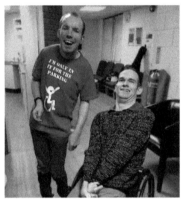

Without wanting to make a sweeping generalisation, throughout history, entertainment has struggled to fairly represent disability and diversity in our society and despite priding ourselves on being an inclusive nation, it's the one area that entertainment has slightly fallen behind in. And I should know after coming to terms with the fact that, due to my Cerebral Palsy and speech difficulties I'll never be top of the bill on *Live at the Apollo*. Yet in recent years there has been somewhat of a significant sea change in comedy and Light Entertainment which has helped to shine a light on diversity like never before. It's difficult to pinpoint a defining moment as the catalyst for such a positive revolution but when Channel Four secured the license for the London 2012 Paralympic Games, this was heralded as a breakthrough in entertainment. It spawned the entertainment series *The Last Leg* presented by Australian comedian and amputee, Adam Hills and fellow comedian and amputee, Alex Brooker alongside Devonshire's own Josh Widdicombe. This paved the way for more disabled comedians to join the circuit and in the subsequent years comedy boldly went to places it had never gone before.

Writer and comedian Lee Ridley had always had his sights firmly set on a career in comedy yet having Cerebral Palsy from birth made this seem almost impossible. Relying on sign language as his predominant method of communication didn't lend itself to being able to entertain an audience. Yet the adoption of an iPad would change everything for Lee and promptly put him on the path to success. In 2014 he won the prestigious BBC New Comedy Award which gained him notoriety amongst comedy circles and pushed his career forward. By this time, Lee had already been lucky enough to support fellow Geordie, Ross Noble on his UK tour following correcting him on his inaccurate impression of Stephen Hawking. As a huge fan of the long haired comedy powerhouse, touring with Ross Noble was a great achievement and invaluable experience for the upcoming comedian.

In 2017 Lee Ridley now preferred to be known as his stage name Lost Voice Guy and had his sights firmly set on world domination. On a particular occasion, his agent recommended that he should audition for *Britain's Got Talent* following the subtle change in attitude toward reality television amongst the comedy fraternity. Merely as a result of the original manner in which he delivers his material, Lee realised the opportunity could be extremely fruitful and he wasn't wrong! Yet Lee is always quick to sarcastically highlight the more important reason for auditioning and that was to meet fellow Geordies Ant and Dec! So it was that Sunday 3rd June 2018 would be the best night in the comedian's career to date as Lost Voice Guy reigned victorious as the twelfth winner of *Britain's Got Talent*. This transformed Lee from a jobbing stand-up comedian to a recognised household name and gained him a spot at that year's *Royal Variety Performance.*

Performing at the Royal Variety was a real honour for Lee and he successfully managed not to swear in front of Harry and Megan. This success led to his critically acclaimed nationwide tour *I'm Only In It For The Parking* which spanned the latter half of 2019. When I realised that Lee was playing a gig near my hometown on the Isle of Wight I realised that this could be my opportunity for something very special. For obvious reasons Lee hadn't made many appearances on interview based programmes apart from the obligatory BGT coverage on ITV's *Lorraine* and *BBC Breakfast* so I knew that if I could do him justice I would be in for somewhat of an exclusive. Therefore I contacted his agent and explained my plight and how great it would be if we could attempt a podcast with two people who can't speak! To my amazement, Lee's agent also shared my enthusiasm for the concept and arranged a short interview prior to the show.

Normally if my subject asks to see my questions beforehand, I'm a little pensive to oblige. Yet in this instance I knew it was vital as just like me, it takes Lee a considerable amount of time to type out his answers on his iPad. Using just one finger, this is Lee's preferred method for 70% of his communication and has clearly served him well. As an iPad user myself, I have great empathy for Lee and the sheer dedication and determination to his craft. So I was more than happy to send my questions in advance and honestly got a lot of enjoyment from attempting to shape the interview in a way that would suit this original method. Instead of relying on a hunch that my subject would intrinsically know my line of questioning, I was required to be both clear and concise with my questions in order to avoid miscommunication. I believe such an experience has encouraged me to be a better interviewer and can only thank Lee for that.

Arriving at a theatre armed with recording equipment is no longer a daunting experience for me. In fact I had done so many interviews at Medina Theatre in the three years leading up to this that all the staff were familiar with me and what I did. On this occasion I was under strict instructions to meet Lee in his dressing room, an area of the theatre I had never been in before. The only dressing room I had previously visited was at the Mayflower Theatre in Southampton where I had gone to see Jimmy Tarbuck when he was appearing with Des O'Connor. Yet this was different and felt more like a school changing room. As me and my PA Will were shown in, we saw Lee dressed in casual attire sitting on a small sofa. With the now famous iPad by his side, it was obvious that he just wanted to get down to business and I got Will to fire away with the first question.

It's a strange experience trying to interview someone with a speaking device as it becomes devoid of natural pauses and chit-chat. Once Lee had selected the text that he wanted to be projected, all that was left to do was sit back and listen to the iPad's delivery. As Lee explained, voice synthesisers have improved massively over the last decade and don't sound as robotic as they did back in the nineties (I should know because I used to have one!). Ridley has since turned this on its head and frequently makes jibes about being the voice of post office queues, British Rail and Radio 4. This addresses and highlights the political elephant in the room and immediately puts his audience at ease. That robotic RP voice has now become synonymous with Lost Voice Guy and is a flawless comedic device.

At the end of every interview I like to get my photo taken with my subject so that I can use it on the website and Lee Ridley was no exception. As soon as we asked him for this he signalled over to his wardrobe where the now iconic *"I'm Only In It For The Parking"* t-shirt was hanging. His assistant then promptly fetched the shirt before a quick change occurred. It was clear that here was a guy who knew about style and the t-shirt was his shorthand.

Now in demand from both comedy bookers and TV producers, there's so much in the pipeline for one of the most exciting performers on the comedy circuit. Successful comedy devices are extremely difficult to perfect but Lee Ridley's iPad synthesiser has become one of the most valuable gadgets in entertainment and the world is now his oyster. It was a great pleasure to meet and interview Lee Ridley aka Lost Voice Guy and it's exciting to see where his unique comedy journey will take him next.

# Steve Hewlett

Throughout history, the art of ventriloquism has marvelled audiences up and down the land and remains a staple of any variety show. It's clear that Britain's fascination with a comic and his plastic or wooden talking doll is enduring, spawning a whole host of familiar faces who we love to see bringing inanimate figures to life. Yet the art, a staple of nearly every Variety bill as little as half a century ago, almost disappeared from the bedrock of Light Entertainment in a bizarre sea change which saw variety struggle to find its purpose in modern Britain. However, the rise of interactive content during the late nineties and into the new millennium would soon return this ancient artform to the top of the showbiz tree.

Comic and ventriloquist Steve Hewlett first discovered he had the rare talent to throw his voice when he saw Jimmy Tamley on the grand final of *New Faces* in 1987. At only twelve years old, Steve realised this was what he wanted for himself and spent the next twenty years making it happen. These were the days before Facebook and Twitter and it was more difficult to interact with people from the world of entertainment but Steve managed to track Jimmy down and literally knocked on his door to ask his advice on how he should make it in showbiz. Not that he had expected it, but Steve would spend the next ten years touring Britain as Tamley's roadie; a great introduction to the world of entertainment.

I got in touch with Steve through Social Media following his highly celebrated induction into the prestigious Grand Order of Water Rats in July 2017 to ask him if he would be interested in the possibility of doing a podcast interview and to my delight he instantly accepted. He kindly invited me to a farm guest house in Eastbourne where we would do the podcast face to face. Having never ventured to this part of the south coast before, I always associated it with the affluent retired and Summer Seasons. This guesthouse echoed the traditional values of great British hospitality with all the staff wearing quintessential waiting attire. My PA Will and I were guided to a reception room where we waited patiently.

Soon the big vintage oak door to the reception room opened, revealing Steve holding a substantial briefcase containing a selection of his best loved comedy characters from Little Simon Cowell and Sunita to longtime sidekick Arthur Lager. It was truly remarkable that in a matter of seconds we could go from polite conversation to finding ourselves interacting with various pieces of fabric! It was now I realised that I was in the presence of a consummate entertainer at the very peak of his powers. Unlike most entertainers, there's something rather shy and reserved about Steve; a soft voice, gentle tone and laid back charm would make you think you're in the presence of a trainee doctor or librarian. It's only when he puts one of his comedy counterparts on the end of his arm, you realise that Hewlett is an accomplished performer of the highest order.

Attempting to emulate his hero Jimmy Tamley, Steve made his television debut on ITV's *The Big Big Talent Show*, a show that had launched the career of Charlotte Church. Steve was placing his hopes on lightning striking twice as fellow ventriloquist Paul Zerdin had won the series in 1996. Unfortunately he didn't reach the final rounds and returned to working cruise ships and playing summer seasons. He also used this time to write a body of material which formed his early routines. Then in 2006 Steve was honoured to be asked to be the new voice of Archie Andrews in a special tribute to the legendary ventriloquist Peter Brough. Renowned as being a ventriloquist on radio, surely one of the strangest acts in Light Entertainment history, Peter Brough's move to television was disastrously unsuccessful as a result of his not being able to control his lips from moving. This failure was a vital lesson for the whole entertainment industry, but despite this, Brough remains one of the pioneers of British ventriloquism and to step into his shoes was a fantastic accolade for Steve.

Just a year later, Steve found himself auditioning for yet another talent show in the form of *Britain's Got Talent*. There seems to be a misconception that reality talent shows are solely for amateur members of the public, yet established professional performers can also use them as a platform to reinvent or boost their own careers. By the time Steve found himself on the famous BGT stage, he'd already enjoyed a twenty year career and had worked alongside giants of entertainment including Ken Dodd and Bruce Forsyth. Yet Simon Cowell and *Britain's Got Talent* gave Steve a platform to gain success on a nationwide scale which in turn helped put ventriloquism back on the entertainment map. Despite coming fourth in the 2013 final, BGT made Steve into a star and opened an endless array of opportunities.

Steve Hewlett's rise to fame coincided with the rediscovery of ventriloquism thanks in part to performers like Nina Conti and Paul Zerdin. There seems to be a significant boom in the popularity of what was considered a dying art only ten years ago. Yet it's not necessarily on mainstream television or radio, instead it's found another home online via YouTube where lots of Steve Hewlett protégés can post endless hours of content. Maybe this is the new path for Variety of this nature? Steve finds himself in the transition stage, where ventriloquism is still an important part of theatrical Variety and he is justifiably proud of being able to make a living from something he loves.

In 2015 Steve was honoured to support The Osmonds on their UK tour. This was a proud moment for a man who grew up watching shiny floor spectaculars and now was supporting the legendary group every night to packed out theatres all around Britain. The success of the show made him realise that there was an appetite for a live show dedicated to ventriloquism. His first live show *Thinking Outside The Box* toured the country in 2014 and featured his long-time stooge, Arthur Lager. Apart from Arthur Lager, Steve maintains a healthy array of puppet friends from Simon Cowell to The Silver Fox and it's incredible how quickly each of them come to life. This is absolute testament to Steve's talent as a writer and performer

My interview with Steve was a complete revelation for me. In a world where reality television has completely overwhelmed the television light entertainment landscape, it would be easy for talent show protégés like Steve to be rather nonchalant about both the history and legacy of traditional British entertainment. Yet the enormous reverence and respect which radiates from him illustrates that irrespective of his talent show connections, Steve Hewlett remains a traditional performer and a fantastic ambassador for the wonderful art of ventriloquism and the formidable legacy of Variety in this great nation.

## Shirley Ballas

In 2017 former dancer and competition judge Shirley Ballas came to national attention when she was unveiled as the new head judge on the BBC's heavyweight *Strictly Come Dancing* replacing the outgoing Len Goodman. This was just another accolade in a glittering career which has spanned four decades. A soaring passion for dance from the age of seven encouraged Shirley to realise her calling and she was quick to make moves in the dance arena. At such a tender age, Shirley had no idea what her dance potential would have in store but simply knew that dance was something which captured her imagination. Fascinated by the *Cha Cha Cha* and the *Waltz*, never missing a dance lesson, Shirley knew that if she wanted to make waves as a dancer she would have to work incredibly hard. Her mother instilled a good work ethic into her which Shirley has never forgotten.

I contacted Shirley through her agent and over the space of a few months we worked to find the perfect opportunity to do a phone interview in amongst her hectic schedule. On receiving one particular email, I noticed that Shirley had been directly copied into the correspondence. Never being one to miss an opportunity, I promptly emailed Shirley directly and was delighted when she instantly replied accepting my request but suggested it might be better to do it in a few weeks when she could find some spare time.

After those few weeks I emailed again, not expecting a response for at least a couple of days so went about my everyday business. I clearly remember it was a Sunday and me and my PA Will had decided to go to the supermarket to stock up on essentials for the week. Strolling through the vegetable aisle, I heard my phone vibrating in the back of my wheelchair and had an inkling who would be on the other end. Will explained to Ms Ballas where we were and asked if she could call back in twenty minutes to give us enough time to get home and set up the equipment. Dumping our items in the corner of the supermarket, we made a quick getaway in preparation to interview the new queen of *Strictly!*

At the age of fifteen, Shirley moved to North Yorkshire to unite with dance partner Nigel Tiffany. Two years later she was persuaded to audition to partner Sammy Stopford; a union which would prove successful both personally and professionally as the couple married in 1985. Together with Sammy, Shirley owned her first dance studio where she was able to teach for the first time. Proving a successful partnership both on and off the dance floor, the pair came second in the 1982, 1983 & 1985 Professional World Latin Dance Championships and won the 1983 International Latin American Dance Championships. They were also the 1984 UK Open Champions in Professional Latin. Being in such a competitive world taught Shirley the vital lessons that come from defeat and that this seemingly negative experience could in fact be a very useful and worthwhile process to go through. This gave her the determination to succeed.

Having been right at the top of her game, Shirley then met dance partner Mark "Corky" Ballas and relived the highs and lows of competitive dance all over again. Surrounded by a powerhouse of dance talent including Marcus Hilton MBE, Karen Hilton MBE and Bill and Bobbie Irvine, it would take over a decade to return to the top of the dance world but in 1995 and again in 1996 Shirley and Mark won the Professional Latin American International Championships. This meant a great deal to Shirley, making her the only professional dancer to win a major competition with two different dance partners. Less than a year later, Shirley decided to retire from competitive dance and enter the world of coaching. At the age of thirty six, Shirley knew that it was time to hang up her dancing shoes and made the decision to bow out in probably the greatest dance arena of Blackpool's Tower Ballroom. She had a great run and cherished every moment of being surrounded by great friends and support but knew that it was the right time to bow out and concentrate on her coaching career.

The offer of replacing Len Goodman on *Strictly* in 2017 came as a substantial shock to Shirley. It was a role she wasn't expecting, especially being a woman in her mid-fifties in an industry dominated by inequality.

Having known Len for the entirety of her working life, the idea of superseding such an iconic figure in dance seemed an impossible task. Yet as she likes to think, her dance slippers sit nicely alongside Len's and while it's clear that there will never be another Len Goodman, Shirley believes that she has put her own stamp on the show and was looking forward to the prospect of her second series which of course was won by the journalist and broadcaster Stacey Dooley.

It was a great pleasure to speak with the undisputed queen of the ballroom Shirley Ballas and I wish her the very best of luck with the rest of her glittering career.

## Chapter Eight - Sum up


After profiling over forty of my greatest interviews with some of the most prolific figures from the last sixty years of British entertainment, how do I sum up this fascinating journey? The simple answer is that it's almost impossible. Despite having loved meeting these incredibly fascinating individuals and been blown away by their contributions to entertainment, I hope this story goes so much deeper than merely a book about the people who I've met. In fact it only occurred to me when compiling this information that this story may not actually be about the interviews themselves. Nor is it about the stars who kindly gave up their invaluable time to take part in a short podcast interview for *Beyond The Title* but maybe for something much bigger. The aim of developing a podcast series was to attempt to create an insight into the entertainment landscape in post millennium Britain and having laid my interviews out in this manner, I guess I have achieved my goal.

Interviews are like nothing else and solely rely upon the unique ability of two people to have a conversation. Celebrities are rare creatures who have become accustomed to the spotlight and in most cases, talking about themselves comes as second nature. The very fact that they are famous would indicate that they have a very interesting story to tell and it's up to me as the interviewer to glean the story in the most natural way possible. The phenomenon of the television interview rose from the audience having a considerable desire to learn more about the stars they saw on their television screens. However, over time the interview has been increasingly used to plug and promote celebrity's upcoming ventures. In my view, this compromises the talent's ability to tangent off into a repertoire of anecdotes which brings the audience closer to the stars themselves. When I embarked on my journey with *Beyond The Title,* I was adamant that this would not be just a platform for PR companies to advertise star endorsements. To me, I thought I had a bigger story that I wanted to tell.

It was my ambition to trace the story of British entertainment through the stars and influential figures it had spawned. I wanted to chart the ever changing face of Britain, celebrating and revisiting the television fads and fashions of our time. In doing this I hope to have highlighted the substantial changes in our cultural history which I believe have become a significant part of our national identity. Anyone who has contributed to the enigmatic world of showbiz over the last sixty years is someone worth celebrating. Who cares how many Twitter followers they have or if they are on trend? If they've had an extensive career within the Arts, then they are surely worth interviewing and by doing so you may obtain an original insight into the business today.

The first change which I have been lucky enough to chart is the evolution of comedy. Comedy legends Barry Cryer and Jimmy Tarbuck spoke fondly of their early experiences on the circuit where entertainment was still split into regional areas where executives would drop in to see if there was anyone who would aptly fit the new medium of television. If they liked what they saw then you could find yourself on the Palladium stage within the week and fame was assured. This meant that it was possible for entertainers to go from obscurity to nationwide stars overnight. Yet unlike the disposable entertainment of today, should figures be lucky enough to find themselves in the glare of the spotlight, it was easier for them to remain there. As time went by and the history of the medium grew ever more invaluable, so did the pioneers who helped to define it.

Yet as soon as television had developed its own momentum, television executives no longer needed to rely upon theatrical variety to fill their schedules and instead looked to the working men's clubs in northern parts of England for the next chapter in the story of Light Entertainment. Notorious for being brutally honest, such clubs proved to be the perfect grounding for the next generation of entertainers and offered them experiences that they would never forget. Thrown objects, threatening behaviour and constant heckling was normal for performers who braved this unpredictable world. If they could survive this raw grounding then it seemed a lifetime of success awaited them. Once they transferred to television and were comfortable with the new medium, it was only a matter of time before these entertainers made it their own.

Like all industries, entertainment relies upon financial backing in order to thrive. Frequently looked upon by senior government ministers as a disposable luxury, the entertainment landscape is somewhat hindered by lack of budgets and limited resources. The only guarantee of financial security is for entertainers to embark on huge nationwide tours similar to Summer and Christmas seasons from yesteryear. For such highly talented performers, they may long for the safe confines of a TV studio (which ironically have all been sold to developers in the midst of a housing crisis) but instead they are forced out on the road playing to a different theatre every night. Such news is music to the ears of entertainment journalists like myself as with the influx of comedy tours it substantially increases access to these stars. So what used to be looked upon as a stepping stone to television success is now an extension of a successful TV career.

Perhaps the most understated and fascinating subjects are the writers who are new to the pragmatics of interview for the simple reason that they have spent an entire career hiding behind the larger than life performers who they've helped shape. Most of these subjects had never been in this kind of interview setting before and were somewhat unfamiliar with the situation. The ironic thing is that once they were accustomed with the format, most became some of my most successful podcasts. Prompted by my questions, they were able to elaborate on subjects which they felt passionately about and actually liked being the ones in the spotlight for a change as opposed to their performing counterparts.

In possible contrast to this, the broadcasters I have been lucky enough to meet have all been cast into the national consciousness as they report on the world events which ultimately define our time. In this case, anonymity is not an option as trust is of paramount importance when attempting to establish a bond between broadcaster and television audience. The familiarity of seeing the same individual presiding the events of the day means a lot to the television watching nation and the ability to inform and educate us in an informal manner is absolutely necessary to maintaining such a trust.

When explaining to people about *Beyond The Title*, there are two questions that I'm frequently asked. Therefore in drawing this book to a close, I thought it would be the perfect opportunity to provide some answers. The first question is, if I had to single out a favourite guest who would it be? At the risk of slightly swerving the question, it would be impossible to just name one. Instead I believe there may be a definitive formula for being a successful guest of *Beyond The Title*. The successful candidate would require the eloquence of Alistair Stewart, the unpredictability of Brian Conley and Joe Pasquale, interspersed with the cultural heritage of Jimmy Tarbuck and Barry Cryer. In short there is no such thing as the ultimate guest but I have been lucky enough to meet some truly remarkable people each with their own enthralling story to tell.

The second question I'm frequently asked is who would be my perfect interviewee and again I always struggle to provide a definitive answer. The entertainment industry is so vast with so many unique and interesting characters that it's impossible to narrow it down to just one. Therefore in conclusion I would like to take the opportunity to provide a shortlist of my future ideal subjects and who knows, I might even be lucky enough to meet them in the coming years:

## Sir Michael Parkinson:

The broadcasting legend who has the potential to strike fear into almost every other interviewer on the planet. Michael Parkinson's journey through television spans the early stages of the genre to the new stars of the twenty first century. With assistance from the legendary TV executive Sir Bill Cotton, he helped create the formula for the chat show format which has inspired each and every interview styled show since. I would love to explore how the programme changed over time and how they managed to maintain the original concept of having three well known figures who would never otherwise meet, taking part in a shared conversation.

His interviews with cultural icons Muhammed Ali, George Best and Peter Sellers have been explored many times and arguably there isn't much left to add to the analysis of them. Just like Parkinson himself, these interviews have become part of the fabric of our culture and now are shorthand for the best in 1970's factual entertainment. And all of this from the son of a miner who escaped the family working tradition to become a leading journalist in Fleet Street during the early sixties before becoming a junior producer on the Granada magazine programme *Seen at 6:30*. At the epicentre of the musical revolution of the time, Parky had unrivalled access to the stars and these interviews have become a vital component of capturing the zeitgeist of the time. Who can forget Mick Jagger's prediction that the Rolling Stones would be lucky if they lasted two years? It seems that Parkinson has been present at almost every cultural landmark in modern British history and it would be fascinating to hear his side of the entertainment story.

## Liza Tarbuck

Born into entertainment, Liza Tarbuck grew up knowing her father was one of the most famous faces in Britain, often mixing with showbiz royalty and the real thing from time to time. It's difficult to comprehend just how big a star Jimmy Tarbuck became during the sixties and seventies and how his fame impacted upon the rest of his family. Having interviewed Jimmy on numerous occasions, he remains extremely philosophical about both his vast achievements and the downsides of fame and since obtaining this side of the story it would be fascinating to learn how Liza felt about her father's fame.

Obviously being a star in her own right, she has forged a career for herself in entertainment and remains one of the most versatile stars around. Graduating from drama school, Liza secured a role in the eighties ITV sitcom *Watching* alongside the actress Emma Wray. Throughout the nineties, she made her name on Light Entertainment shows including *The Big Breakfast* before staring in her own BBC1 comedy drama *Linda Green* surrounding the sexual exploits of a forty something club singer. The series culminated in a shocking revelation that her father was not who she thought and instead was her long lost Uncle Vic played by Liza's real dad Jimmy.

Now a weekend presenter on BBC Radio 2, Liza has a union of followers who appreciate her gentle irreverent perspective on everyday life and her warmth and humility transcends the airwaves. There's so much I would love to ask her and her story would make for a fascinating podcast.

## Michael McIntyre

The current undisputed doyen of Light Entertainment has almost single-handedly brought Variety back to Saturday nights thanks in part to his hugely popular *Big Show*. Equally at home headlining *The Comedy Store* or *Live At The Apollo* as he is addressing a theatre full of people or presenting *The Royal Variety Performance*, this all round entertainer has the ability to do anything he sets his mind to. Obviously entertainment is in Michael's blood with his late father Ray Cameron being one of the leading writers on *The Kenny Everett Show* during the 1970's and as a result gave the young comedian an invaluable insight into the workings of the business. I would love to know what it was like to grow up amongst comedy legends and how that was able to influence his later career.

## Anthony Joshua OBE

The champion boxer has transcended his sport to become one of Britain's biggest stars. Ever since claiming a gold medal at London 2012, Joshua has allowed his personality to shine through everything that he does. Yet like most sportsmen, the ever-present lingering cloud of defeat remains something which has threatened to thwart his career and which he only recently tasted for the first time. This concept is extremely difficult for sportsmen to compartmentalise as by their very nature, they are trained to win and failure isn't an option. So how do they pick themselves up following a massive blow and get back on the metaphorical horse?

Arguably Anthony Joshua was the first sportsman to fully embrace the phenomenon of Social Media and had the foresight to use it to its ultimate potential. Today fans are able to watch his vlogs, read his tweets and see his stories on Instagram, bringing them closer to the preparation to a fight than ever before. This in turn allows fans to have more of a vested interest in the outcome of the fight which extends AJ's appeal. It's quite clear that this is a highly intelligent guy who forever remains one step ahead of the game.

As an athlete, Joshua adheres to a regimented training regime which maintains his physicality to be literally, fighting fit. Such a process must occupy hours and hours of everyday and would undoubtedly affect everything. This sacrifice is one which not many could achieve but if done right could earn you worldwide adulation. I would love to establish whether this feeling is always enough to motivate him to adhere to such a strict schedule each and every day.

## Claudia Winkleman

Before obtaining her Saturday night sparkle, Claudia Winkleman was a nineties television presenter who was right at the centre of ladette culture. Presenting Sky One's dating series *God's Gift* which was responsible for the television debut of Paddy McGuiness, Claudia aptly fitted the cheeky, relaxed mood of the time and it wasn't long before appearances on the BBC's *Holiday* programme came calling. Daughter of legendary broadcaster and journalist Eve Pollard, the young Claudia grew up surrounded by entertainment and it wasn't surprising that she wanted a slice of showbiz action for herself.

Now a firm fixture on one of the most successful Light Entertainment shows on British television, Claudia remains as in demand as ever both on TV and radio. Yet it would be fascinating to learn what she has made of her career so far and as someone with a showbiz heritage, does she feel a responsibility to maintain the entertainment tradition?

These are just a handful of figures who I would thrive on the opportunity to interview over the coming years but there are so many more who I can't wait to welcome into the *Beyond The Title* 'family'. In the coming years I hope to extend my own profile within the Arts to build my reputation as a trusted and consummate interviewer. By raising my own profile, hopefully it will increase the draw of celebrities to want to feature on my podcast. That's my ambition and something I wish to conquer in the years to come.

Avid listeners of *Beyond The Title* will know that I like to end each and every interview with the same two questions and I felt it was only right to bring this book to a close by answering these two questions myself.

**What's your proudest achievement?** Taking into consideration everything I have done throughout my life, the creation and development of *Beyond The Title* undoubtedly remains my proudest achievement in many different ways. Ever since I can remember, I have longed to play a part in the enigmatic world of entertainment. Due to my disability, I always knew that it would be extremely difficult for me to participate in this world but since creating the podcast series, it has finally fulfilled the inner entertainer in me who has that glowing desire to shine on a stage. In many ways, *Beyond The Title* has been my stage, acting as a platform for me to achieve my hopes and dreams. Beyond everything, I believe that to be my proudest achievement.

**And what's next for Josh Barry?** For both Josh Barry and *Beyond The Title*, well you'll just have to wait and see but if I continue to meet such fascinating, talented individuals who are willing to give up their valuable time to offer me their insight into the industry which they love, surely I can't go wrong.

If anyone reading this book has taken inspiration from the platform which I have attempted to create, I would really urge you to start one of your own as it may turn out to be the best journey you have ever had. What better way to spend the early part of your career than by getting up close and personal with the people who you admire. If it's been my greatest achievement then why couldn't it be someone else's too? On a personal note, I would like to thank every figure who has contributed to *Beyond The Title* and for making the impossible seem possible.

However, the last word of this book can't go to any of those highly talented figures. My life is all about teamwork and I couldn't have achieved such a great project without a devoted and professional team around me who are ever present at my side going above and beyond the call of duty just to see me shine. Above all, they have been and still remain the true heroes of *Beyond The Title* and to them and for them I am extremely grateful.

Thanks for purchasing a copy of this book and always remember to drop in each and every Friday to www.beyondthetitle.co.uk to listen to the next chapter of my rich story interviewing the greats of entertainment.

Josh Barry
Isle of Wight
2020

## About the author

Josh Barry is a freelance writer for the screen, stage and page from East Cowes on the Isle of Wight. He graduated from Bournemouth University in 2010 with a MA in Writing for the Media, which was preceded by a BA in Scriptwriting for Film and Television. While he has lived with the physical limitations of Athetoid Cerebral Palsy since birth, Barry's razor-sharp wit and inimitable way with words has seen him carve out a rich and eclectic media career over the past decade.

Whether he's producing radio documentaries and screenplays about the enchanting world of Light Entertainment, podcasting with industry icons like Jimmy Tarbuck, Barry Cryer, and Ben Elton, or authoring books like this one, Barry has consistently shown that a disability is no match for bucket loads of passion and even more talent. However, while the bright lights of showbiz may be calling, Barry remains happiest when he's back home, in the company of friends and family, enjoying a leisurely summer evening's stroll along the Cowes seafront. You can also find Josh's autobiography "Adapted" for sale online or by order from all good bookstores.

Lightning Source UK Ltd.
Milton Keynes UK
UKHW051226140920
369756UK00008B/89